History in the early years

Until recently, history was sometimes seen as being inappropriate for young children. Increasingly, however, teachers are discovering that children enjoy finding out about the past, yet teachers are often unsure about what counts as 'real' history. Hilary Cooper here explains the strands of thinking involved in historical enquiry at any level, the extent to which pre-school children can think in this way and how teachers can build on this thinking once children are in school, making history an integral part of good practice. The book includes case studies to illustrate points and activities through which historical thinking can be developed.

Hilary Cooper is Director of Professional Studies in the Department of Teaching and Education Studies at Lancaster University. She has also spent many years as a class teacher in a variety of primary schools and has published widely in the area of primary history.

Teaching and learning in the first three years of school
Series Editor *Joy Palmer*

This innovatory and up-to-date series is concerned specifically with curriculum practice in the first three years of school. Each book includes guidance on:

- subject content
- planning and organisation
- assessment and record keeping
- in-service training

This practical advice is placed in the context of the National Curriculum and the latest theoretical work on how children learn at this age and what experiences they bring to their early years in the classroom.

History in the early years

Hilary Cooper

London and New York

First published 1995
by Routledge
11 New Fetter Lane, London EC4P 4EE

Simultaneously published in the USA and Canada
by Routledge
29 West 35th Street, New York, NY 10001

Reprinted 1998

Typeset in Palatino by
Ponting-Green Publishing Services, Chesham, Bucks
Printed and bound in Great Britain by
Biddles Ltd, Guildford and King's Lynn

Printed on acid-free paper

British Library Cataloguing in Publication Data
A catalogue record for this book is available from the
British Library

Library of Congress Cataloging-in-Publication Data
A catalogue record for this book has been requested

ISBN 0–415–10100–X

Contents

Illustrations

Editor's preface

Each book in this series focuses on a specific curriculum area. The series relates relevant learning theory or a rationale for early years learning to the practical development and implementation of subject-based topics and classroom activities at the infant level (i.e. Reception, Y1, Y2). It seems that the majority of existing books on primary education and the primary curriculum focus on pupils aged 7–11 years. It is hoped that this series presents a refreshing and much needed change in that it specifically addresses the first three years in school.

Each volume is intended to be an up-to-date, judicious mix of theory and practical classroom application, offering a wealth of background information, ideas and advice to all concerned with planning, implementing, monitoring and evaluating teaching and learning in the first three years in school. Theoretical perspectives are presented in a lively and interesting way, drawing upon recent classroom research findings wherever possible. Case studies and activities from a range of classrooms and schools illuminate many of the substantial issues related to the subject area in question.

Readers will find a similar pattern of contents in all the books in the series. Each discusses the early learning environment and the transition from home- to school-based learning, and addresses the key questions of what this means for the early years teacher and the curriculum. Such discussion inevitably incorporates ideas on the knowledge which young children may have of subjects and an overview of the subject matter itself which is under scrutiny. As the thrust of the series is towards young children learning subjects, albeit in a holistic way, no doubt readers will wish to consider what is an appropriate content or rationale for the subject in the early years. Having considered young children as learners, what they are bringing into school in terms of prior knowledge, the teacher's task and the subject matter itself, each book then turns its attention to appropriate methods of planning, organising, implementing and evaluating teaching and learning activities. Crucial matters such as assessment, evaluation and record-keeping are dealt with in their own right, and are also referred to and discussed in ongoing examples of good practice. Each book concludes with useful suggestions for further staffroom discussion/INSET activities and advice on resources.

As a whole, the series aims to be inspirational and forward looking. As all readers know so well, the National Curriculum is not 'written in concrete'. Education is a dynamic process. While taking due account of the essential National Curriculum framework, authors go far beyond the level of description of rigid content guidelines to highlight *principles* for teaching and learning. Furthermore, they incorporate two key messages which surely underpin successful, reflective education, namely 'vision' and 'enthusiasm'. It is hoped that students and teachers will be inspired and assisted in their task of implementing successful and progressive plans which help young learners to make sense of their world and the key areas of knowledge within it.

Joy A. Palmer

Acknowledgements

We are only beginning to explore the ways in which young children can find out about the past, and to recognise their need to do so. Our greater understanding will depend on teachers who can translate questions about the past into stories, play and activities which allow young children to grapple with them in embryonic but genuinely historical ways, and who reflect on children's responses and share them with others. I am therefore greatly indebted to the students and teachers who have worked with children to investigate questions, illustrate points and exemplify ideas suggested in this book. I am grateful to the PGCE students whose dissertation studies investigated children's responses to stories, artefacts and pictures, and in particular to Lyn Clarke, Hilary Croft, Joanne Edwards, Virginia Hunt and Shelley Moore. I am grateful to the class teachers who undertook case studies to illustrate a variety of approaches to planning and assessment, Helen Ingham, Angela Kinsett, Julie Giles and Rosie Alston, and to Teresa Clark, Humanities Inspector in Lewisham. My thanks are due to the National Curriculum Council for permission to publish teachers' work prepared as part of a project contracted by the NCC. I should like to thank teachers who have shared their ideas through projects, especially Ann Dingdale, co-ordinator of the Women in History Key Stage 1 Biography Project, Jonathan Barnes, for infectious enthusiasm and expertise in teaching Medieval history to 5- and 6-year-olds shared at Historical Association workshops, and Liz George (Another Tale) for sharing her knowledge of children's books. And I am grateful to teachers who have found the time to publish their ideas and their practice in the journals *Teaching History* and *Primary History*. I am especially grateful to Joan Blyth who has done so much to initiate and support the teaching of history to young children, for the encouragement and help she has given me over the last decade.

The examples on pp. 69, 88–90, and 100–2, 152–60 are from case studies undertaken as part of a project contracted by the NCC and are reproduced with permission of the NCC.

I am indebted to Margaret Taylor, a third-year Education student, for her work on case study 4 (Chapter 12). I received Margaret Taylor's lesson plans and evaluation the morning after I had spent an evening with a 'colleague' from a prestigious university, who spent the entire time telling me that teachers are academically limited and second-rate individuals, that teacher education is worthless and that state schools provide a travesty of education. When I read these notes, I wept in anger for the teachers I know all over this country who give their all, their spirits, their time and energy and above all professional expertise in often very difficult circumstances, because of a strong moral commitment to what they consider good and right, for *all* the children, whatever their background or difficulties.

Stimulating, creative teaching as a basis for professional development has never been more crucial. I hope that the questions raised in this book will encourage further reflective and shared practice.

Finally, I am grateful to Sally Vetch who typed a virtually indecipherable manuscript with patience, good humour and meticulous care.

Introduction

With so much current emphasis on testing, and on literacy and numeracy, many teachers may feel that there is no time or need for history during the first three years of school. This view is based on long-standing arguments which need to be re-examined.

First, it is often argued that teaching 'subjects' is inappropriate for young children because it fragments their learning. The *Plowden Report* (DES 1967) advocated a broad, rich curriculum but did not pay particular attention to history. Yet the importance of learning the thinking processes and concepts which lie at the heart of each discipline from the very beginning in their simplest form, then in an increasingly complex way, has been accepted ever since Bruner (1963) developed the ideal of a spiral curriculum. Each subject, he said, must be rewritten and teaching materials revamped in such a way that pervading, powerful ideas and attitudes relating to it are given a central role. 'The more elementary a course and the younger its students, the more serious must be its pedagogical aim of forming the intellectual powers of those whom it serves' (Bruner 1963: Ch. 4). The National Curriculum may be regarded as an attempt to make a broad spiral curriculum a reality. Indeed, by attempting to define progression in thinking central to each discipline, topics can be designed which both recognise links between curriculum areas and allow for progression within each discipline. There are clear overlaps between history and the other aspects of the curriculum because history is concerned with finding out about all aspects of societies in the past: with art, music, science and technology. Historical enquiry, and communicating findings, can involve many aspects of language and of mathematics, in stimulating and meaningful contexts.

Second, history has been considered inappropriate for young children because research has shown that they learn best through their own experiences, whereas history is concerned with abstract ideas, the causes or effects of changes over time and the behaviour of adults, and involves understanding that the past is constantly reinterpreted, by making inferences about incomplete sources. Yet the past *is* a dimension of children's social and physical environment and they interact with it from birth. They hear and use the vocabulary of time and change: old, new, yesterday, tomorrow, last year, before you were born, when mummy was little, a long time ago, once upon a time. They ask questions about the sequence and causes of events: when did we move here? Why? What happened in the story next? Children encounter different interpretations of past times in nursery rhymes and fairy stories, family anecdotes, theme parks, films and pantomime. They encounter historical sources: old photographs, a baby book, an ornament, a statue, a church, maybe a closed-down factory or a derelict cinema being replaced by new roads and flats. They ask questions: who is in the photograph, or who is that statue? Why did the factory close? Before children start school there are many contexts in which they are implicitly aware of the past.

Third, many adults' experience of history is a passive memorising of large numbers of apparently irrelevant facts, with no opportunity to ask and investigate questions which interest *them*. I recently discovered a prize presented to my grandmother at Cosgreaves School, when she was 5, in 1869. It is called *A Day at the Seaside* by Mrs Barnard. It begins with Emma Somerton mending her stocking. This inspires her mother to spend the next 140 pages instructing her in the whole of European and Asian history, all commendably linked to the history of stockings. 'The Ancient Britons painted themselves red and blue before stockings were invented. . . . However, in the reign of Edward VI, knitting was a common employment. Cotton had not yet been brought to England and things were made of wool.' By page 10 Emma learns that silk was taken to Spain by the Arabs, 'during the reign of Adderhaman III who ruled Cordova from AD 912 to AD 961'. On page 11, she is reminded that 'the Emperor Tacitus made it unlawful for men to wear silk unmixed with ordinary substances', and that 'silk comes from the caterpillar *Phaloena Mori* which was domesticated in China . . .'. Fortunately for 5-year-olds today, the emphasis is on *doing* things to investigate their own questions: talking to older people, finding out how things work, making drawings or models of places they have visited, listening to stories and exploring them through imaginative play.

Finally, although it was argued recently that history means 'facts, dates, major personalities and the study of national identity' (*The Times*, first leader, 3 October 1992), many people today question the original national-istic and moralistic reasons for the teaching of history to young children. In 1905, *Suggestions for the Consideration of Teachers and Others Concerned in the Work of Public Elementary Schools* stated that history should be taught in order to teach children their rights and duties and to compare Britain's heritage with that of other nations, by holding up to them the example of good men (Board of Education 1905). In 1927, a *Handbook of Suggestions for Teachers* (Board of Education 1927) viewed history as an instrument for moral training learnt through good and evil personalities. *Teaching of*

History, a Ministry of Education pamphlet of 1952, emphasised the difficulty of teaching history to younger pupils; the cover was decorated with portraits of kings and queens of Britain and it recommended a diet of well-told exemplary stories.

However, it is recognised now that history develops moral awareness, and social and emotional as well as cognitive growth, not through didactic teaching but by encouraging children to ask questions, to discuss and to speculate about the reasons for people's behaviour, attitudes and values in other times and in other places. Jones (1968), whose work was based on the psychodynamic theories of Erikson (1965), felt that children can and must be encouraged to understand both themselves and the behaviour, ideas and feelings of people in different societies, and that the humanities provide an ideal means of doing this. He saw it as essential that cognitive development should be related to emotional and imaginative growth. He said that Bruner never understood how the free flow of creative fantasy and the rational process of proof can be related through the educational process. 'It is necessary that children feel myth as well as understand it' (Jones 1968: 49). *History in the Primary and Secondary Years* (DES 1985) acknowledged that the great myths of North America, Africa and Asia, as well as European myths, are likely to play an important part in the experience of young children. It also said that children between 4 and 7 can begin to relate judgements about people to evidence and to identify with the predicaments and points of view of others. It saw history as part of self-knowledge and the development of moral awareness. Thinking historically constantly involves the questions: 'What is it like to be someone else?' and 'How do I know it is true?' These questions are assertions of intellectual independence.

The cross-curricular themes and dimensions of the National Curriculum (DES 1989a; NCC 1990) explicitly require children, from their earliest years in school, to discuss values and controversial issues. In history, young children can talk to older people about social, economic and technological changes in the home and in workplaces, or changes in their local environment, in food or in health care, or in attitudes to women, and how they have been affected by, and feel about, the changes. Through oral history, children can find out about the experiences, attitudes and values, thoughts and feelings of people from different social, ethnic, religious and cultural backgrounds.

History, then, is not only appropriate for young children; it is essential. This book aims to show how history, taught as a dimension of an umbrella theme such as 'houses', or through history-focused topics, can give coherence to a broad curriculum and a purpose to investigations and presentations. History makes links between child and home, between school and the wider community, between past and present. It links deductive reasoning and imagination. It can be an enriching context for stories, play-reading, writing, talking, drawing and model-making. It is central to social, emotional and cognitive growth.

An awareness of the past is as important for an individual as it is for a society. Through history we can find out about, share and become part of the record of the human race. It is an awareness which, nurtured when young, grows throughout life.

> In childhood it may have the same appeal as a fairy story or a tale of adventure; in later life it may come to have a philosophical meaning . . . a subject that is capable of interesting you as a child and does not fail to reward you, has ever deeper interest for a grown man.
>
> (Rowse 1946: 49)

Part I reviews research which suggests the embryonic but genuine historical thinking which children are capable of when they start school and how this can be developed during the following years. Part II considers the nature of history and how research in cognitive development discussed in Part I can be related to the processes of historical enquiry in school. In Part III, issues concerning whole-school, long- and short-term planning and assessment are discussed and examples of possible formats given. Case studies in Part IV describe history topics which were planned and assessed in different ways, illustrated by examples of children's work. Part V gives suggestions for workshops for teachers which could help them to write and implement a school policy document which suits the needs of their school. The workshops are intended to be stimulating and fun, for exciting teaching is the product of confident, informed, reflective practice by teachers who are constantly developing their own interests and expertise and, above all, enjoying themselves.

Part I

Children's early learning: a context for history in the first three years of school

There are three interdependent strands to historical thinking. First, historians are concerned with tracing changes over time; changes may be rapid or gradual. They analyse the various causes of change and the effects of change on people's lives. Changes may be political, economic, social, technological or cultural; changes in one area affect other aspects of life. Some changes are more significant than others.

Second, historians construct accounts of past times. Their accounts depend on the preoccupations of the times in which they live, on their own interests and perspectives, and on the sources available to them. These may be artefacts, buildings, pictures, archaeological sites or a variety of written sources ranging from statistics and laws to diaries and contemporary literature.

Third, in order to construct accounts of the past, historians make deductions and inferences about sources, the traces of the past which remain. Because sources are often incomplete, or because their status is unknown, it is often possible to make more than one valid supposition about a source. Validity depends on whether the supposition is likely, in the light of what else is known of the period, and whether there is other supporting evidence. These three interrelated aspects of historical thinking will be examined in more detail in Part II. In Part I, we shall consider the ways in which young children may be aware of the past when they begin school, and research in cognitive psychology related to each of the three aspects of historical thinking which suggests the extent to which they may be capable of thinking about the past in a genuinely historical way.

Chapter 1

Understanding change over time

MEASURING THE PASSING OF TIME

The measurement of time involves complex interacting concepts which emerge slowly: concepts of speed, space and number. Our lives are measured in hours and days, which depend on the rotation of the earth on its axis, in months recorded by the moon's orbit of the earth, and in seasons and years, governed by the earth's orbit of the sun.

To the Ancient Greek philosophers, the nature of space, time, matter and motion was deeply problematical. Our everyday conception of time is a product of the scientific world view created in the seventeenth century by Newton, who discovered a theory which relates these concepts. Central to Newton's theory is the hypothesis that material bodies move through space along predictable paths subject to forces which accelerate them in accordance with strict mathematical laws. Therefore, Newton wrote that absolute true and mathematical time, of itself and from its own nature, flows equably without relation to anything external. This was time told by cosmic clockwork, the time by which motion was to be gauged and events determined. This is the basis of our preoccupation with precision time-keeping. After Newton, time became more than merely our stream of consciousness; it began to play a fundamental role in our description of the physical world. Newton did for time what the Greeks did for space: he abstracted it into a measurable dimension. Journeys of exploration in the seventeenth century required accurate clocks in order to determine longitude, so the tyranny of the clock began. Three centuries later we have atomic clocks accurate to a billionth of a second and satellite navigation which can pinpoint a boat to within metres. As a result we can now see that Newton's image of time, though suitable for most human purposes and still the basis of commonsense reality, is flawed. Newton showed that time is mathematical and measurable, but time is also relative to the observer's frame of reference. My time and your time may be similar but they are not identical. If I live at the top of a high building, my time runs slightly faster than yours.

Piaget (1956) investigated children's developing understanding of the measurement of time. He showed how developing concepts of speed, space and time interact. In one experiment children were asked to draw a succession of pictures showing water pouring from one container into another container below. He found the first competence to emerge was the ability to match pictures of water in the upper and lower containers and to put the pictures in order showing an understanding of events occurring in ordered succession. Next, children understood that the drop in one container and the rise in the other took the same amount of time to occur; they could understand a scale for measuring the passing of time. At the third stage Piaget found that children could understand that events can occur at the same time, and also that units of time can be added together. Only then could they understand the measurement of time in equal intervals. In other experiments he showed that children had to reach a certain developmental level before they could understand that if two trains enter tunnels of different lengths and emerge at the same time, the train travelling through the longer tunnel must be faster, or that if two snails take an equal time to move along tracks which begin and end at parallel points the snail moving along a bending path must move faster than the snail on a straight path.

Children only learn gradually that time can be measured using standard scales of equal intervals: minutes and hours, days, years and centuries. It has often been assumed that young children are not interested in the past because they cannot measure time. Yet their ability to understand that time can be measured develops, piecemeal, through relating their subjective experience of the passing of time to standard scales of hours, days and years. In fact, children are immersed in concepts of time. They are part of their developing identity and must be nurtured. Days have patterns, passing years are marked by birthdays, seasons remembered in relation to festivals, holidays and weather.

However, concepts of time are subjective and cultural. They depend on children's experiences, on language and opportunities to listen to and talk about stories and rhymes concerned with the passing of time and with other times, and to relate events in their own lives to the passing of time: 'When I am 5 I will go to school', 'When I was 2 our baby was born', 'My birthday was in June, last summer', 'The bus will come in half an hour.' Awareness of past times depends, too, on the family unit and on where the children live and how long they have lived there. Few children today live with adults extending over several generations, or among furniture and ornaments from previous generations. Often they have recently moved to new estates, or from another part of the world. Bernot and Blancard (1953) showed that people who have lived all their lives in a community where the people and way of life have changed little have an awareness of time which goes beyond their personal experience; they remember older people's shared tales of events, buildings, occupations and folk memories from before their own times. People who have moved into the community from different places have less sense of the past because they do not have shared memories which are related to their present environment.

Not all children are surrounded by physical remains of the past which are also part of their present in the way that George Mackay Brown so poetically describes in Orkney.

> There are stories in the air here. . . . These islands are a microcosm of the world. They've been continuously lived in for about 6000 years, and the layers of cultures and races are inescapable and unavoidable wherever you go. . . . History has not been parcelled up into Heritage in Orkney. The past is the present.
>
> (*The Times*, 25 July 1992)

Understanding of the relationship between subjective time and measured time develops through understanding other dimensions of the concept of time – chronological sequences, duration, changes over time, similarities and differences between now and past times – and the vocabulary of time.

CHRONOLOGICAL SEQUENCES

Piaget (1952) traced children's ability to place objects in numerical sequence and to recognise ordinal numbers. If this competence is applied to an historical context, before they start school children are becoming able to sequence events in their own lives, and possibly artefacts and photographs related to their own experience, and to retell stories in chronological sequence, recognising conventions such as 'once upon a time' and 'they all lived happily every after'. When Susan Mead read her nursery class a story in which the teddy said, 'You have to come from somewhere to have a family,' 4-year-old Adam spontaneously remarked, 'Everyone has a life story. It means when you're a baby it starts.' She followed this by suggesting that the children made their own 'family snakes'. She wrote the name of each family member on a flag and asked the children to stick them into plasticine snakes, in order, from the oldest to the youngest. Although the flags had no clear order Adam, for instance, grouped the 'nanny' flags together and insisted on a flag at the other end of his snake for the unborn baby.

Holdaway (1979: 62–3) showed how pre-school children, through shared bed-time reading, try to repeat and retell the sequences of events in a story with increasing self-conviction. They develop the ability to follow a plot describing events over time and learn to create images which have not been experienced in sensory reality, perhaps because they belong to other times: city gates, cinders, pitch-forks, pumps. Waterland (1985) described a sequence in children's ability to retell stories which precedes decoding text. At first the child listens to the story and watches the pictures, then listens to the story and observes the text. Next, the child tells the story with the adult. When children know a story well, they will 'make up' the story, at first without accurate recall, then with more accurate retelling and finally with complete accuracy. Children can also relate, poetically, the passing of time to standard units of time through nursery rhymes.

> A sunshiney shower
> Will last half an hour.

> Rain before seven
> Fine before eleven.

> March winds, April showers
> Bring forth May flowers.

> Monday's child is fair of face . . .

> Solomon Grundy, born on Monday . . .

Old nursery rhymes are part of our heritage – a primary source – and in a rapidly changing world it is satisfying to hand them down. 'We feel part of human progression as we see our children swept into the dance as we were before them' (Butler 1988: 70).

DURATION

Smith and Tomlinson (1977) found that children of 8 could not compare intervals of time in the past because they did not recognise the need for an independent calendar scale. They had little understanding of what is meant by 'a long time' or 'a short time' and would equate an interval of time with the number of events, wars or kings and queens linked to it. However, more research needs to be done. It seems likely that much younger children can compare intervals of time if they are given a time line marked in equal intervals, particularly if their first experience of time lines is linked to events in their own lives.

CAUSES AND EFFECTS OF CHANGES OVER TIME

Crowther (1982), investigating concepts of change in children between 7 and 11, found that they regarded change only as a result of a direct action or as the substitution of one thing for another, taking little account of the time factor. But again the focus of the research was on older children, and the material they were asked to respond to was unlikely to produce a refined analysis of very young children's understanding of changes over time: of cause and effect, of motive, or of different kinds of change. More research is needed. However, young children's understanding of stories shows that they are able to discuss how people's behaviour influences events. They ask questions and make predictions; they learn grammatical structures (if . . . then). Children between 2 and 3 years old learn about cause and effect, motives and rules through stories with consistent and dependable characters which move steadily towards a predictable out-come. Peter Rabbit is told in precise Victorian parlour language not to go into Mr McGregor's garden, and ignores the advice with predictable consequences. Rosie the Hen (Hutchins 1973) is almost overtaken at every point on her walk through the farmyard by the fox but, in her case, behaviour which ignores the rules just avoids the predicted effect in the end. By 3 years old, many children enjoy more complex stories and enjoy shades of meaning. They use the word 'perhaps' and they ask why people did things. They may begin with stories in which rigid rules apply and those in peril ultimately emerge safely ('The Three Bears' or 'The Billy Goats Gruff'). In these stories, motive is important; Goldilocks is curious and the billy goats go up the hill 'to get fat'. Between 4 and 5 years old, children begin to see things from points of view other than their own and to share the hopes, joys and fears of others. Gradually they develop greater insights about people. Although fairy stories are not about historical characters, they develop in children the ability to consider motives, causes and effects, which can later be transferred to myths and legends, heroes and heroines and to stories about people who really lived and events which really happened.

Harpin (1976) showed how growing maturity in children's syntax reflects their increasing ability to use conjunctions related to time, and to cause and effect, instead of 'and'. 'Autumn came and the leaves fell' becomes 'because the autumn came the leaves fell'. Instead of 'he finished work and went to bed' they may say, 'after he finished work he went to bed'.

However, Donaldson (1978) showed that young children are often prepared to accept, and not to question, illogical situations; they need to be encouraged to question the sequence and causes and effects of events in a story.

SIMILARITY AND DIFFERENCE BETWEEN PAST AND PRESENT

Piaget (1952) showed how children learn to form sets of objects with shared characteristics. The process will be discussed in the section on the language of time (p. 12). In the context of history it means that children can begin to sort 'old' and 'new' and to discuss the reasons for putting an object into either set.

When Susan Mead read her nursery class the story about an old teddy this led to a discussion about which of two dolls was the older. The children concluded that the older doll must be the one with 'the china head and a body full of fluff' because the other doll had 'a plastic head. A long time ago they didn't have plastic.'

Children from 2 years old or earlier can become curious about how the past was different through illustrated nursery rhyme books. Greenaway illustrations (1991) introduce children to worlds where people wear clothes which are different from their own: long dresses, buttoned breeches, feathered bonnets and mob caps. Their toys are different: hobby horses, skipping ropes, fishing lines and see-saws. They are gently introduced to the occupations of a rural pre-industrial society:

> Down to the meadow to milk the cow . . .

> Elsie Marley has grown so fine
> She won't get up to feed the swine . . .

> Little Bo Peep has lost her sheep . . .

They learn about bakers, and pipers, and chimney-sweeps. And they are introduced to the vocabulary of other times: looking-glass, Sabbath, scholar, parlour.

THE LANGUAGE OF TIME

Learning about the past involves learning vocabulary which is to some extent specific to history. Blyth (1990) pointed out that there is no clear agreement about what is meant by 'historical concepts'. Some are concerned with recording the passing of time (year, decade, generation, century), or with changes over time (old, new, the same, different, cause, effect). Some concepts describe the shared characteristics of periods of time (Roman, Victorian). Some concepts describe organising ideas which run through all societies and which are not exclusively historical (agriculture, trade, communication, beliefs). Others describe buildings, technology or groups of people belonging to former times (castle, villa; galleon, spinning wheel; Roundhead, knight). There are also concepts concerned with the processes of interpreting sources.

A concept may be a noun or an adjective, a verb or an adverb. It is a word, a symbol, which represents groups of objects or ideas which have one or more shared attributes. Some concepts are concrete; they refer to objects which can be borne in mind as images or as specific examples (king, castle). Other concepts are abstract (ruler, defence) and depend on an understanding of subordinate concrete concepts.

Children learn concepts not through ready-made definitions but by learning, in an active, problem-solving way, through trial and error and through discussion, to abstract their shared characteristics. In this way they gradually refine their concepts. Vygotsky (1962) showed the sequence in which concepts develop. At first, objects and ideas are linked by chance (all stone buildings are castles). At the second stage, they are linked by a characteristic which can change as new information is added (all castles are built on a mound, until we see one built on a cliff; all castles have a rectangular keep until we see one with round towers). Gradually pseudo-concepts develop which are deduced from context but are still unstable (a castle is a fort; a castle is a lord's big home; a castle has a moat). Children's and adults' words may coincide, but the child may be thinking of the concept in a different way from the adult (a castle was built to keep the baddies out; a castle represents feudal social structure). At the final stage, it is possible to formulate a rule which establishes a relationship between concepts and so creates an abstract idea (a castle is the fortified home of a feudal lord).

If children sort objects into 'old' and 'new', at the first stage they may not be able to offer any explanation for their groupings, which are random. At the next stage they may make sets of worn objects and of undamaged objects, but the defining attribute will have to change when a pristine object, which is known to be very old, is introduced. They may redefine the sets as 'things which are precious' and 'things which are not precious' until the teacher explains why her old threadbare teddy is very precious to her. Finally, the children may agree on a shared attribute for the 'old' and the 'new' sets, such as 'the old things are all older than we are', and 'the new things were made in our life-time'. Concepts of time are particularly difficult to engage with because they are relative, and subjective. People of different ages have different concepts of an old person, a long time or long ago. Yesterday and tomorrow can only be defined by an abstract rule.

Klausmeier *et al.* (1979) showed how concrete tangible concepts are learnt through verbal labelling and through storing images; children become increasingly able to recognise similarities and differences.

They may, for example, increasingly extend and refine their concept of a castle by first visiting a castle, then collecting pictures of castles built in different places and in different periods, and discussing the similarities and differences between them. They may explore the concept of 'prince' by listening to stories, true and fictitious, about good princes and bad, strong and weak, powerful and powerless, who lived in different times and places.

Children may be introduced to the abstract, organising concepts which run through all societies, and to the subordinate concepts related to them, through myths, legends and folk tales, for these stories revolve around central ideas: power and social organisation, beliefs, trade, journeys, communication, agriculture.

Research has shown that children learn new concepts best when they are selected, used and discussed (Vygotsky 1962). Language is the tool for unlocking the past. Children need to discuss, explain and justify with each other and with adults the reasons for the chronological sequences they form, to suggest the causes and effects of changes the sequences represent, to explain and refine the categories they form and the similarities and differences between examples – between a windmill they have visited and other examples seen in pictures. They need to discuss vocabulary used in stories. Donaldson (1978) found that young children rarely question new vocabulary; what is meant by 'fair' or 'brave'? In their play, too, they need to explore and use the new concepts they have been introduced to in stories.

Virginia Hunt, a student, described how her son, aged 2 years and 8 months, enjoyed *Bill and Pete Go Down the Nile* (de Paolo 1988). He repeatedly asked to have it read to him and questioned the alternative meaning of 'mummy'. On each reading he remembered and identified the sarcophagus and the sphinx. Given a selection of books about the past, he chose a book on Ancient Egypt and searched for a sarcophagus, then pointed out sarcophagi and sphinxes in other books! This is an excellent example of how to use children's experience of stories as a familiar foundation from which to explore new concepts related to other times.

As children get older, language becomes increasingly important in refining concepts. What kind of soldier is he? What type of wood, or metal or fabric is it made from? What was it used for? If it was used to make work easier it is a tool. If it was used for fighting it is a weapon.

THE CONCEPT OF TIME

In helping young children to be curious about and to find out about the past, how important is a concept of time? Certainly, children's understanding of the relationship between subjective and measured time develops slowly. Their knowledge of the past and experience of time is limited. The measurement of time involves complex concepts. Concepts of time change with age and circumstance.

However, Lello (1980) argued that a grasp of chronology and the fixing of events in context and time are not synonymous with developing an understanding of past times. Certainly, many games devised to teach children about chronological sequence would not seem to develop their understanding of the past at all.

This game will not a little contribute to make the Players acquainted with the Genealogy of their own kings. We hope the young Player will not think much of Exercising his Memory to Acquire a Perfect Knowledge of it.

('The Royal Genealogical Pastime of the Sovereigns of England', published by Edward Wallis, London, 1791)

Marbeau (1988) argued that a child of 6 has a very narrow and discontinuous grasp of his own duration: 'History at first is historicisation of a child's own existence.' Children build continuity into their existence by reciting it to others (and to themselves). However, difficulty with the measurement of time does not impair children's interest in history. Marbeau saw this as a reflection of their interest in 'the problem of origins'. One 6-year-old, Lisa, constantly asked her mother, a student history teacher, to repeat the order in which their household had come together (mum, cat, dad, dog, Lisa), but remained confused by the fact that dad was clearly older than the cat. A time-line helped, but Lisa continued to believe that she would eventually be the same age as her mother. She still talked about things she did quite recently as 'When I was a baby', but told stories about things which had happened some time ago as recent events. A video recording of all her birthdays helped her to sequence events in her own life.

Penelope Lively, who is a history graduate as well as a novelist, wrote poetically about how a child's sense of time is different from that of an adult.

> He [the father] perceived in an instant the perpetual flow of childhood, the interminable present from which, eventually, we escape, and which we can never retrieve. We cohabit with these mysterious beings who occupy a different time zone, who share our days, and move with us through them, but whose vision is that of aliens.
>
> (Lively 1991: 183)

Yet even for adults, time is not always best understood on a chronological, equal interval scale, and it is sometimes possible to feel closer to people long dead than when they were alive.

> Time present and time past
> Are both perhaps present in time future
> And time future contained in time past.
>
> (from 'Burnt Norton', in Eliot 1986)

A fascination with time runs through all Shakespeare's writing. In different ways, time permeates all cultures. The Jamaican poet Dennis Scott (1986) wrote:

> Uncle Time is a spider-man, cunnin' an' cool,
> him tell you: watch de hill an' yu se mi.
> Huh! Fe yu yi no quick enough fe si
> how 'im move like mongoose; man, yu tink 'im fool?
> . . .
> Watch how 'im spin web roun' yu house, an' creep
> inside, an' when 'im touch you, weep . . .

Or, in the words of a popular Bengali song:

> This bank erodes
> Another bank emerges:
> Such are the whims of the river.
> You are a wealthy *Amir* in the morning
> A penniless *Fakir* in the evening
> Such are the whims of the river.

It is not surprising that children get confused. Of course chronology and dates and measured time are central to history as a discipline, but for young children whose understanding of time is embryonic, a curiosity and excitement about other people, other lives and other times are more important than dates.

Chapter 2

Interpretations of the past

Historians write different accounts of the past. They differ because of the preoccupations of the age in which they live, because of their own interests and perspectives, and because historical evidence is frequently incomplete. There is no single correct view of the past. We all reconstruct our own views of the past, depending on our knowledge, political stance, class, race, gender and interests. Doing so enables us to reflect on our own position in relation to the present and to the past.

Selecting, piecing together and interpreting evidence in order to construct an account of the past requires imagination. Trevelyan (1919) said that at bottom the appeal of history is imaginative; truth is the criterion of historical study but its impelling motive is poetic. Elton (1970) saw historical imagination as a tool for filling in the gaps when facts are not available. Lee (1984) defined it more precisely as the disposition to make a range of valid suppositions based on evidence. Historians do not aim to identify with people in the past or to project themselves into the past because this is not possible, but they attempt to understand and explain on the basis of likely possibilities the thoughts and feelings which underpinned the actions and behaviour of people in the past. This is difficult because people in the past had attitudes and values different from our own, because of their different knowledge bases and the different political, social and economic constraints within which they lived.

Young children can begin to understand why there may be more than one version of a story about the past. In order to do so they need opportunities to create their own interpretations, based on what they know, and to see how and why they may differ.

UNDERSTANDING INTERPRETATIONS

Piaget (1956) suggested that young children are incapable of holding more than one perspective at a time. This implies that they cannot compare two different versions of a story. Others have said, however, that their ability to see a situation from more than one viewpoint depends on how involved they are, and on their understanding of a situation.

Donaldson (1978), Borke (1978) and Flavell (1985) found that children are capable of seeing more than one viewpoint but that they do not often see the need to do so. Recent research has differentiated between visual perspective-taking, conversational role-taking and pictorial representation, and in each instance young children appear to be underestimated. Cox (1986) said that in their verbal interactions, young children do develop inferences concerning the points of view of others, although more research is needed. It will be interesting, then, to investigate to what extent they are able to recognise different versions of a story, different illustrations of the same story, or a story told from different perspectives, and whether they can explain what is the same and what is different. Two-year-olds can learn that there are different versions of stories and nursery rhymes. A traditional *Mother Goose Treasury* with Victorian-style illustrations (Hague 1984) contrasts strongly with the purples and scarlets of Brian Wildsmith's (1987) *Mother Goose*, and with the meticulous dignity and quiet colour of Katherine Line's *Lavender's Blue* (1989). Nursery rhymes translated into different languages can be compared (Chinese nursery rhymes, translated into eight languages, from Haringey Multicultural Resource Centre, see p. 193), or different versions in bilingual books (e.g. Wasu 1986). In *Mother Goose Comes to Cable Street* (Stones and Mann 1987) English nursery rhymes are brilliantly illustrated in the context of contemporary East London street scenes; traditional pictures of 'I do not like thee, Dr. Fell' can be compared with amusing pictures of a doctor's waiting room today. In *The Baby's Catalogue* (Ahlberg 1984) the babies illustrate the similarities and differences in the lives of five different families. Young children could make comparisons between the experience of a baby in their own family and in their friends' families.

Thomas (1993) showed how nursery-age children can detect contradictory meanings in books. She introduced children who had previous experience of browsing and talking about illustrations to books which explicitly invite the reader to find meanings in pictures which are different from those in the text, for example, *If at First You Do not See* (Brown 1982), *Lights On, Lights Off* (Taylor 1988). Then they progressed to books where text and pictures do not conform: *Time to Get Out of the Bath, Shirley* (Burningham 1985), *Not Now Bernard* (McKee 1980), *Rosie's Walk* (Hutchins 1973), *Never Satisfied* (Testa 1982). In the text of *Never Satisfied*, children constantly restate how boring everything is while the pictures show all kinds of incredible happenings: a woman tightrope-walking on a washing line and monsters appearing over walls. The seven children listening to the story all insisted that there *were* things happening but the characters didn't appear to notice. Cameron said that much of the story was unseen. The children only paused when the pictures became ambiguous, showing the characters' eyes apparently directed at unseen events. This caused Thomas to re-examine her own preconceptions; is the story about people who do not look, or about looking but not seeing, or about seeing but not being impressed? Thomas found that the children could recognise and discuss contradictory meanings irrespective of their ability to decode the text, that being able to read between the lines includes the recognition of different possible interpretations of meaning, and that adults should be wary of imposing their own presuppositions on children. She concluded that children need to hear alternative versions of the same story in fiction and later to be aware that different newspapers may present conflicting accounts of 'the truth', as do different historians and different scientists.

> Nursery-aged children are not too young to be offered play and literary experiences that will help them to develop the ability to look for alternative views and viewpoints later in their development, and to start to think about character and motive.
>
> (Thomas 1993)

CREATING INTERPRETATIONS

Through 'let's pretend' imaginative play children, alone or together, can create their own interpretations of past times, based on stories, visits and pictures. There is no single, all-embracing explanation of what or how children learn through play, but each theory suggests different ways in which play can help children to interpret the past.

At the beginning of this century play was seen as a way in which a child reproduces the early experiences of humanity: wandering tribes, hunting, war, building shelters and fighting. Certainly shelters, tree-houses, tents, caves, defending the 'hide-out' and preparing food often feature in spontaneous play.

Bruner saw play as a means of exploring the uses of basic technology. Free play often involves, for example, making castles (making moats and dams and bridges, moving loads with carts and pulleys), sailing boats, exploring materials central to human societies (wood, stone, metal, wool, leather, synthetic materials), and taking things apart to see how they work and what they are used for.

Others have stressed the psychodynamic nature of play. This may involve exploring relationships changing over time within the family unit, for example, as a new baby is born, or coping with the loss of a grandparent. It may involve exploring motives, a family decision to move house for example. Such play could explore stories told about what life was like when grandparents were young, or re-enacting stories from other cultures. These may all be ways of relating what children find meaningful and significant in their own lives to changes over time, and to life in other times and places.

Erikson (1965) found that if children were asked to reconstruct exciting scenes from folk tales through 'let's pretend' play, the stories they acted out seemed to be metaphors for their own lives, concerns and interests. Such play, he said, helps children to engage with the mainstream of human emotions in the context of times and places other than their own.

Winnicott (Bruce 1991: 77) suggested that adults are able to relate to powerful events, hero figures, music and paintings as part of the external world if they have related to them and merged with what is important to them, through play. Singer and Singer (1990) traced a continuum between such childhood play, fantasy in adolescence and creativity in adult life.

In imaginative 'let's pretend' play, then, children reconstruct their own versions of stories (Warlow 1977: 93). Play about stories from the past involves experimental dialogue about materials, places and people in other times (Garvey 1977: 32). It allows children to explore emotions, attitudes, relationships and situations outside their direct experience. They can make 'suppositions' about alternative worlds which are imaginative, creative and innovative. Such play brings together what children already know, feel and understand and allows them to explore situations which they will not meet in their real lives until later.

Moyles (1989) suggested that play in the context of a pretend castle, an old kitchen, a Victorian classroom for dolls, a palace or a workplace helps children both to understand themselves and their own self-worth, and also explore what it might have been like to be somebody else. The ability to pretend helps children to learn about something without experiencing it for themselves. Through role-play children can wear different 'hats' in different situations, imitate gestures, movements and expressions, and explore what it might have been like to wear a hooped skirt or knee breeches, to milk a cow or ride a horse. They can investigate what it might feel like to use a flat iron, scrub a floor, sight a new land from a crow's nest or keep watch from the battlements. A child looks in the mirror and fits, in manner and gesture, the picture in the mirror. Garvey (1977) found that re-enactments are created from concepts of appropriate behaviour and are most likely not direct imitations of people.

Children who have heard stories about the past spontaneously re-construct them in play. A student described how a 3-year-old who had seen a film about Robin Hood on television continued long afterwards to re-enact whole scenes in solitary play, quoting verbatim and with great relish such phrases as 'Seize the fat one!'. Younger children in a group often find themselves in the play without knowing too much about it but the older children negotiate in advance a general script or statement, then 'tell them the story'. Bruce (1991) described how a group of 5-year-olds heard stories about the Black Prince and about King Arthur which led to extensive play about princes and princesses. On another occasion, Hannah, aged 5, and Tom, aged 3, used a rough script based on the story of George and the Dragon as an agenda for play. Children's toys can stimulate stories about the past which will extend their play. Bruce (1991) showed how one teacher added wings to 4-year-old Sukvinder's 'My Little Pony' and used it as a prop to tell children the story of Pegasus. Although the children were under no pressure to take up the myth, they were enthralled by it and it reappeared in free-flow play and in their paintings. From the age of 2 children, in their play, can take on a role, create a context, use symbols and negotiate a narrative. They are able to exist in two worlds, the real and the imaginary, at the same time, by creating symbols which are the pivot between the two worlds: a table may become a cave or a horse.

Play stimulates language development, clarifying new words and concepts, motivating language use and encouraging verbal thinking, for language cannot occur in a vacuum. It is about the reconstruction of meaning. In play children can make inferences about behaviour, consider alternatives and probability, and use different tenses and complex sentences related to causes and effects. Such language is essential in the development of historical thinking. Sources can tell us nothing about the past until we know how to interpret them and how to communicate our interpretations.

Of course children's imaginative play, stimulated by stories about the past, or by a visit to a sailing ship or a castle, has very little in common with the processes by which historians construct accounts of the past. Genuine historical imagination depends on careful consideration of what seems likely in the light of known evidence. This requires both the maturity to consider how adults in the past may have felt, thought and behaved, and extensive knowledge of the times in which they lived. Historians do not project themselves into a past time, or identify with people in the past. They can only try to explain the past with circumspection and humility (Cooper 1992: 136–7). Young children have neither the maturity, nor the knowledge, nor the circumspection to do this in a way that is historically valid. Links with evidence, with what is known, are slight and play is dominated by fantasy rather than by genuine historical imagination. However, in play, children do attempt to identify with people in the past and to project themselves into past times. In play set in an historical context, children are, in an embryonic way, embarking on the process of finding out about and trying to understand and reconstruct past times. This can be the beginning of a continuum in which, with maturity, fantasy will gradually diminish and a search for what is known will become increasingly important.

Chapter 3

Deductions and inferences from sources

Historians find out about the past through asking questions and making inferences about sources which remain: buildings, sites, pictures, artefacts and written sources. How was it made? Why? How was it used? What did it mean to the people who made and used it? Sources are often incomplete, and their status may be unknown. (For example, was the bone pendant in a bronze age grave an ornament or symbolic object?) Therefore it may be possible to make a number of different and equally valid inferences about a source. Inferences are valid if they conform with what else is known of the period and if they assume that people in the past acted rationally. It is necessary to support inferences with arguments and also to listen to the arguments of others. To what extent, then, are young children able to make valid inferences about historical sources, to support their inferences with arguments, and to listen to each other's suggestions?

INFERENTIAL THINKING

According to Piaget's posited sequence in cognitive development, the thinking of young children is dominated by trial and error and by their own experiences and feelings. Gradually they take in more information about the tangible and visible world, sometimes needing to adjust their own mental patterns to accommodate new information. Piaget (1951) traced the development of children's increasing awareness of what can be known and what can be reasonably supposed. Through his work on language (1926) and on logic (1928) a pattern in the development of argument can be traced. At first the child is not concerned with interesting or convincing others and leaps from a premise to an unreasonable conclusion in one bound. Next the child tries to communicate intellectual processes which are factual and descriptive and show incipient logic, but these are not clearly expressed. This leads to a valid statement of fact or description. From this follows 'primitive argument' in which the statement or opinion is followed by a deduction going beyond the information given, but the explanation for the deduction is only implicit. At the next stage, the child tries to justify and demonstrate the assertion using a conjunction ('therefore' or 'because'), but does not succeed in expressing a truly logical relationship. Eventually, through frequent attempts to justify his or her own opinion and avoid contradiction, and also as a result of internal debate, a child is able to use 'therefore' or 'because' correctly, and to relate an argument to its premise. Others have found that children's capacity for deductive and inferential thinking is influenced by their interest and involvement, and by their understanding of what kind of thinking is required.

Donaldson (1978) examined the dichotomy she recognised between children's capacity for deductive reasoning in informal, everyday situations and Piaget's conclusion that children under 7 have little reasoning ability. She found that young children are capable of deductive reasoning, that their problem-solving depends on the extent to which they can concentrate on language, and that language development is related to other non-verbal clues which are also brought to bear on problem-solving. She found that children find reasoning difficult because they rarely spontaneously discuss the meanings of words, they are easily distracted and they do not always select relevant terms in problem-solving. She concluded that their level of deductive and inferential thinking depends on whether the reasoning stems from the children's immediate concerns, or whether it is externally imposed. It also depends on the child's expectation of what the questioner wants.

Wright (1984) found that 7-year-olds could draw their own conclusions from pottery finds and there is evidence that 8-year-olds can learn to make complex inferences about artefacts, pictures, archaeological plans, maps and written sources (Cooper 1991).

So far, however, there has been no systematic study of younger children's ability to make inferences about historical sources. But there is increasing awareness that young children can ask questions about artefacts from everyday life in the past which involve looking, listening, touching and smelling. *Under Fives and Museums* (Ironbridge Gorge Museum Trust) gives useful suggestions about how the Ironbridge Gorge Museum site can be used to help pre-school children make deductions and inferences about the past. Donaldson (1978) argued that they must be helped to make inferences, and to understand the nature of different disciplines, as early as possible, in order to recognise the abstraction of language.

DISCUSSION

Dialogue which allows children to make deductions and inferences, to speculate, to consider possibilities and accept that there may be no single right answer, to discuss causes and effects and to retell stories is essential for the development of historical understanding. Lee (1984) suggested that the capacity to generate a number of suggestions makes mature historical imagination possible.

Some pre-school children have more opportunities for interactive dialogue than others. Much has been written about the importance of spoken language and social interaction from birth (e.g. Bruner 1983). Doise (1975, 1978) saw cognitive growth as the result of either conflict of viewpoint or of interaction at different cognitive levels, although no sensitive measures for assessing the effect of social interaction on cognition have been achieved. Light (1983) concluded that there will be rapid development in our understanding of these issues.

Most children have more opportunities at home than they do in school to talk to an adult one-to-one, to ask open-ended questions and to initiate discussion, because in school there is a different ratio of children to adults and different social relationships. Maclure and French (1986) found that children are more likely to correct their parents than their teachers. However, there is more continuity between patterns of language interaction at home and in school than has sometimes been assumed. Both parents and teachers sometimes ask closed questions to which they know the answers in order to monitor children's understanding: 'After spring it will be . . . ?' After summer it will be . . . ?' 'So how many seasons are there altogether?' (Wells 1986). But in school, children are also encouraged to make suggestions. Maclure and French (1986) found that teachers are more likely than parents to want children to offer alternative interpretations, rather than to correct them. Often they do this by making a general statement, then asking individual children a series of questions related to it. This requires on-going attention in order to participate and so to share ideas. They may begin with a question about the physical environment which will produce a positive response, then extend the discussion. Or they may begin with a shared experience: 'Did you look inside?' 'What did you see?'

Children need to learn the kinds of questions to ask and appropriate ways of answering them, and to take turns. There is evidence that if they do, their talk among themselves may be more dense, discursive and reflective than when an adult is present (Prisk 1987).

Open-ended discussion in the school, then, can build on and extend patterns of interactive language at home, so that children gradually learn to talk to each other in a purposeful and focused way, without continuous adult support. They learn to share ideas about how artefacts or buildings may have been made and used, and how they may have affected people's lives, and to make up and compare stories which may explain pictures, photographs, artefacts or statues.

Part II

History during the first three years of school

In Part I it was argued that when children start school they are already capable, in an embryonic way, of historical thinking. They have some awareness of the passing of time, of causes and effects in sequences of events, and of differences between present and past times. They are able to recognise and to construct different interpretations of stories. They are capable of deductive reasoning in informal situations.

In Part II, we shall consider how teachers can build, in a structured way, on the embryonic capacity for historical thinking and the awareness of the past which children already have when they come to school. Each of the strands of historical thinking introduced in Part I will be examined in turn, although it is important to remember that they interact; they are not discrete and they need to be learnt through coherent activities related to a particular theme (discussion of how this may be done is in Part III). First, we shall consider how we may develop children's understanding of concepts of change, then how we can help children to learn how and why accounts of the past may be different and, finally, we shall explore how children can learn to find out about the past from sources, the traces of the past which remain.

Since state education was introduced, the nature of history as a discipline has evolved, the rationale for history in education has changed and our understanding of the ways in which children learn in general has increased. However, limitations in recent practice have been identified which show that these developments have not generally been reflected in the teaching of history to young children. Provision has been uneven and progression in children's understanding has been difficult to sustain and monitor. An HMI survey found that historical material is often introduced incidentally into the curriculum of children (4–7) or it arises in an unplanned way (DES 1989c). Themes such as 'Our Village' or 'People who Help Us', 'Homes', 'Customs', 'Leisure' and 'Transport' are recurrent, but activities associated with them rarely make children aware of aspects of the past. The survey found that occasionally historical material comes from 'news' or television programmes, or is associated with important local or national events, but is therefore intermittent and sometimes limited in scope. Few teachers see the potential of selected themes for introducing historical material into the activities provided for young children and for building up with them an historical picture which has relevance and meaning.

Where work of quality has been found (DES 1989b) it has been identified as dependent on documentation with clear aims, in terms of teachers' understanding of the nature of historical thinking and how this can be related to and build upon children's existing knowledge and understanding, through active learning.

Chapter 4

Teaching children to understand concepts of time and change

History in the National Curriculum requires children at Key Stage 1 to learn about chronological sequence, motive and causation, and similarities and differences between now and past times, and to use language associated with the passing of time. During the first three years of school, they should learn to recount episodes from stories of the past, to sequence events and objects, and begin to develop an awareness that the past is divided into periods of time. Children are expected to consider the reasons why people in the past behaved as they did, and to identify reasons for historical events or developments. They are expected to make distinctions between past and present in their own and in other people's lives, then to begin to recognise similarities and differences between different periods in the past.

Yet it was argued in Part I that understanding standard measurements of time and relating them to subjective understanding is complex and piecemeal. It is a broadening rather than a hierarchical process. There are many levels within each of the National Curriculum statements of attainment and the statements are not hierarchical. Children gradually build up a map of the past which is constantly changing as new information and new processes are added. It is a map which children carry in their heads just as they build up a map of their locality in their heads. This militates against the easy view of a chronological map as a framework of facts. The more a chronological framework becomes merely a framework of 'basic facts', the less it will be used and remembered. If children are to be genuinely equipped with a chronological map, they also need a set of themes and concepts for handling the past.

A recent television programme offered a good example of how 6- to 7-year-olds can learn procedural concepts of history, cause and effect, continuity and change, similarity and difference in the context of a theme they could assimilate into their own, existing chronological maps ('Watch, Forty Years On', BBC TV 1990). The film showed evidence of changes typical in many localities since the 1950s: bomb sites replaced by new flats, Victorian schools by modern buildings, the corner shop by the supermarket. West Indians were seen leaving their Caribbean islands to look for work in Britain. The *causes* of these changes were explained: new materials and inventions led to new styles of building and of home decoration, and to new household appliances. The 'baby boom' after the war led to more schools being built. West Indians came to Britain because they were needed to work on trains and buses and in hospitals. Children had the opportunity to consider the different *effects* of these changes. Gran explained why she did not think the new supermarket was an improvement while mum appreciated the benefits of the washing machine. Two West Indian women talked of their contrasting feelings when they first came to Britain. Children, too, reacted to change in different ways; when a girl discovered a book called *Electricity for Boys* she said with incredulity, 'Surely they would share it?' The programme ended with a question which challenged the children to continue to discuss *continuity and change, similarities and differences*: 'Holidays are still the same, aren't they?'

Research has suggested that understanding historical time is dependent on an understanding of personal, clock and calendar time. Jahoda (1963) and Friedman (1978) suggested that children of about 4 years old become aware of time through events specific to themselves and to people in their immediate surroundings; the past and present are differentiated by words such as 'before', 'after', 'now' and 'then'. At about 5, events are ordered into earlier and later ones, and the succession of events becomes apparent. Harner (1982) showed that understanding these words depended on an understanding of the varied linguistic structures for the past tense, and also of adverbs such as 'yesterday', 'before', 'already', and 'last week'. Thornton and Vukelich (1988) found that between 4 and 6 years old, children begin to order daily routines chronologically, from early morning until bedtime. Bradley (1947) identified a third 'time distinction', beginning at 6 or 7 years when 'clock' time skills appear to develop from larger to smaller units (hour, to minute, to second), while 'calendar' time appears to work in reverse (from days, to weeks, to months).

The activities in Box 4.1 will help to develop children's understanding of the measurement of time and relate this to chronological sequences, to the causes and effects of changes they represent, and to similarities and differences between now and past times. Concepts central to investigating changes over time are discussed. However, since there is little research investigating young children's understanding of historical time, the numerous questions arising in planning activities will be discussed in the hope that teachers will approach them in a spirit of genuine enquiry, rather than simply regard them as replicate activities devised as assessment tasks; this could restrict both children's opportunities for real historical enquiry and teachers' professional understanding of children's capabilities.

CHRONOLOGICAL SEQUENCES: CAUSES AND EFFECTS

Children begin to sequence events by describing the pattern of their own lives. Loader (1993) quoted a nursery child, working on a topic on 'Ourselves'.

> I could only crawl when I was tiny. And I can walk when I was a bit older. And when I was 3 I was happy enough. And I didn't drink out of a bottle any more, and I didn't play with rattles any more, and I didn't cuddle toys any more (sometimes I do).

Salma, in year 2, was able to consider not only her own recollections but how her life was linked by her family to other times before she was born, and to other places.

> My Mum's Mum is the oldest person I know. I never got to see my Mum's Dad. He lived in Bangladesh. When I first got here everyone was carrying me because I was so small. My Mum was crying because her Dad had died. I was about 3. . . . Grandads and aunts tell about how things were before you were born. They have photographs . . .

Carl, aged 6, also became aware of past times through the death of a grandparent.

> You can look in the churchyard cemetery – look at the gravestones. My Nan always goes to the cemetery because they built my Grandad a bench and his stone is by his ashes. She's always talking to him. She thinks he's alive.

Describing events in their own lives can help children to describe the sequence of events in stories. This, too, is not straightforward. It depends on the complexity of the story, the number of events, on whether they are clearly sequential, on the complexity of causes and motives, and on a child's ability to recognise and describe these. The text of these 4-page books, in which two reception children retell the story of 'Snow White', record images of key events, but if they see the causal connection between them they do not see the need to make this explicit.

> *Snow White, by S.J.*
> Snow White is in the glass coffin.
> The wicked queen is in the castle.
> Snow White and the Prince got married.

> *Snow White Got Married, by S.G.*
> Snow White ate an apple and fell to the ground.
> Snow White is in a glass coffin.
> Snow White and a prince got married.

Box 4.1 The measurement of time

Units of time	What the children will do	Possible questions
1 Night/day	• Collect and draw or make sets of day-time and night-time pictures (use great paintings, magazines, children's books) • Read and write (picture) stories about getting up and going to bed. Read 'Wintertime' and 'Bed in Summer' (R.L. Stevenson, in Opie and Opie 1973)	• Describe each picture: colours, feelings, activity. How are they the same/different? Why? • What do you do when you get up/go to bed? In what order? Why is it candlelight in the poem? How is the poem the same as/different from what you do? Why is it dark at bedtime in the winter?
2 Day: morning, afternoon, evening	• Sets: things we do in the morning, afternoon, evening • Zig-zag book, 'My Day' • Make cards: getting up, breakfast, going to school, etc. Can you put cards in the right order?	• What does everyone do, and what things do only some people do? • Read your zig-zag book to a grown-up. Ask about their day • Does it matter which order the pictures are in? Is that true for all the pictures? Why not?
3 Days of the week	• Talk about/look at class timetable. Make pictures sequencing activities during a day showing 'Us in PE, assembly', etc. • Rhymes (e.g. Solomon Grundy)	• Are the days all the same? What is different? (Learn days of the week.) What happens today/tomorrow/yesterday/next week/last week? • Make up your own rhyme for days of the week

4 Months of the year	• Make a bar chart or time-line for birthdays each month
	• Learn Victorian rhyme:
	   January brings the snow,
	   makes your feet and fingers glow.
	   February brings the rain,
	   thaws the frozen lake again
	      (Sara Coleridge in Opie and Opie 1973)
	• Look at calendars from different cultures (e.g. Muslim, Chinese) and from different times (e.g. Medieval agricultural calendar)
		• How many birthdays in, e.g. June or in summer?
		• Make up a couplet for this month
		
		• Make your own calendar with pictures for each month. What is the same/different about calendars from other cultures? Why was the 'agricultural' calendar important?

	• Make devices for measuring sun, rain, wind. Keep records	
5 The four seasons	• Collect paintings from different periods showing summer, autumn, winter, spring (e.g. Breughel and Monet snow scenes) • Collect poems about seasons • Make a spinner game • Make a picture showing seasons (four groups?), e.g. a picture of a familiar tree in each season • Make a collection of clothes for each season • Design dolls' clothes for each season	• Are all the pictures of winter the same? How are they the same/different? What comes before/after/next? • How do you know which season this is about? • When it lands on summer, say a word to do with summer before the count of ten. Collect words for word bank • Make up music to go with your picture. Can others match the picture and the music? • Do some things belong to all the seasons? Which? Why? • How do we keep warm/cool?
6 Measuring time	• Make devices for measuring time (sun sticks, sand clocks, water clocks, candle clocks, marble and bagatelle clocks) using non-standard units • Collect instruments for measuring time (digital and analogue clocks, chronometer, sundial, egg-timer)	• Use them to measure time taken, e.g. for a child to wash hands for lunch. Compare them with an egg-timer/stop-watch. Are they reliable? Why not? • How do they work?
7 Standardised units: seconds, minutes, hours	• Devise games: how many times can you run across the playground, jump on the spot, say a word, in 30 seconds? Can you be quiet for 1 minute? Keep records	• Can you guess how many times? Who was fastest, slowest? By how many seconds?
8 Telling the time	• Make timetables and clocks showing times for let's pretend play: house corner shop; bus journey play; doctor's waiting room and surgery time; timetables for pretend police or fire station or any workplace	• When does it open? Close? How long does it take? When will it be open again?

Children in a year 1 class were helped to consider the structure of the story of Cinderella by discussing causes and effects of changes in the story: how did she change? Into what? Why? Was she happier? They wrote a story-board as a class. Then they worked in groups on each stage of the story and made a Big Book. From this they frequently retold and shared the story. This led to discussion about how they would like to change and whether they thought the change would make them happier, and why. This led to work involving other curriculum areas: discussing Cinderella's shoe size, then sequencing their shoes in order of size; dancing at the ball, with a partner, to music; happy and sad role-play; drawing pictures of Cinderella and the Prince in modern clothes and comparing the drawings with traditional illustrations; designing clothes for different occasions; testing the fabrics used for appropriate durability!

Lynn Clarke, a PGCE student, investigated the ability of a group of year 2 children, who were beginning to speak English, to explore the passing of time in relation to family history and to their own lives through story. First, they looked at the pictures in *Once There Were Giants* (Waddell and Dale 1989). These pictures show in sequence the life story of 'me', who is seen as a baby at the beginning of the book and at the end of the book is seen looking after her own baby in the same room, surrounded by the same members of her family, all altered to some extent by the intervening two or three decades. At the end of the story, the children, after some confusion about whether 'me' was the teacher, since she had introduced the session with a picture of herself as a small child, realised that 'me' was both the baby at the beginning of the book and the mother at the end. The extract from their discussion which leads to this conclusion shows how the children gradually focused on the fine details in the two pictures of the 'me' as a baby and as a mother, and discussed the similarities and the differences between them.

Teacher   Are these two pictures the same?
Aminur   Yes.
Teacher   Are you sure?
Aminur   No, there are different people in them.
Teacher   Who is different?
Sehrish   The mum. She had a red jumper and her hair is tied back.
Teacher   Is it the same mum?
All   Yes.
Sehrish   No, it isn't. It's 'ME'! 'Me' is the baby's Mum.
Group   Oh yes – she's grown up hasn't she? [etc.]
Koiesur   That's Uncle Tom. He's still got a beard.
Teacher   That's right. Is there anything else you recognise in the picture?
Aminur   The carpet.
Ayesha   It's a bit pink [faded] now.
Koiesur   There's a mirror on the wall, but it's a bigger mirror.

They went on to discuss the differences in clothes and in hair styles and hair colour; the replacement of cloth nappies by disposable ones, of frilly pants by leggings; and the different styles of lighting. However, Sehrish noticed that the baby's toys, the teddy bear and the rabbit, were still the same.

In a second session, the children read 'Jill's history' (Shutter and Reynoldson 1991). Each page they turned showed Jill as a progressively younger child until in the final picture they saw her mother when she had been pregnant with Jill. This led the children to identify with Jill on each page, and to discuss their own similar experiences, moving sequentially back in time. They talked about their birthday parties, the sequence of teachers since they had begun school, their first day at school, their nursery school experience, shopping as a toddler and playing at home as a baby. Their sense of duration varied; Aminur correctly sequenced all his teachers, the rooms they had been in and the kind of work he had done, from the nursery school to year 2:

> In the nursery we did scribbling and played with water. Now we do writing and read books and do puzzles and play nicely. We did paintings then and we still do painting, but now we do close drawing.

Ayesha condensed two years of schooling into one day!

Children can also learn about chronological sequence by ordering photographs or artefacts, or listening to oral accounts. Selection of the sources which children are given raises a number of questions which it will be interesting for teachers to investigate. It will also be interesting to consider the best questions to ask children in order to examine the reasoning by which they arrive at their sequence.

Are some aspects of change easier than others to illustrate or to understand (technological, social, aesthetic)? What is the best mode of representation for sequence of change (artefacts, photographs, stories, oral accounts)? How should sequencing activities be structured to involve different periods of time (from the child's own life-time, to living memory and beyond, to the distant past; from family to impersonal affairs)?

How should sequences be extended from the simple and obvious, with limited examples, to larger numbers of objects, photographs or sequences which are ambiguous? How can simple stories be extended to stories with more events, with more complex causes, involving greater understanding of human behaviour? What knowledge do children bring to bear on their reasoning in these contexts? How do children read pictures, in order to compare similarities and differences? What sorts of pictures and how much detail do children of different ages enjoy? What reasons do children give for changes, and how do they suggest that changes affected people's lives? Teachers need to consider such issues in planning activities and, through observation and discussion, to discover the kind of thinking which children bring to bear on these tasks.

Loader (1993) found that reception children, asked to sequence photographs of themselves, had idiosyncratic ways of doing this. Clare put her 'now' photograph (of her in school uniform) first, then the picture of her at 1 day old, then the rest chronologically. Séan arranged his in a circular pattern in chronological order.

A group of year 3 children in Joanne Edwards' class, given five of her family photographs to sequence, dating from 1880, 1912, 1946, 1960 and 1970, could all put them in chronological order, but they used different reasoning to do so. One child sequenced them correctly on the basis of quality and technology. Another child recognised the same person at different ages in four of the pictures. Three children used other clues in the pictures, particularly clothes.

Clearly, helping children to sequence photographs or artefacts will not be an isolated activity, but part of a broader topic. Boxes 4.2 and 4.3 contain suggestions for sequencing activities and questions related to typical Key Stage 1 themes.

Scott (1994) described how year 2 children were able to put a toasting fork, an old electric toaster, a new toaster and a sandwich-maker in chronological order, although they were predictably unclear about the last two items. One child, Jane, then chose to draw and number the sequence in a circular, clock-wise rotation. (This led to a subsequent discussion among the students working with the children about the possibility of reflecting with them on the need to show some sequences in linear form – since we do not return to using a toasting fork at regular intervals – whereas it may be appropriate to record months, seasons and years in a circular form.) Jane was able to say confidently that the object she labelled 'one' was the 'oldest' and 'four' was the 'youngest'. With much prompting and encouragement, she was able to say that 'two is a bit younger than three' and 'three is more younger than two and one'. She explained the changes in terms of efficiency.

> The toasting fork takes longer than the toaster, because you have to turn the toast over. The new toaster is quite like number two. The sandwich-maker can cook more toast, so a family can all eat at once and it can make a sandwich.

Routh and Rowe (1992) have identified picture books which provide experiences of the many facets of time: night-time, day-time, special days, week by week, festivals, the year round, time and change and astrological time. Cox and Hughes (1990) showed how concepts of time and other aspects of historical thinking can be developed through story, and list examples of stories about childhood, grannies and more distant times. Stories are a traditional way of involving children in other places and

Box 4.2   Chronological sequences (1)

Theme	What the children will do	Possible questions
1 Personal history	(a) • Children bring photographs of themselves when they were babies and a recent photograph	(a) • Who is it? What are they doing and wearing? How big are they? Where are they? Who is with them? How have they changed? Are all the baby photographs the same/different? Why?
	• Make a book of 'Things I can do', and 'Things a baby can do' • Collect and sort sets of baby clothes and 5-year-olds' clothes • Collect and sort sets of baby toys and 5-year-olds' toys	• How have you changed since you were a baby?
	(b) • Bring in photographs for each year, 1–5. Read stories about birthdays, e.g. *Happy Birthday Bini* (Bhatia 1988) • Write a questionnaire for parent about what you were like, etc. Write about each year of your life based on the questionnaire results • Make a time-line for years 1–5 and put writing and photographs on the time-line	(b) • Can you put them in order? Put each other's photographs in order. How do you know if you are right? • e.g. When did I have my bike? My grommets? When was my sister born? Where did we go to . . . ? Move house? • Can you explain or suggest why events described on time-line happened. Is this photograph earlier or later? Is it newer or older? Are you older in the new photograph or the old photograph?
	• Collect photographs of children of 1–5 years from old newspapers and magazines (e.g. Royal Family)	• Can you put these in order? Why do you think this is the right order? Can you put them on a time-line? Is the child older in this photograph than that one? Why do you think so?

Theme	What the children will do	Possible questions
	• Draw pictures (make sets) of what has stayed the same in your life and what has changed since you were a baby	
2 Living memory	(a) • Children are shown photographs of a child of 1–2 years old and of its mother at the same age (e.g. the teacher as a 2-year-old and the teacher's mother as a 2-year-old) • Compare two toys or books belonging to each of the children in the photographs • Interview mother in photograph about when she was little. Ask her for more 'evidence' of her past	(a) • How old are the two children? Who are they? Has the mother changed since then? How old might she be now? Which photograph was taken first? How do you know? • Which belongs to which photograph? Why? How are they the same/different? • Write an article for a newspaper or make a tape-recording for a radio programme about this mother's life story
	(b) • Make a class museum. Collect photographs, books, toys, belonging to 'great grandparents', 'grandparents', 'parents'	(b) • Write labels for the exhibits. Find out their dates • Which photographs belong to each generation; can you sort them to find out? Does this tell us which things are oldest? Can we use the dates to put them on a time-line? (This illustrates the need for a standard measure)

Box 4.3 Chronological sequences (2)

Theme	What the children will do	Possible questions
1 The locality • Shopping street	• Choose a shop. Find out from interviews and local history library what it was like/sold in past times. Write/draw the history of the shop for display by present owner • From old photographs find out about transport: horses/buses/cars/lorries/vans in the street in past times. Put the photographs in order • Visit a supermarket and a corner shop. How are goods and jobs organised in each? Draw a design for a supermarket layout and a corner shop • Street furniture: collect and identify initials on post boxes • Collect street lamps/coal hole covers, horse troughs	• Sequence and explain changes in what was sold, in display, advertisements, packaging, work conditions, customers' needs, ways of paying • Describe, explain the sequence. How would the changes affect people's lives? • List advantages of supermarket and of corner shop. Why were supermarkets 'invented'? • Can you put them in order on a 'kings and queens' time-line? Can you find the stamps for each king and queen? • Can you sequence these? How would they affect people's lives?
• Farm	• *Tools* Visit a farm: collect hand tools. Find out how same work is done today • *Buildings* Sort into old and new. Look for clues • *Maps* Look at old map(s) and contemporary map	• Move a load (e.g. of fodder) by hand on a barrow/cart. Compare with how much a tractor can move in the same time • How are materials, structures, purposes different? • Look for and explain change in name, paths, field size, crops
• Seaside	• Collect and sequence seaside postcards	• What changes can you see in entertainments, clothes, food, buildings, transport, station?

Theme	What the children will do	Possible questions
	• Compare three views, e.g. eighteenth-century or early nineteenth-century painting or engraving before holiday industry; early seaside holidays; recent • Listen to popular seaside music from three periods, e.g. nineteenth century ('I do like to be beside the seaside'), 1950s and today	• In three groups pretend you are a person in one of these pictures. Make up a play about what you are doing • How have the words, sounds and means of playing music (e.g. piano, 78 record, CD) changed?
2 Clothes	• Collect old photographs/ paintings/advertisements/ dress and knitting patterns. Can you put them in order? • Collect pictures of sports clothes, wedding clothes, work clothes, hats or shoes. Order them • Sort fabrics into natural (fur, wool, leather, cotton, linen) and synthetic • Experiment with natural dyes and man-made dyes • Borrow children's clothes from local amateur dramatic club or drama college for children to try on, or buy replicas or make them for play corner	• Why do you think this is the right order? Describe/ explain changes • How have they changed? Why? What can we work out about how people's pastimes/attitudes have changed? • Find out about methods of spinning, dyeing, weaving in the past and now. Describe/explain changes • Can you match the style to pictures in books and put them in order? What could you do/not do wearing these clothes? How do they feel different from your own clothes?
3 Homes	• Collect pictures of houses and order: new, old, very old • Draw or photograph three houses from locality (e.g. 1980, 1930, 1880)	• Why have you put 'this house' in this set? Did you have to change the sets when you found new pictures? • What is different? Why? Find out about the families who lived in each home when it was built (census or street

Theme	What the children will do	Possible questions
	• Collect old domestic appliances or ornaments from families, junk shops.	directories). Use books to find out about heat, water, light, games, music, their clothes, furniture. Make up stories, plays, pictures about each family • Can you put them in order? What changes in people's lives do they show?
4 School	• Collect pictures of your school. Can you put them in order? Can you link other evidence to each picture (oral history, school log or punishment book, old school books or exercise books, timetables)? • Collect and sequence old children's books • Sequence, e.g., slate, steel pen, felt tip, word-processing disk	• Describe changes in building, furniture, display, way children are organised, what they are doing/wearing. What can you work out about changes in schools, in how children felt, behaved? Can you explain the changes? • Describe and explain changes in type, text, pictures • What difference would each make to children's life in school?

times, of exploring other people's minds and encouraging children to decentre. They stimulate the imagination and the emotions, and help children to reflect on their own experiences and on the way they view others. Narrative underlies both story and history. It holds children's attention and provides a framework for asking 'Who?' and 'Why?'

SIMILARITIES AND DIFFERENCES

Virginia Hunt, a student, examined children's understanding of similarities and differences between now and past times, through text and illustrations in stories. When she read a group of bilingual year 1 children *Bill and Pete Go Down the Nile* (de Paolo 1988), the Museum of Ancient Egypt illustrated in the story led them to discuss what they knew about the past. Ayodele said that, 'History [referred to in the text] means "a long time ago" or "the olden days".' 'In the olden days', she said, aeroplanes were 'not like they are now', they were 'funny and flapping around'. (She went on to say that her granny was old and lived in Africa and was born 'before the war came.)' She thought that the crocodile in the picture might be old because it was crinkly like her gran, but Shellie thought it was more likely crinkly because it had been too long in the water! There is evidence of reasoning here, although the children's limited knowledge prevents them reaching a correct conclusion. Ayodele's next remark, though, was subtle and accurate because her reasoning in this case was supported by knowledge. The Sphinx, she said, was very old, but it looked new because it had been cleaned; she knew this because she had seen a television programme about it. This led Shellie to talk more about the way buildings changed colour as they aged; she, too, had seen a programme about this on television. Aaron knew about the olden days because he had visited 'a dinosaur museum'. The group displayed rudimentary maps of the past based on incidental knowledge they had acquired. Egyptian mummies were from a long time ago, before Shellie's mum was born, but dinosaurs lived in the olden days before even people were here, but they 'got killed off'.

When these children were read *Joseph and His Magnificent Coat of Colours* (Williams 1992), they again related the story to knowledge acquired from television. Shellie knew from a programme she had seen that the pyramids were built a long time ago and that they still exist, and Theodore developed her point to add that they were in Egypt because the River Nile was mentioned. He thought that probably Canaan was therefore a real place too. From evidence in the pictures, the children thought that the story happened a long time ago in Egypt, 'before I was born; before everyone was born', because 'there are chariots – you don't see them today' and because of the furniture – 'you don't get those things no more'. However, the circumspection of their reasoning was surprisingly sophisticated: 'But people in Africa might still wear clothes like this. I've seen them on telly.'

When the children were read a story about the more recent past, about *Princess Victoria* (Mitchellhill 1991), they again used their limited know-ledge, from their own experience and from television, to consider the possible differences between 'then' and 'now'. Theodore thought the king was old, 'like my Grandad and my friend Jack. He's 70 and has got a stick'. However, he decided that the king had probably lived before his grandad and worked out why he thought so.

> The coach is from the olden days, like in cowboys. I saw a coach like that on telly. You don't get cowboys now, only on the telly. They lived about two hundred years ago. Also the globe in the picture is different from my teacher's globe.

He tried very hard to support his argument and this led to the rest of the group finding many other differences in the illustrations, between then and now: the clothes, the furniture, the chalkboard and the toys, including wooden dolls. Again, they tested their conclusions. 'You don't get a lady to teach you now, you have to go to school.' 'But you might get one if you were a queen.' Focused observation like this shows how year 1 children, some with little English and with very limited knowledge, supported their statements with arguments, and both developed and questioned each other's ideas. It would be interesting to find out the level of sophistication they could have achieved if they had been taught in a coherent way about the past.

Warton (1993) asked year 2 children to compare two pictures, to encourage them to discuss similarities and differences between the milkman today and in the past. This was part of a project on 'where we live'. Their discussion illustrated how children need to learn the kind of question they are being asked and the type of answer that is expected in an historical context.

Matthew and Colin were confident that they knew what was required:

Matthew   That's easy. The old one's black and white.
Amy   Did people used to have cars and horses because electricity wasn't invented?
Matthew   The milk's not in bottles. It's in big metal pots.
Colin   And there's no roof on the cart. That's why the milkman's wearing a hat.

Amy, however, was less sure!

Amy   Both milkmen have got moustaches. And our milkman hasn't, but he's got a dog and it's called Bones.

Children can learn to consider similarities and differences between past and present times by sorting pictures and artefacts into sets of very old, old and new, for example. This again raises questions which it will be interesting to investigate. What reasons can they give for their choices? What vocabulary do they use or need to? Do they concentrate at first on evidence of ageing: if it is worn or dirty it must be old? Do they consider reproductions as old and if so, why? Can they sort pictures better than artefacts? Are they prepared to listen to the arguments of others and change their decisions? Do some categories overlap? Do they consider materials or technology? Do black and white pictures appear older than coloured ones? Can they discuss the effects of the changes on people's lives? What sort of changes are easiest to perceive?

Hilary Croft, a student, began to investigate some of these questions, while working with a year 2 class. She found that when they were asked to sort into very old, old and modern they were at first hampered by the terminology. They did not understand modern, and when this was replaced by 'new' they assumed that this meant straight from the shop. They thought at first that 'old' was the equivalent of worn; therefore they classed relatively new trainers as old. However, they refined their understanding of the concept as they took clearly older things from the box, and as they did so they also resorted the artefacts into different categories.

The teacher explored the children's reasoning as she observed them by asking them questions: 'Why do you think it belongs there?' 'What made you decide that it was old?' 'Do you think this is older than that?' She recognised the need to extend the children's thinking, but not to intervene too much, because she noticed that the children did not contradict her and were very anxious at first about giving the right answer. Carl expressed this initial anxiety: 'But how do we know if it's right if you don't tell us or help us?' Children need to *learn* to accept uncertainty, to make possible inferences, to support them with arguments and to listen to the arguments of others.

The following extract, in which they were discussing a sepia photograph of the teacher's family dressed up as American pioneers, shows how they gradually learned to revise their categories.

D   It's a very, very old photograph because it's black and white, and
        they're wearing funny clothes.

Teacher Let's look at it more closely. Do you recognise anybody?
S   It's you, Hilary!
E   It can't be old then.

They all agree that it is not *very* old, but could be either new or old.

Similarly, the children at first thought that lace underskirts they were shown were new until they found similar clothes in old photographs in which people were wearing very long skirts. They decided that the underskirts must also be very old because they were very long and similar to the skirts in the photographs.

S at first said, 'I don't think they would have had hats like that in the old days', but then she found similar hats in old photographs and decided that they did. Children also began to give reasons for their suggestions and to use 'because'.

E   It's old because it's wrinkly.
D   It's new – they didn't have plastic in the olden days.
S   Yes it's old, because, look at the buttons – they're made of bone.

They began to consider alternative possibilities. In discussing a pair of new platform sandals which were similar in style to platform shoes of the 1960s and 1970s, E said, 'they're old fashioned'. But D said they were similar to those currently worn by 'Betty Boo' (a 1990s singer). This led them to examine the bottoms and find that they were clean and so to agree that 'they are probably new'.

Gradually the children were learning to form hypotheses, to reason, to look for supporting evidence, to discuss alternatives and so to change their hypotheses and to refine their understanding of concepts of very old, old and new.

In a second session, the children chose an old hat or a new hat, or an old or a new shoe, to draw. This gave rise to further discussion of 'old' and 'new' while they were drawing. In the final session, they brought their own 'old things'. The teacher found that they talked far more extensively about their own artefacts and pictures than they had about the things she had brought in previously, because they had background knowledge about them which they could share with others and use to answer questions. She concluded that although children need to learn to accept uncertainty, some knowledge and personal experience made them more confident in asking questions and considering possibilities.

CONCEPTS RELATED TO UNDERSTANDING CHANGES OVER TIME: ORGANISING CONCEPTS

It was said in Part I that there is no clear agreement about what is meant by historical concepts. Some concepts, which have already been discussed, are concerned with changes over time, with similarities and differences, continuity and change. Others are organising ideas which run through all societies: conflict, beliefs, agriculture. Some special vocabulary relates to particular periods in the past: Roman, Medieval. Other concepts are concerned with the process of interpreting sources. We shall consider in turn ways of introducing each type of concept to young children.

First, we shall consider those concepts which are central to all societies. Children need to learn to understand such key concepts in order to place detail in a structural pattern so that it is not forgotten. This enables them to compare similarities and differences between times and places (Bruner 1966). Concepts such as trade, communication, power and government are abstract and complex. But young children can be introduced to simpler, concrete concepts, selected because they relate to and will eventually lead to an understanding of the over-arching, abstract concepts (Vygotsky 1962; Ausubel 1968; Gagne 1977; Klausmeier 1978; Klausmeier et al. 1979). Vygotsky suggested that concept understanding is promoted by careful use of language. He found that concepts which are specially introduced because they belong to a particular discipline and are not acquired spontaneously are learned more consciously and completely, and that the significant use of new vocabulary promotes intellectual growth. Bruner (1966) suggested that children need opportunities to learn new concepts through physical experience and sensation (handling and using an old artefact, for example), through images (pictures and models), and through relating these to language (in stories and poems, and by labelling). There is evidence that if young children are introduced, in these ways, to selected concrete concepts, they gradually learn to use the more abstract over-arching concepts related to them.

Furth (1980) traced children's growing understanding of concepts such as government, social roles, money and community. He found that at 5 years old children had an image of government as a 'special man' (sic). From this they developed the concept of a ruler, then of a job-giver or owner of land, until at 9 or 10 they understood that a government provides functions and services in return for taxes.

Suggestions in Box 4.4 show how subordinate concepts related to key concepts may be selected and introduced through traditional topics.

Box 4.4 Concepts and topics

Organising concept	*Related concepts*	*Possible topic*
Agriculture	Farm: farmhouse, barn, dairy Crops: yams, corn, tobacco, coffee, ground nuts, cassava, maize, rice, barley Animals: horses, sheep, pigs, chickens, buffalo, oxen Tools: sickle, plough, windmill, tractor, watermill, combine harvester Sow, reap, winnow, thresh, store Milkmaid, goose girl, shepherd	Farming A farm visit, or visit to a reconstruction of rural life. Folk tales about crops, farming, e.g. *The Village of Round and Square Houses* (Grafoni 1989) (Cameroon villages); *Shaker Lane* (Provensen and Provensen 1991); *Mufaro's Beautiful Daughters* (Steptoe 1992); *Where the Forest Meets the Sea* (Baker 1991) Stories about real people
Manufacture	Cloth: tailor, weaver, spinster, loom, spinning wheel Pottery: potter, kiln, clay Metalwork: mine, smelt, mould Leather: cobbler, cordwainer Buildings: carpenter, stone-mason Energy: machines, tools, weapons, water power, wind power, steam power, (nuclear) factory	Jobs people do Buildings Visits to sites, workplaces, e.g. windmill, watermill Visits to a reconstruction of an industrial site or workplace (the Tin Smith, the Mine, Foundry, Candle Factory at Ironbridge Gorge Museum) True stories about real people Folk tales (e.g. *The Tailor of Gloucester*, Beatrix Potter)
Trade	Exchange, buy, sell, weight, money, price, fair, market, merchant, rich, poor	Jobs people do Visit to local shop, shopping street, market, other workplace

Organising concept	Related concepts	Possible topic
Communi-cation	Transport: track, road, coach, car, steam train, diesel, tram, bus Ship: oars, sail, steam Oral: folk tales, stories, laws, proclamations Writing: glyph, wax, quill, print, fax, disk Media: radio, record, film, television Symbols: religious symbols, logos, paintings	Visit a reconstruction, e.g. The Bank, Blists Hill (Ironbridge Gorge Museum) or Black Country Museum, Dudley Stories about real people Folk tales (e.g. Dick Whittington), *The Emperor's Dan-Dan* (Agard 1992) Folk tales and true stories about journeys, inventions Stories about real people (e.g. King Alfred, The Highwayman, Mary Seacole (Blyth *et al.* 1991) or consult local history library for journeys made by people from or to your locality (Collicott 1993) Visit to printers, toll house, canal at Blists Hill (Ironbridge Gorge Museum)
Power/ social structure	Attack, defend, conflict, weapons Ruler: king, queen, prince, princess, government Rich, poor, peasant, knight, lord, servant Laws, obey, fight	True stories Folk tales (e.g. Robin Hood)
Beliefs, values, attitudes	Religious buildings: church, mosque, synagogue Religious writings Symbols of belief systems Ceremony: festival, faith, prayer, praise, worship, good, evil, hope, fear	Festivals Stories related to belief systems Stories related to statues, stained glass, religious paintings Folk tale

CONCEPTS RELATED TO PARTICULAR PERIODS

The second type of historical concept to which young children may be introduced through visits, pictures, stories and imaginative play is associated with different periods in the past. Young children relish using 'special words', such as 'portcullis' or 'gargoyle', usually accompanied by appropriate body language, although refined use, as Vygotsky showed, develops piecemeal, through trial and error. A group of 5-year-olds, sharing their knowledge about castles, confused me by describing the Spitfire they were adding to their model, until I saw it demonstrated, rotating a paper ox over the fire; and the parents of a reception child were mystified by a lusty rendering of 'wind the poppy up' accompanied by wild twisting and pulling gestures, until the teacher explained that a visitor had brought a bobbin to school and taught the class an old weavers' song! Examples of labels used by historians to describe society in a particular time and place are shown in the first column of Box 4.5. Words describing characteristic aspects of that society are in the second column.

Box 4.5 Historical vocabulary

Roman	Villa, fort, centurion, legion, standard, toga
Medieval	Monastery, cathedral, castle, knight, battlements, portcullus, moat, tournament, spinning wheel, bow and arrow, tunic, hose
Elizabethan	Explorers, galleon, treasure, pirate, ruff, wig
Victorian	Carriage, coalman, flat iron, hotwater bottle, oil lamp, button hook

CONCEPTS ASSOCIATED WITH MAKING DEDUCTIONS AND INFERENCES ABOUT SOURCES

A third group of concepts which children may learn is concerned with describing historical sources and with recognising different levels of validity and certainty in interpreting sources: I am sure, I think, I can guess; probably, perhaps, maybe; because, therefore. Box 4.6 shows activities through which children may explore, discuss and use probability language.

Box 4.6 Activities which allow children to become conscious of levels of probability

Activity	*Possible questions*
• Piece together broken tool, pot, plate, with parts missing. Draw possible original. This could be deliberately broken, or a genuine fragment	• What shape do you think it was? Why? Who do you think used it? What do you think the writing/ picture was like when the pot/ plate was complete?
• (Photo)copy a complete (old) artefact. Cut it up into a jigsaw with pieces missing and ask your friend to put it together again	• How many ways could you remake the jigsaw? Why do you think this is the best answer?
• Class museum. Collect old things. Research, using books, asking adults questions, making reasonable guesses about what cannot be known. Write labels, or a guide for the museum or make an oral tape	• What do you know about this? What is it made of? How old is it? Who used it? What for? What difference did it make to their lives? Are there others?
• A class dig. Measure off a square metre of rough ground. See what you can find. Measure and draw finds, put them on a time-line. Draw a plan to show where they were found	• Label finds. What can you work out about the people they belonged to? Can you find out more? Why were they buried?
• Make a stratified model in a fish tank by burying a few objects every day in layers of soil, sand, gravel, etc. Put a dolls' house on top	• Can you make up stories for each group of people who lived on this 'site' before the dolls' house was built?
• Extend a photograph: attach it to a large sheet of paper and draw what the camera did not record	• Why have you added this? Why do you think it is certainly/ probably true?
• Read extract from account in old newspaper of interest to children	• Why do you think this happened?
• Participate in an excavation. Harrison (1993) described an infant archaeology project at Battle Abbey in which children mixed colours to match the shades of the stone, did wall rubbings, observational drawings of pottery shards, measured walls, doors and keys, decorated tiles and looked for layers and gargoyles	• Can you draw the whole pot from this piece? Can you draw the building when it was new? How was it built? Can you make up a play about building the abbey?

Chapter 5

Interpretations

Historians' accounts of the past may be different but equally valid if they conform to what is known, if they are reasonable, and if there is no contradictory evidence. Historians construct accounts by selecting and interpreting sources which are often incomplete. Accounts differ, first because they reflect the values and preoccupations of the times in which they are written. Historians in Ancient Greece and Imperial Rome were preoccupied with the idealised views of glorious conquests. Victorians were concerned with the origins of common law and parliaments. In the twentieth century, the emphasis has been on the perspectives of 'ordinary people' and most recently on the role of women and on non-Eurocentric history. Second, accounts vary according to the interests of the writer. History today encompasses all aspects of human activity: industry, religion, arts, literature, folk lore, great individuals, key events and groups and movements, in-depth studies and broad brush strokes. Third, history is rewritten as new evidence is discovered.

We are also surrounded by reconstructions of the past, of varying status, which were not produced by historians: historical drama, fiction, theme parks and re-enactments.

Our view of the past is dynamic. It is constantly being reinterpreted, just as we continually reappraise our personal histories throughout our lives. History is many faceted; no simple framework or perspective or truth is possible. For this reason, it is important to learn history in order to develop a questioning understanding of values and attitudes and of our own place in a changing society (Jenkins 1991).

There are many ways in which young children can begin to learn that there are different interpretations of the past. They hear different versions of stories set in the past. Their families have their own histories and views of the past. They come from different parts of the British Isles and of the world; they come from different social backgrounds; they consist of men and women. Children can learn from the beginning to be aware of, to build on and to evaluate these perspectives, for this is what history is, and they need to find their place in it. Fryer (1989) quotes Ayi Kwei Armah ('The Healers' 1979).

> The present is where we get lost
> If we forget our own past and have
> No vision of the future.

In *History in the National Curriculum* (DES 1991) at Key Stage 1, children are expected to begin to show awareness that the past is represented in different ways. As the working group wrote in its final report, historical objectivity is an ideal always to be pursued though it may never be completely realised; historical theories are there to be constantly re-examined; there is no final answer to any historical question and there are no monopolies of the truth (DES 1990: 11). It is of vital significance that this strand of historical understanding has been included in the revised version of the National Curriculum (DfE 1995). Learning that the past is represented in different ways is a protection against the exploitation of history, and is also central to the understanding of the nature of history. Any study of the past will lead to an interpretation, but this will change as perspectives change, and according to how one period in the past is represented by a subsequent period. Children will eventually learn how and why historians' accounts differ if, from the beginning, they are given opportunities to: (1) develop awareness of different ways of representing past events, for example: pictures, written accounts, film, television programmes, plays, songs, reproductions of objects in museums, museum displays; and (2) distinguish between different versions of events, for example: different accounts by pupils of the same events. Children can learn that stories may be about real or fictional characters, that different stories about the past give different versions of what happened.

Interpretations of events and of behaviour, and different versions of stories, are part of everyday life. Young children may begin by discussing different versions of events in their own lives during the day or week (different accounts of their shared experience of the morning, of the concert, of a playground squabble) before they consider different accounts of family events, of oral history, or events in the distant past. Children may go on to learn about different interpretations, both by considering existing reconstructions of the past and by constructing their own versions of a place, event or person.

COMPARING INTERPRETATIONS

Physical reconstructions

There are many exciting opportunities for children to see reconstructions of past times. They are made for different purposes and have differing levels of validity. Museum 'still life' reconstructions, for example of an air raid shelter, a Roman kitchen or a neolithic site, or replicas of museum exhibits, are based on evidence and research. They may well raise questions such as: 'How did they know?' 'Are there others?' 'What might it have felt like when . . . ?' Reconstructions of sites, homes, streets and workplaces, such as West Stowe Anglo-Saxon village in Suffolk, Butser Iron Age Farm in Hampshire, the Yorvik Viking Centre, Ironbridge Gorge Museum and Morwellham Quay Copper mine at Tavistock in Devon, have an educational purpose and a foundation in serious academic research. They can inform, but will also stimulate questions for children as well as for researchers: how do you know what crops the Iron Age people grew, or how Saxons made their homes? How do you know how a Viking village smelt? Why do you think a maid may have talked or dressed like that? Would the streets and the air really have been so clean? Reconstructions of events, made primarily for entertainment, are, to differing degrees, authentic. The National Trust and English Heritage Events diaries list exciting historical re-enactments and demonstrations: mummers, tournaments, feasts, dances, music, parades of Roman Imperial troops, civil war battles, archery and falconry.

Other reconstructions are made predominantly for commercial reasons: cartoons such as *Asterix* or *The Flintstones*, musicals and films such as *Oliver* and *Robin Hood*. Young children who have learned to ask 'Why?' and 'How do we know?' can begin to discuss why reconstructions have been made, whether it might really have been like that, why, why not, and why they think it might have been different.

Different versions of stories

Stories are important. They are as central to everyday life as they are to historians. 'There is conflict of characters, the natural likes and dislikes, loves and hatreds . . . the conflicts, the irrationalities . . . the divided loyalties, complexity of motive . . . drama and tragedy' (Rowse 1946: 47).

Young children are comfortable listening to stories. They broaden their experience and their knowledge. Stories affect children's intellectual growth, for they do not listen passively; they are called upon to create new worlds through powers of imagination. Holdaway (1979) described how stories enable children to escape from the bonds of the present into the past, and to explore emotion, intention, behaviour and human purpose. Stories extend first-hand experiences of the world, giving access to more experiences than any one person can have in their life-time, and so extending perceptions of the world.

In listening to stories about other times, children are required to react, to confirm, to modify or to reject their existing ideas. Listening to different versions of stories, then, helps children not only to learn about times and places and people outside their own experience, but also to understand that there is no single 'correct' version of the past. Alternative versions of stories may battle with one another, marry one another or mock one another in the listener's mind (Bruner 1986: 7). They represent models of our world which we carry in our mind and which allow us constantly to redefine our views of the world. Until recently, the only history in many societies was oral history and, in some cultures, the oral tradition has remained alive to the present day. A society with no history would be like an individual with no memory; the oral tradition perpetuates stories of a people's past, shared folk memories, beliefs, values and social customs. But unlike the story in a written text, the story in oral tradition is ephemeral and elusive because it is created by a particular teller, for a particular audience, in a particular place and time. Therefore, stories change their form in response to different audiences. Philip (1989) recorded twenty variations of the Cinderella story which illustrate its development through the centuries, from ninth-century China to the seventeenth-century French court. Children can also compare versions of the same story told in different languages: 'The Hare and the Tortoise', for example, in English, Hindi, Gujarati and Turkish (Douloubakas, 1985).

Anthony Enahoro described his own experience of the living oral tradition, as the son of a schoolmaster in West Africa in the 1930s:

> Women were ever our historians. Singing, spinning, now one, then another, now in parts, now in unison, they told of the old days before the coming of white men, of the founding of the clan, of tribal wars, of families, of the great deeds of our forebears, in their small world.

He told how,

> Those young children of the very large family, who were not already asleep lay on mats listening to stories told by the women of the household. Such stories might be folk lore, myth or history, and such themes had been enacted thousands of times in every family in the Ishan sub-tribe of the Binis, from time immemorial. This was the story of the tribe of the clan, of the family, passed on from generation to generation, from the time when the Ishans settled in that part of Nigeria . . .
>
> (Hulton 1989: 83)

West African stories analyse the problems as well as the advantages of communal living and the extended family; they describe the buildings and the compound of the universal family village, an institution which has existed in West Africa since time immemorial. Osoba (1993) has collected folk tales and legends from his oral tradition in Edo State which blend fact and fiction, and keep alive and share the values and history of the Bini people who live there. In Thailand and in Indonesia, through Nat Yai shadow puppets, stories pass on the religious mythology of the people, the community's shared wisdom and values, their explanations of the world and of the behaviour of the people in it.

In native American oral culture, stories tell of journeys of nomadic progress, the cycle of time and the rhythm of the seasons. Australian stories deal with family patterns, government and tribal organisation. When stories from the oral tradition were finally written down, a variety of different versions was recorded.

In Europe, the oral tradition remains only in 'fairy stories', the stories of the peasant and the nurse, written down in the nineteenth century by, for example, Perrault, the brothers Grimm and Hans Andersen. The European oral tradition, therefore, became part of the nursery by historical accident. Children's understanding of history cannot be assessed through fairy stories because they have become divorced from real events and contain elements of fantasy. But fairy stories introduce children to powerful perennial ideas and emotions which run through the oral tradition. Evil is not suppressed, but is omnipresent with virtue, and children are offered new dimensions of imagination which they could not discover on their own. Such stories help them to examine the relationship between fantasy and reality, to recognise what is likely or possible and what is not, based on their own experiences, and to look for causes of events and reasons for behaviour. Fairy stories, because they come from an oral tradition, can also help children to see that there may be more than one version of a story. (For a brilliant analysis of fairy stories, see Warner 1994.)

Versions of fairy stories

Some would argue that many fairy stories are not suitable for children starting school because they are still not able to differentiate between fact and fantasy. Susan Isaacs (1930) thought that they might therefore be damaging to children under 7. However, Tucker (1981) argued that stories which are in tune with modes of thought which are not logical may in fact help children to examine the relationship between fantasy and reality and so build their intellectual confidence. Stories which explain natural phenomena in terms of human intervention long ago reflect Piagetian levels of autistic thought in which everything in the Universe is made for the convenience of man, and human thoughts and feelings are attributed to most things in the Universe. There is also often a Piagetian concept of 'immanent justice' in fairy stories: the bridge broke because it *knew* the boy crossing it had stolen the apple. When they listen to stories which reflect this stage of thinking, children may *expect* success for the good and doom for the bad because at this stage a child's view is subjective and is constructed around what he or she thinks ought to be true rather than what is. Nevertheless, the stories encourage them to begin to question and ask *why* things happen as they do. Applebee (Tucker 1981) found that 41 per cent of 6-year-olds had firm expectations about characters and predicted the outcomes of situations.

Children observe deductions being made in stories, and these deductions are based on concrete, logical analysis of the evidence. Children also identify with characters making deductions in the story based on their own level of experience – either with those who are, or those who are *not*, in control. For example, the story of the 'Three Little Pigs' mirrors the progress of a child's own thinking, and children identify with the pigs according to their own level of learning from experience. This process is interesting for those who have arrived at this level of inductive reasoning and those who have not can begin to see what it is about. Thus the little billy goats went up to the high pastures *because* the grass was sweet; the pigs perceived *from the rough voice* that it was the wolf.

In this way, the bridge between fantasy and reality is gradually crossed. Applebee (Tucker 1981: 70) found that at about 6 years old children thought that Cinderella existed, but few thought that she could be visited, either because she lived too far away or too long ago. Some stories reflect this intermediate level of thinking. Inanimate objects cannot *always* talk; in some stories only animals can talk; in some stories only some animals can talk. This intermediate level is shown by a 5-year-old who, asked if he thought 'Jack and the Beanstalk' was a true story, said that he knew the giant was not real because he knew there were no giants, but that he thought Jack's mother was real 'because my mum talks to me like that'!

After experience of different texts, one teacher found that her 6-year-olds were quite confident in sorting books into 'reality' and 'fantasy' sets: 'The Knights and Armour books are about what happened long ago. *Willy the Wimp* – that's not true. The knights and the racing car books are true. . . .' As Meek (1988: 18) pointed out, you cannot be given a rule in advance. You learn by joining in.

Cook (1969) argued the need for the reinterpretation of fairy stories for a modern audience. Since then there have been many 'modern versions' telling the same story but with inverted gender roles: the competent, combative princess rescues the vain, passive prince. In other reinterpretations, the story is retold from the point of view of the villain; or the essential story is retold in a modern context. Sometimes the traditional version is illustrated in different styles.

Shelley Moore, a PGCE student, investigated the ability of her reception class to decentre and so to differentiate between, and account for the differences between, two versions of a story. She was attempting to teach these 4- and 5-year-olds the rudiments of historical thinking by going with the grain of their interests. First she read them *The Pain and the Great One* (Blume 1988), two stories of an ordinary day told from a brother's and a sister's perspective. The children were spontaneously very interested.

They appeared to empathise with one or with both of the characters and tried to explain how two contradictory interpretations were possible. Next they were read a traditional version of 'Little Red Riding Hood' and a second version told from the wolf's perspective ('Little Red Riding Hood', in Wilson 1988). She was careful in her choice of language when she introduced the second story and did not refer to it as 'a different story' or 'another story'. The children appeared to be operating on two levels at once, on the one level recognising that it was the same story about the same wolf told from different viewpoints, and at the same time thinking that there were two wolves, a 'good wolf' and a 'bad wolf'. Jordan said, 'He told us his own story because the two was different', but then went on to say later, 'There was one wolf in each story, a good wolf and a bad wolf.'

Brogan also at first seemed to think that the same wolf was telling his own version of the story, 'I think the wolf's good. He didn't eat her.' Joanne accounted for the alternative version by explaining that there was one wolf, who had lied to create the second version, while Lan produced an alternative, sophisticated argument, 'Little Red Riding Hood was lying; she made her story up.' Jordan then made the amazing remark, 'They might be different because they're reported differently.' However, as the discussion continued, it revealed two powerful influences which changed the children's fragile attempts to explain the two versions: first teacher intervention, then peer group pressure. In the middle of the discussion, the teacher asked if they thought it was 'the same wolf in each story'. On listening to the tape-recording of the discussion, the teacher decided that this 'leading question' caused the children to lose confidence in their own reasoning. Joanne and Brogan went on to make statements apparently contradicting their previous arguments and to accept that there were two different wolves. They contested Lan's argument that Little Red Riding Hood had made up her story, and Lan, possibly because English was her second language and she felt unable to explain or defend her view, gave in to peer group pressure.

In a second session, the teacher therefore tried to eliminate peer group pressure by talking to the children individually, and to eliminate teacher influence by asking open questions. In this session, she confirmed her original impression that both Joanne and Jordan understood that they had heard two versions of the same events. Both the children were more confident, and began to identify motives, and looked for possible reasons for the different versions and to develop arguments.

Jordan   They were the same story because the last one was the real one, because the wolf didn't want to eat her and the granny lied.

Joanne   The wolf isn't bad. I believe the wolf. The wolf told us his own story. The wolf did want to eat granny. He was hungry. Granny lied.

These discussions are a good example of how a perceptive teacher can look for the reasoning and complex thinking that children are often struggling to clarify and express. It shows the significance of the questions teachers ask, in influencing expectations, as well as the influence of peer group pressure on children's fragile reasoning. These 4- and 5-year-olds were operating at two levels, but one of them was a very sophisticated level which they could not quite achieve. It shows, too, the limitations of assessing children's thinking on the basis of one example.

In a third session, Shelley Moore read the children a traditional version of 'The Three Little Pigs' and a second version which was clearly stated to be 'the wolf's version of events' (Sciesczka 1991). She wanted to see if this quite explicit statement would make it easier for children to understand that there were different versions of the same story. It was interesting that Jordan again understood initially that these were different versions of the same events and began to develop arguments as to why. But when Jordan and Joanne again insisted that there were two wolves, one good and one bad, he again became uncertain and ended up saying, 'No, yes, I don't know . . . got no idea.' This seems to reinforce the idea that the qualitative differences in children's inferential thinking occur gradually through constant opportunities to reason and to discuss in different contexts.

Susan Jarvis, another PGCE student, told her year 1 class the traditional story of 'Little Red Riding Hood', then read them 'newspaper interviews' which she had written, telling the story from Red Riding Hood's point of view (at first she had assumed it was Granny in bed), from Granny's perspective (the wolf locked her in the cupboard), and the wolf's story (he had popped in for an aspirin because he had a headache, then fallen asleep on the bed). The children were able to select one of these stories and draw an appropriate picture and caption. Most of the girls identified with Red Riding Hood because they 'liked her cape'; Jamie concluded that Granny's story must be true because 'Grannies don't tell lies.' But the children's discussion of their pictures showed that they understood that there were three explanations of the story.

Claire Turnbull's case study illustrates the considerable difference between the groups of 4- and 5-year-olds described above, and her group of 7-year-olds, in their ability to differentiate between fantasy and reality and to understand that there may be different versions of a fairy story.

The 7-year-olds said that as 'babies' they probably thought fairy tales were true but that now they realised that they had been made up a long time ago. They contrasted them with true stories and with cautionary tales, as told by the visiting policeman. They offered sophisticated insights as to what is meant by real and by fantasy. Ryan said that he liked fairy stories because: 'They're *more* like real than real life. They're about really important things.' They thought that *Prince Cinders* (Cole 1987) was *not* like real life 'because it was modern'.

The 7-year-olds had no difficulty in extracting the common moral theme from different versions of a story and thought that the moral is the reason why people enjoy them. In the story they had been read, Ryan defined the moral as: 'Never boss other people around and make them do all the work.' Jason said the story meant, 'don't be unkind'. And Laura added: 'Don't be unkind because you'll probably get it back.'

Because they could extract the common theme in different versions, the children were also able to understand the differences between versions. *Prince Cinders* is not the same as the traditional story of Cinderella because: 'It's about a man instead of a girl.' Laura liked *The Paper Bag Princess* (Munsch 1988), which is not a version of any particular fairy tale, but differs from the traditional genre because the princess *tackles* the dragon. 'Normally in the books I read, when someone gets captured, it's usually the girl', she said. However, when the adaptation was more subtle, as in 'Little Red Cap', the Grimm version of 'Little Red Riding Hood' (in which the wolf dies), and in 'Little Red Riding Hood' (Ross 1991) (in which the wolf repents, the woodcutter has a 'quiet smoke', Gran drinks stout and Little Red Riding Hood rides a bike), the children seemed unaware of the details in the modern version; the similar story line was what they recognised as being important.

Myths, legends and folk tales

The distinction between myths, legends and folk tales is not clear. A myth is defined in the *Oxford English Dictionary* as purely fictitious narrative involving supernatural persons, actions or events and embodying some popular idea concerning natural or historical phenomena. Legends depend more on folk memories of events which have really happened although there is clearly overlap. In Medieval times, legends were the life stories of saints, but later came to mean stories, histories or accounts which were not authentic but were handed down by tradition from early times and regarded as authentic. They are therefore folk tales; the *Oxford English Dictionary* defines folk as a people, a nation or a tribe.

When children are able to distinguish between what may be real and what is fantasy in fairy stories, they will find a fresh challenge in understanding the complex dual role of fantasy and reality in myths, legends and folk tales. These stories were not created for young children, but they are important to children who are already used to fairy stories. First, they are full of metaphor, symbol, imagery and oblique meanings which express the complex interaction of 'pretend' and reality. Bruner (1989) suggested that such stories offer the opportunity of reconciling 'here and now' reality with the reality of the imagination. Second, myths and legends help children to look outward, to value differences between now and past times, and between different societies in the past. They learn new ways of thinking about the world, to change perspective and, as Booth (1985) put it, 'to try on other lives for size'. By questioning traditional stories and trying to resolve issues, children learn to speculate and hypothesise about behaviour and beliefs. Third, myths and folk tales from Africa, the Caribbean, India and China are most important for children who have no experience of cultural and ethnic diversity, because they open up to them values and attitudes other than their own (Klein 1989).

Finally, myths in particular are important because they grapple with the big matters of existence: life and death, the after-life and other worlds. Often they deal with morality and the relationship between the super-natural and everyday life.

Myths, legends and folk tales may need to be challenged and this can draw children into a discussion of alternative versions of stories. First, because they are rooted in the oral tradition, there is often more than one version of a story – of a Greek myth or of creation stories in different cultures, for example. Second, folk tales in different cultures often have a common theme. This may be because of communication between societies. Aesop recorded in Greek the allegories about jackals and lions which belonged to his own culture in Africa, and versions of the West African Anansi stories are well known throughout the Caribbean and Britain. In other cases, there is no known link between the places. The idea that knowledge of a person's name gives power over the person is found in stories in the Kalahari Desert, among the North American Indians, the Vikings, in Celtic Britain and in Germany. Third, folk tales are often found in dual language books (or in the language of the country the story comes from). A child explaining it in one language, and another child retelling it in a second language, may provide two versions of the story which can be discussed.

Most importantly, because folk tales flowed through the oral tradition, they evolved around the key organising concepts which lie at the heart of all societies. They deal with values and beliefs: heroism, compassion, self-sacrifice, jealousy, courage, betrayal, rough justice, creation stories and spiritual power. They describe social structure. Kings, princes, black-smiths, tailors and peasants may occasionally change status, but rank itself is not challenged. They are concerned with agriculture and with economic systems; markets in West Africa are full of yams, cassava and sweetcorn, and in Europe there are turnips, potatoes, cows and pigs. Stories tell of threats to society from wind, fire and flood. They tell of journeys, of communication systems, by sea and land. These central organising con-cepts – values and beliefs, social structure, economic and communication systems – provide a framework. Within this conceptual framework children can compare similarities and differences between societies. Do they all have rich and poor people, rulers and subjects? Do they all grow things and make things and buy and sell them? Do crafty people, jealous people, compassionate people exist in all societies? Do they all have hopes, fears, gods? How are they different in their rules, the things they grow and make and in their daily lives?

Myths, legends and folk tales offer opportunities for comparing different versions of a story or similar themes in stories from different cultures. They provide a framework for seeing similarities (and differences) in attitudes, values and behaviour, and in social and economic systems, in different societies. 'King March's Secret', for example (History Box, National Language Unit of Wales, see p. 196), is the Welsh version of Midas and his ass's ears. Different versions of the same folk tales have been collected by folk lore societies. The Folklore Society at the University of Edinburgh School of Scottish Studies and the Nigerian Folk Lore Society, Ibadan, for example, publish versions of myths, legends and folk tales for use by teachers.

Virginia Hunt, a student teacher, investigated the reasoning of a group of year 1 children who were discussing whether, and in what ways, myths, legends and other stories which she read them were true. They all thought that *The Turtle and the Island*, a creation myth from Papua, New Guinea (Ker Wilson 1990), was made up, apart from Ayodele, who thought it might be true because Papua, New Guinea, was on the globe and 'therefore it's a real place, so you could go there, and you might see the turtle – but you wouldn't get purple crabs!' But Theodore argued that the purple crabs, 'and the other colours', showed that the story was not true. He supported this argument by adding that he had seen a turtle in Granada, 'and it couldn't carry a woman or make an island'. Shelley accepted this, and added that 'if it tried, the shell might crack and the person would fall off'. These 5-year-olds were reasoning logically, based on their own experiences and knowledge, and were listening to, considering and developing each other's points. They used similar arguments in discussing whether *Joseph and His Magnificent Coat of Colours* (Williams 1992) was a true story. Shelley said that she thought it was not true because of the colours of the pyramids and the trees, 'so they must be made up'. But she recognised the subtle distinction that Egypt was a real place because she had seen it on television, and that part of the story was probably about Egypt because 'it said about the Nile'. Therefore Canaan, also mentioned in the story, was probably a real place too. Aaron and Ayodele decided, on the basis of their own experience, that the bit about Joseph's brothers would not be true because brothers would not be that horrible to each other.

The children again made reasoned distinctions about the parts of *Bill and Pete Go Down the Nile* (de Paolo 1988) which might be true, and the parts which they thought were not. Aaron knew 'the sphinx and pyramids are true', because he had seen them on television, and in pictures, 'so you *could* probably see them in a museum'. Theodore agreed; he had learnt about sphinxes from his mum. So, as Ayodele concluded, 'parts are about real things, but crocodiles and birds can't talk!'

Princess Victoria (Mitchelhill 1991) was generally agreed to be 'true', and the children were able to explain why. Ayodele had seen a picture of Queen Victoria which looked like the one in the book and she had been to a museum about Queen Victoria; she thought it was the 'Victoria Museum'. She had also noticed the word 'history' on the cover: 'That means it happened a long time ago?' Shelley thought you could find out more about whether the things in the pictures were 'true' by 'going to an old-fashioned shop where they had things from the olden days'.

These year 1 children were able to differentiate between degrees of probability, in different aspects of each story and in different types of story. They could support their views with arguments based on their existing knowledge and experience, and listen to, endorse or disagree with each other's arguments.

Different versions of stories in pictures and artefacts

Barnes (1993) showed how he helps Key Stage 1 children to discuss different interpretations, through looking at different representations of Christian festivals and of Christian saints. His workshop for teachers took place in the Medieval Rooms of the Victoria and Albert Museum, but he also takes his children to Canterbury Cathedral. Many children already know the stories of the Nativity and the Crucifixion, and can look for different images of these stories. They may also be introduced to and become familiar with stories about St George and other Christian saints, and learn the symbols associated with them in Medieval images. For example:

- St Michael has wings, a shield, a dragon.
- St John is young and beardless, with a book.
- St Peter has a beard, a book and the keys of Heaven.
- Mary, mother of Jesus, has a halo, covered head, long clothes and a baby.

When they arrive in the museum or the cathedral, children can see how many different images they can find of the Nativity, or how many examples they can find of their chosen saint. They can then compare the way the scene, or the saint, they discover is depicted in different poses and in different media. In the Victoria and Albert Museum there may be examples in wood, stone, ivory, metal, stained glass or embroidery. Close observational drawing, using the 'view finder' (a small piece of card with a rectangular hole cut in it) to isolate their chosen example, will encourage children to look very carefully at detail. Back in school, children can discuss similarities and differences. With very young children, it might be best to select just two examples, an altarpiece carving and a stained glass window, for example.

Older children could note the dates of their images and where they come from. In school they could display them in chronological order and find the places on a map. This would help them to recognise and explain differences between styles and periods, between austere early Medieval, Byzantine and Baroque (even if they did not use this terminology).

Powerful images in metal, ivory, glass, wood and stone taught people in Medieval Europe, through symbolic stories, about the Gospels and the lives of the saints. These were embodied in an oral tradition. For this reason, different images tell different stories, and tell stories in different ways. By collecting different examples of dragons, or of the Nativity, or of a particular saint, children become aware that there may be many versions of the same story. This stimulates them to begin to ask questions which will help them to understand the complex relationship between fantasy, reality and symbolism; they will begin to discuss whether characters may be real or fictional and to be aware of the difference between a fact and a point of view. There are lots of dragons in the Victoria and Albert Museum, in the Medieval and the Chinese rooms, so did dragons really exist? Is this story likely to be true? Were the saints from the Gospels white? Why do they look white?

Different versions of stories in comics

Children enjoy comic strip stories, and they can be as important in learning history as they are in the reading process. They are important in reading because they are easy to read. You can tell the story with the bubble voices. They offer children choice in styles of reading. They make the experience of reading meaningful and purposeful. Seven-year-old Chris said of a comic strip of 'Maid Marion and the Merry Men': 'I like the way you can see the writer . . . his hand with his pen . . . and they climb out of the pictures when they escape with the knight.' He liked the humour and the colour. Comics are important because they do not rely on an adult to reinforce the meaning.

Such comic strips can be important in beginning history too, in helping children to understand that there are clearly different versions of stories, and that these are of varying status. Chris used the word 'proper' to show that he noticed the different status and level of acceptability of comics and 'proper' books: 'The people aren't rich. In the *proper* story they don't eat *that* much!' Meek (1988: 27) felt that there is a danger that if children are taught to pay attention only to words in books, 'This particular kind of multi-consciousness, apparently so natural in childhood, yet culturally and specifically learned, is passed over.'

Discussing the captions in a humorous cartoon book such as *The Normans are Coming; The Truth About 1066* (Clements 1987) could help older children, in a zany way, to begin to see how accounts of a period may be written through the anachronistic blinkers of another age. The Normans, depicted in Bayeux tapestry style, refresh themselves with frogburgers and snail sorbet at William's wine bar in Hastings! Certainly, *The Truth About Castles* (Clements 1988) combines lots of graphically shown factual information about how castles were built and defended, and about the lives of people living in a castle, with humorous speech bubbles; this would make a wonderful comparison with the images of life in a castle in *Sir Gawain and the Loathly Lady* (Hastings 1992) which is illustrated with rich, elegant and detailed pre-Raphaelite-style paintings.

Comparing interpretations in illustrations

It is important to help children to explain how different illustrations can express different ideas and feelings about a story. They enjoy talking about what an illustration means and go back to their favourite pictures again and again, searching out details and constructing and reconstructing meanings (Doonan 1993). In order to explain why different pictures express different ideas and feelings, children need to talk about how colour, shape, composition, scale, pattern and the rhythm of lines convey different feelings. They can also begin to understand that styles change with society and with technology, and that they reflect society's values. Nineteenth-century illustrations in children's history books are different from those of the early twentieth century, and from those in modern books.

Different versions of stories about real people

There are recently published stories for young children about real people (Shuter and Reynoldson 1991; Blyth *et al.* 1991) in response to the requirement of *History in the National Curriculum* (DES 1991) that children should learn about famous men and women and events. However, it seems doubtful whether stories about complex events, told in necessarily simple language, are as suitable for young children as stories about the lives of 'ordinary' people.

The Women's History Network Key Stage 1 Biography Project (see p. 196) has involved teachers in researching biographies of well-known women which involve more than one interpretation and they have been tried out with Key Stage 1 children.

The biography of Mary Anning, for instance, has raised some very interesting issues about the way that she has been presented. She has been remembered for the fossil discoveries she made as a child in the early nineteenth century, while playing on the beach at Lyme Regis. Stories about her childhood exploits appear to be untrue, while her very real achievements as an adult appear to have been seriously undervalued.

Fictional stories set in the past

Many stories explore changes over the generations in family life. *Minnie and Ginger* (Smith 1990) tells, with beautiful illustrations, of the lives of Minnie, who began work as an assistant milliner, and Ginger, who worked in a soap factory, and how they had married before Ginger was called up, fought in and survived the Great War. *Timothy's Teddy* (Harrison 1992) describes Teddy's life over two generations; Great Grandpa's memories are humorously treated in *My Great Grandpa* (Waddell and Mansell 1991), and Burningham's *Granpa* (1984) interprets ideas simultaneously through the eyes of a little girl and her grandfather:

> 'If I catch a fish we can eat it for supper.'
> 'What if you catch a whale, Granpa?'

In the end, we are left with the empty chair. The life and death of another Grandpa is sensitively told in *Grandpa's Slide Show* (Gould 1990). Grandmas seem blessed with greater longevity. *When I Was Little* (Williams 1991) tells, in beautiful, humorous, detailed strip cartoons with speech bubbles, of Granny's rosy recollections of her childhood when 'ice cream tasted of cream' and 'babies never cried'.

Such stories are a wonderful way of making children aware of changes over time, within living memory, in their own lives and families. This can lead to investigating the lives of their own grandparents and great grandparents and finding that there are many versions of the past.

Children could make their own books about their Teddy or Grandpa, or when Gran or an older person comes to visit, then compare their books. Gran, Grandpa or older friends could help to draw things for the pages 'We didn't have these' and 'We did have these'.

Children could sort statements written on cards about things Granny says which may be true and things which may not be true: 'we did sums on the blackboard'; 'the sun always shone'. There may be all sorts of opportunities for cross-curricular extensions: science – how many days will it rain *this* summer, or snow *this* winter; how long *do* lollipops last? When *did* the first man land on the moon? Sorting materials – Granny didn't have these, but she did have these. Maths – 'We walked four miles to school.' Is this true? How far is this? Do we do our sums differently from Gran? How far do we walk? Geography – what food do we have that Granny didn't? Why?

CONSTRUCTING INTERPRETATIONS OF THE PAST

Children can begin to learn how and why interpretations of the past differ by constructing their own accounts. They may do this through play, both in 'let's pretend' play, model making and drawing, and by telling and writing stories. Their interpretations must be based on evidence, on what is known. This could be learnt through a story, or a visit to a site. 'Storytelling at Historic Sites' (see p. 196, English Heritage entry) is a selection of myths, legends and folk tales told on audiotape, which are linked to sites. Children's own interpretations could be stimulated by a museum or living history reconstruction, by discussing artefacts or pictures, or by talking to older people. Nevertheless, with very young children, there will be a greater emphasis in their reconstructions on imagination than there is on evidence. Their imagination will involve more fantasy than historical validity, if we take validity to mean conformity with what is known of the period (Lee 1984; Shemilt 1984), because they are immature and their knowledge is limited.

Yet it is important that from the beginning children have the opportunity to develop their imagination about past times. As they get older and their knowledge increases, they can rely more on finding out what is known. Through the process of making a variety of suppositions about the past, children can gradually, with increasing maturity, learn valid historical imagination. This may lead eventually to the achievement of historical empathy, to understanding in a coherent way that people in the past may have thought, felt and behaved differently from us, because of their different knowledge bases and the different social, economic and political constraints of the societies in which they lived (Cooper 1992: 137). Generating hypotheses cultivates multiple perspectives, and possible worlds to match the requirements of those perspectives. This process lies at the heart of history from the very beginning. The eventual aim is that hypotheses will be 'true to conceivable experience: that they have verisimilitudes' (Bruner 1986: 52).

Constructing interpretations through 'let's pretend' play

Children need to explore the world in which they live and their relation to it through play. Yet if play in school is to be valued and justified as central to education, we need to be articulate about how it can be related, in an embryonic way, to the disciplines which constitute a broad curriculum, and about the role of the teacher in supporting such play. Tough (1976: 79) believed that imaginative play enables children to think in an historical way. O'Toole (1992) showed how Dorothy Heathcote's model for distance framing can be developed by teachers in historical contexts.

First, we shall consider how historical thinking can be developed through play and why play is an important way of introducing young children to history, then we shall consider the role of the teacher in interpreting, observing, structuring and extending such play.

Historical thinking can develop through play about people, places, events and stories from the past, because such play involves making inferences about how artefacts (a candle, an old mangle, a bow and arrow) were used, and how they influenced people's lives. This will involve considering how the past may have been different from the present (in the things people did, the way they dressed, the situations they found themselves in); it will involve constructing and explaining sequences of events and the reasons for actions. Through such play, children can explore the difference between what is known, what might be supposed and what cannot be known; they learn that stories may be about real or fictional characters and that there may be different versions of what happened.

Play is an excellent way of introducing children to history. First, it helps them to make sense of what they have learned, to explore and develop it, and to integrate it with what they already know. Before new knowledge can be used it has to be integrated into existing knowledge, and young children find it difficult to integrate 'impersonal' information. Stories about the past have a structure which children can reinvent through play and so recreate and internalise their meanings. Second, play allows children to explore the boundaries between imagination and reality, which are, in any case, blurred for young children. This is particularly so in history, which is concerned with reconstructing, from incomplete traces, a past reality which no longer exists. In play, children are able to live in several worlds at once, the everyday and the imaginary. By recreating myths, legends and stories about the past, children can explore and speculate; wonder what would happen if. . . . 'Through metaphor, chairs and tables can become mountains and caves and a young child can become a powerful adventurer' (Bearne 1992: 147). Children find it difficult to deal with abstract information, but in play they can move from the anecdotal to the formulation of hypotheses. Third, play can allow children to reject what they are not able to internalise and make sense of. Rosen and Rosen (1973) thought that sliding from reality thinking to fantasy may be an intellectual stage, or that it may be a device for cutting off when the information given by adults is inappropriate or unacceptable. Chukovksy (1968) believed that a child is armoured against thoughts and information that it does not need, which is prematurely offered by adults.

Research has shown that the role of the teacher is essential to ensure optimum value in play (Sylva *et al.* 1980; Bateson 1985), and that the most effective teachers are those who involve themselves as well as the children in problem-solving. Free-flow play does not just happen; the adult acts as the catalyst (Singer and Singer 1990). First, the adult needs to provide materials ('props') and construct an environment related to a story, a visit or a living history reconstruction which children have been to see. The 'props' may be costumes (a mob cap, flowing skirts, breeches, caps, a parasol or walking stick) and old artefacts (a scrubbing board and wash tub, a candle, a besom). Constructing the environment may mean turning the play corner or climbing frame into a castle with a flag and a drawbridge, a ship's cabin, a cave or a Victorian kitchen with a cardboard-box range.

Adult interaction needs to be sensitive, for play and language arise from within the child. It is important that the play is not teacher-dominated and geared to 'let's pretend this story'. Intervention should be based on observation of the children's play, and initiated by the children so that it builds on their own ideas. Children between 4 and 5 years old may, for instance, ask for confirmation of events and experiences through the questions they ask. Teachers should contribute their own ideas and avoid giving brief functional answers. They may ask, for instance, to 'tell me one thing you know about it. Now tell me more . . .' and encourage children to think about hypothetical experiences. Through the context of play, the teacher is freed for real and meaningful discussion, possibly in-role as the play develops: 'What do you think Stone Age people would be frightened of?' 'Where is your ship sailing to? Why?' 'Why have you built your castle there?' 'What are you going to cook for dinner?' Older children may sustain play over a longer period and the questions they raise could lead to discussion and use of information books as a basis for further play, or picture-making and story-writing which is more closely related to evidence and to what is known.

'Let's pretend' play about the past can take place in a museum as well as in the classroom. Tullie House in Carlisle has a 15-foot replica of Hadrian's Wall, replica crossbows which can be fired and Roman silver mines to explore. At the National Waterways Museum in Gloucester, you can build bridges and haul canal boat pulleys; at Madame Tussauds, a £10 million 'Spirit of London' ride whisks you through London's history. In 1988, the National Maritime Museum in London established two temporary interactive history centres, in collaboration with the staff and students of Goldsmiths' College, University of London (Anderson 1989). Their aim was to develop historical thinking: an awareness of evidence and its incompleteness, of primary and secondary sources, of similarity and difference between past and present, awareness that 'causes' are the product of interpretation and that events have many causes. They wanted children to understand how historians, in attempting to reconstruct the past, reconstruct not only the externals of life and behaviour, but also the thoughts, feelings, motives, values and attitudes of people in the past. The Armada Discovery Centre was designed for children from 3 to 8 years old and the Bounty Discovery Centre, which followed it, was for 3- to 14-year-olds and their parents.

In the Armada Discovery Centre, children's play was stimulated by stories and by the construction of the play area. Initially sitting in a rocky corner of a darkened room (7 m x 12 m), children heard the story of the *Gran Grifon* which was wrecked off Northern Scotland in 1588. At the point in the story when the ship was about to be wrecked, the lights went up and the children were invited to explore a 10 m-long reconstruction of part of the upper deck and the captain's cabin, standing out from a painted seascape, complete with replica artefacts, including a gun carriage which could be loaded with canon, a barrel of salt fish, and rations of dried biscuits and chickpeas. The play session ended with the story of the Spaniards' rescue, or with folk tales of shipwrecks.

The Bounty Discovery Centre presented the *Bounty* in Tahiti in 1789, a few months before the mutiny. It was recreated against a painted background. The sounds of Tahiti, of children, chickens, pigs, birdsong and the sea, were recorded. There were replicas of a Tahitian house and its artefacts. These contrasted with a 3 m × 3 m reconstruction of Bligh's cabin and part of the lower deck of the *Bounty*, complete with hoists, hammocks, scattered sailors' belongings and barrels of malt vinegar and salt fish. Student teachers who had specialised in Early Years education interacted with the children. It was decided that they could help to interpret the experience for the children in a way that was more historically honest, and arguably with greater diversity and sophistication, if they did not wear costume. The role of the adults here was not to stimulate play with stories, as in the Armada Discovery Centre, but to respond to questions.

It was interesting that parents and students played a crucial role in the children's play. Most parents and grandparents of either sex joined in the children's play activities with enthusiasm. However, when the student interpreters were not present, learning and enjoyment suffered noticeably, and visits were shorter. When the students were present, children and adults readily appreciated the frame within which they participated. It was concluded that the role of the students was to establish rule structures for imaginative play. Once these were communicated, children showed remarkable ability to move confidently and creatively between play and reality.

Classrooms cannot provide such elaborate reconstructions, but children's play does not require this. A play area can easily be transformed into a ship, a castle, a cave or a Victorian kitchen with a few 'props' and dressing-up clothes. Fairclough and Redsell (1987: 34) give basic patterns for eighteenth-century and twelfth-century costumes. Each of the following play reconstructions was set up in a Key Stage 1 classroom. If teachers set play objectives and provide a framework for children to explore, so that they take responsibility for their own learning, the teacher is free to observe the children's learning in a more incisive and focused way. Unfortunately, Tizard *et al.* (1988: 49) found that in thirty-three London schools children in top infant classes spent less than 1 per cent of their time on such 'free' activities.

Box 5.1 The ship

POSSIBLE STIMULI

- Visits to, e.g.
  - The National Maritime Museum, the *Cutty Sark*, London
  - *The Mary Rose, The Victory,* Portsmouth
  - Chatham Historic Dockyard, Kent ('living museum' with tradesmen at work)
  - Town Docks Museum, Hull (on whales and whaling)
  - Royal Research Ship, *Discovery,* Dundee (Scot's Antarctic ship)
  - Merseyside Maritime Museum
  - National Waterways Museum, Gloucester
  - Stoke Bruerne Canal Museum
- Sea shanties
- Poetry, e.g. 'Nursery Chairs' (the third chair), 'The Island' (in Milne 1979a)
- A visit by a sailor
- Video excerpts or excerpts from stories, e.g. *Treasure Island, Peter Pan*
- Fictional stories set in the past told by teacher in role as a pirate or old sailor, e.g. *Jack at Sea* (Dupasquier 1987), a story with brief text and detailed illustrations about a young boy who has run away to join his friend who was press-ganged into the navy during the Napoleonic Wars; or stories of pirates, e.g. *I wish I had a Pirate Suit* (P. Allen, Penguin, London, 1991).
- Maritime paintings
- 'Ships and Seafarers', National Maritime Museum Resource pack
- Replica posters, National Maritime Museum

PLAY

- Initial resources for free play:
  - *Outdoors:* • Climbing frame, climbing net, monkey run
  - *Indoors:* • Playhouse 'cabin'; deck outlined with benches
    - How could we make this more like a ship?
    - Broom-handle mast, tablecloth sail, flag, gang-plank, wheel, telescope, (skipping) ropes, bucket and mop, life belt, compass, chart, maps

EXTENDING PLAY

(Possible questions which may arise from children's comments, from observing play or being involved in play. These could extend the play and may encourage some children to seek further information from other sources.)

Historical thinking

- *Time and change*

Retell a story	Do you know any stories about sailing ships?
Suggest reasons why people in the past acted as they did	Where are you sailing to? Why? What do you think it will be like there?

Identify differences between past and present times	What jobs do you do on the ship? What do you eat/drink? Why? Where do you sleep?
• *Interpretations*	Is your story about a real ship/person? How do you know that story? Have you made up parts of the story? Why?
• *Deductions from sources*	What do you know about sailing ships? How do you know that? What else can you find out? How do you hoist the sails? How do you know which way to sail? etc.

Cross-curricular extensions

Mathematics

- Calculations, e.g. How far is it? And back?
- Shape of flags, sails
- Measures: time – how long is the journey? Keep a log
  capacity – how much water will fill the barrel?
  weight – how many apples/biscuits? How heavy?
  length – how tall/long/wide is your ship?
  money – what are you buying/selling? Bills, paying crew

English
Speaking and listening, reading, writing:

- Name of ship
- Posters advertising for crew for voyage
- List of crew's names
- List of stores, ship's log, buried treasure map and clues, rules and jobs for crew, letters home
- Reading stories and information books
- Concepts: rigging, prow, cabin, deck, gang-plank, explore, navigate, steer, anchor, crow's nest, 'land ahoy'

Science

- Investigations: wind power, sinking and floating, food preservation, waterproof materials, pulleys (sails), balance (gang-plank – walking the plank!)

Music

- Making wind/water music
- Singing sea shanties

Art

- Making 'props': fish, palm trees, flags, pirate hats, eye patches
- Mixing sea colours: sea finger-paintings
- Looking at seascapes in different styles

Geography

- Graphic skills: make imaginary maps, treasure maps, devise symbols and key, write directions as clues
- Use globe or maps to trace route
- Find out about new country: mountains, rivers, climate
- Keep weather chart on journey: wind direction, sunshine, rain
- Learn weather lore, e.g. 'Mackerel skies and mare's tails/ Make tall ships carry low sails'

PE

- Pirates (home base game)
- Shadow fence with pirates
- Swimming, diving
- Jumping into shark-infested seas
- Walk plank
- Climb rigging
- Scrub decks
- Dance hornpipe

The following example shows how drama was used in a more structured way to introduce historical information about voyages of trade and exploration to year 1 children, as part of a topic on transport.

Stage 1

In the classroom the children were shown the *Westward* poster (Maritime Museum, London) which advertised for able-bodied men to sail on the *Westward* to foreign lands in 1798. Out-of-role they discussed briefly what they knew about sailing ships. How did they go? What would the sailors have to take with them? The children were told that when they got to the hall the teacher would be captain of the ship and would be training them as new crew members for the voyage.

Stage 2

In the hall the first part of the lesson was like a simple movement session. The children practised scrubbing decks, climbing rigging and steering. They were taught the shanty 'Haul Away Joe' and they hauled on the heavy ropes. Detail was added at all times by comments like 'Hold tight up there, don't fall', 'How far can you see from up there?', 'Get on with it, work harder, we don't have any slackers here.'

Stage 3

In the second part of the lesson, they were declared fit to crew the ship. They built the shape of the ship from benches and blocks, loaded the ship with food, fresh water and goods to trade, and set sail.

Again, information was given by comments in role. 'We need all the fresh water we can carry – who knows when we'll see land again.' 'Stow the cargo safely, we must try and get as much as we can for it.'

They had an adventure with pirates during the voyage. But it could have been any of a dozen scenarios.

Stage 4

Back in the classroom, the children wrote up their entries for the ship's log and drew maps of their journeys. They had assimilated a great deal of detail and information in the course of one hour's session.

With all the children working at their own level, the teacher, in role, was able to challenge and extend their understanding by questioning and commenting in the course of the drama. Subsequent drama lessons can move the activity forward and introduce new learning areas. In this case, they could have dealt with being becalmed or storm-damaged, initiating trade with a foreign country or charting lands Europeans had not visited before.

Box 5.2 The castle

POSSIBLE STIMULI

- Visits to, e.g. a castle or a Living History reconstruction of tournaments, jousts, feasts and battles (English Heritage), or reconstruction of a site, e.g. Mountfitchet Castle, Stansted. This is an authentic reconstruction of Richard de Mountfitchet's castle, razed to the ground by King John in 1212 in revenge because Mountfitchet joined the barons responsible for Magna Carta. The building materials are authentic; so, probably, are the noises and smells. Telling the story as the children walk around the site can trigger an imaginative understanding of how these Normans lived, cheek by jowl with their animals, with one eye always on potential attackers from outside (the catapult and the quintain) and from within (the gaol, stocks, mantrap and gibbet)
- Video excerpts, e.g. Ivanhoe, Robin Hood
- Stories set in castles or fictional stories, e.g. *Tim's Knight* (S. Isherwood, Hamish Hamilton, London, 1987), in which a lonely boy finds he can 'magic' a Medieval knight into his own time
- Paintings, photographs, illustrations of castles (posters of castles are available from English Heritage, XR13258)
- Poetry ('Knights and Ladies', in Milne 1979a)

PLAY

- Initial resources for free play

  Outdoors: • Play fort, climbing tower

  Indoors: • Playhouse converted into keep
  - How could we make this more like a castle?
  - Moat, marked with paper, drawbridge, flags, shields, helmets and head-dresses, straw on floor, hobby horses for tournament . . .

EXTENDING PLAY

Historical thinking

• *Time and change* Place events in sequence Suggest reasons why people in the past acted as they did. Identify differences between past and present	Do you know any stories about castles? What happens? Why have you built the castle here? What do people eat? How do they cook? Where does the water come from? Who might attack you? How? Why? A teacher, in role, could introduce the idea of spies in the castle . . . How will you defend yourselves? How did you build the castle?
• *Interpretations*	Is your story a true story? Why do you think that? What part do you know is true/made up? Why?
• *Making deductions from (secondary) sources*	Are you going to have a tournament? a ball? a banquet? Can you find out what it might be like?

Cross-curricular extensions

Mathematics
- Shape and space: body size for making armour, shields, cones for ladies' hats, battlements, round towers, rectangular windows

English
Speaking and listening, reading, writing:

- Proclamations
- Invitations to the ball
- Reading stories (fairy stories, legends, stories about local castle)
- Concepts: keep, battlements, moat, drawbridge, portcullis, siege, attack, defend, tournament, jousting, armour, ball

Science

- Pulleys: drawbridge, flag, well
- Levers: bridge
- Structures: test strength of a thick/thin wall, a tall/squat tower, a long/ short bridge
- Investigate spinning, weaving, natural dyes
- Design and technology: design armour, ladies' hats

Music

- Listen to Medieval music for banquet/tournament
- Compose music for banquet/tournament

Art

- Design and make shields, flags
- Collect paintings of castles in different styles

Geography

- Look at maps of site of a real castle
- Draw pretend plans of castle for spies, with directions
- Draw pretend plans of countryside to decide where to build castle

PE

- Dancing at the ball
- Jousting at the tournament
- Climbing, scaling walls, climbing ropes, crawling through undergrowth, tunnels, passages

Box 5.3 Cave/shelter

POSSIBLE STIMULI

- Visits to museums, to a museum reconstruction of a Neolithic site or to a site where there is evidence of a Neolithic settlement, or alternatively modify plans to base play on a visit to a reconstruction of an Iron Age village (Butser, Hampshire) or a Saxon village (West Stowe, Suffolk)
- Slides of cave paintings, neolithic implements
- Fictional stories, e.g. *Stone Age Magic* (Ball 1989), in which a group of children travel back in time to the Stone Age during a museum visit

PLAY

- Initial resources
  Outdoors:
  - Visit to a local site where neolithic implements (could have been) found
  - Pretend you are neolithic people. Where will you build your shelter? Why here? How?
  - How will you keep warm? Make a comfortable place to sleep? What will you eat? How will you defend yourself?

  Indoors:
  - Make 'cave paintings' by projecting slides on to paper on a wall. Use sticks, feathers, fingers to make 'cave paintings'. Make replica clay pots for storage and cooking
  - Collect nuts, seeds and berries to store
  - Use leather off-cuts, wood, (blunt) stone, twine to design, then make a neolithic tool or weapon
  - Cook a 'neolithic meal' (Renfrew 1985)
  - Make a shelter from tables, covered in hessian, with twigs attached, and a pretend fire

EXTENDING PLAY

Historical thinking

- *Time and change*
  Suggest reasons why people in the past acted as they did. Identify differences between past and present times

  Why do you think Stone Age people made the cave paintings? What things do you think they might have been frightened of?
  What animals are you going to hunt? How?
  What do you eat?
  How do you make your shelter? Your clothes?

- *Interpretations*

  Do you think this could really have happened? Why do you think that? What have you made up? Why?

- *Making deductions from sources*

  How do you think people might have used this tool (e.g. pictures of arrowhead, axe, scraper)? Why?
  Teacher, in role, could introduce the idea of a hunting expedition. . . the teacher may be no good at hunting and afraid of killing. . . .

Cross-curricular extensions

Mathematics
- Sorting collections, e.g. nuts, berries, roots, leaves; or things for shelter, food, tools, weapons; or sorting pictures of tools and weapons; or sorting into wood, stone, bone, plants
- Calculations based on sets

English
Speaking and listening, reading, writing:

- Trying to interpret petraglyphics; making up a Stone Age language and its symbols, for a friend to decode
- Ritual chants for a hunting or healing ceremony
- Stories based on play
- Concepts: power, defend, attack, tools, weapons

Science

- Materials: firing clay, spinning, weaving, dyeing
- Cooking 'neolithic' food
- Growing wheat seeds
- Technology: design (and make) a tool or weapon
- Forces and structures: how might neolithic people have moved/lifted stones?

Music

- Make instruments using natural materials: percussion, wind, strings (?)

Art

- Make pottery decorated with natural objects
- Devise ways of applying paint for cave paintings; mix limited 'natural' colours
- Discuss slides of cave paintings: what do they depict? How were they made? Why?

Geography

- Reasons for selecting your site (protection, drainage, water, wood, crops)
- How were flint and chalk formed?

PE

- Hunting: tracking, crawling, running, jumping, changing speed/direction, stopping and starting, transferring body weight

Box 5.4 The Victorian kitchen

POSSIBLE STIMULI

- Visit to an old house or living history reconstruction (e.g. the Squatters Cottage and The Toll House at Blists Hill Open Air Museum, Ironbridge Gorge)
- Illustrated diaries (Bradley 1974: 70)
- Contemporary book illustrations, e.g. Beatrix Potter, *The Pie and the Pattie Pan*; *Mrs Tiggy-Winkle*
- Artefacts, e.g. old cooking, washing and cleaning utensils
- Photographs
- Video, e.g. 'The Victorian Kitchen', BBC TV
- Recipes, e.g. jelly, blancmange, gingerbread men, jams, pickles, sweets

PLAY

- Initial resources for free play: range made from cardboard boxes, mantelpiece, table, chair, candle, enamel bowl, flat iron, scrubbing brush, mop, floor polish, carpet beater, pastry cutters, basins, boot scraper, tin bath, old ornaments, rag rug, clothes horse, flowers and vegetables from kitchen garden

EXTENDING PLAY

Historical thinking

- *Time and change*

Suggest reasons why people in the past acted as they did	Why do you think people grew their own fruit/vegetables?
	Why did most women only work in the home?
	Did you have to do all these jobs if you were rich? What if you were poor?
Identify differences between past and present	Why did they use a tin bath, beat the rugs, scrub the clothes?

- *Interpretations*   Are all kitchens we have found out about the same?
                          How?
                          How are they different? Why?
- *Making*   Where does the water come from?
  deductions   How was it heated?
  from sources   How do you dry the clothes, do the ironing?
                          Where is the coal kept? Where does the smoke go?
                          Where do you keep the food? How is it packed/stored?
                          Children, as 'themselves', could 'visit' a Victorian
                          kitchen, where they meet a person dressed differently
                          from themselves who is trying to find someone who
                          worked there a hundred years ago

Cross-curricular extensions

Mathematics

- Calculations, e.g. shopping lists using old pennies
- Measures: time – how long does it take to scrub this . . . clean without
              detergent? to polish this candlestick; scrub the floor, polish
              the lino?
              weight – how much does the flat iron/coal bucket weigh?
              cooking – weighing ingredients
              capacity – how much does the jug/basin/blancmange mould
              hold?
              shape and space – rolling out pastry to fit pattie pans/cutters
              length – making paper aprons

English
Speaking and listening, reading, writing:

- Kitchen rules, maids' jobs, samplers
- Shopping lists, recipes
- Victorian parlour games

Science

- Electricity: how does it make things work? Effects on life in the kitchen?
- Food preservation, then and now
- Materials: old and new fabrics/kitchen implements

Art

- Drawing/painting old kitchen ornaments and utensils

Music

- Victorian songs: learn hymns, music hall songs, Gilbert and Sullivan;
  collect and listen to records on old gramophone

Geography

- Draw a plan of the Victorian kitchen for house corner
- Draw a plan of your kitchen at home (differences?)

PE

- Gardening, polishing, scrubbing, balancing trays, lifting loads

It is possible to help children to understand why there may be more than one interpretation of a story through more structured play. Shamroth (1992) described how a teacher, in role as Goldilocks, maintained that Daddy Bear's traditional version of the story was not true, and that he had captured her in the woods. A piece of her dress, found in the woods, was produced! The children, in role as villagers searching for Goldilocks, questioned Goldilocks (the teacher) about what had happened. They compared the teacher's version and the original version. They fed back what they knew, what they thought they knew and what they wanted to find out. Daddy Bear was tried and the teacher eventually confessed to a hall full of intent 'villagers' that her version was not true. With great relief Daddy Bear was released.

In another example (Vass 1993) the teacher began by saying, 'I am going to pretend to be a little girl who lived x years ago and I want you to pretend too'. She then reconstructed the Great Fire of London as a witness, within the conventions of a simulation game. The children became part of the reconstruction and contributed to it with their questions. The key features, the hard evidence of the narrative, were combined with opinions and imagination. Out of role they discussed what was true and what was made up.

Box 5.5 shows how a visit to the Victorian letterbox at the end of the road was developed to involve a wide range of historical thinking and led children to re-enact their own interpretations of a true local story. Children and teacher 'found' a very old letter, in copperplate hand-writing, sealed with wax. Who could have written it? To whom? Why? How?

Box 5.5 The Victorian letterbox

HISTORICAL THINKING	
Communicate information acquired from an historical source. Ask further questions.	Visit Victorian post box. The post box was built in the time of VR. Who was VR? When could you *first* send letters by post? How? (mail coaches, and turnpike roads)
Understand that stories may be about real people or fictional characters.	Stories about highwaymen who really lived, e.g. Dick Turpin, and in fiction, e.g. *The Toby Man* (King Smith 1989), the story of a small boy forced by poverty to follow his father into a career of highway robbery.
Place familiar objects in chronological order. Identify differences between past and present.	Teacher finds out from local history society records that the road (the Brighton Road) had been a turnpike road. Children collect toy horses, carts, cars and photographs and sort into old, very old, new.

	Teacher invited a member of the local history society to talk to class about a true story, found in the society's records, about a boy who drove a cart along the Brighton Road a hundred years ago and did not stop at the turnpike. In his haste, he dropped his oil lamp. The visitor brought the same lamp, which was confiscated, to show the children.
Make deductions from historical sources. Distinguish between a fact and a point of view.	Children examined the lamp, discussed how it worked, and made models to explain this. They discussed the boy's motives for driving through the turnpike (naughty, poor, late/why? how did he feel?).
Awareness of different versions of what happened. Differentiating between a fact and a point of view.	Different groups of children for some time afterwards arranged chairs as a cart and, using the model lamp, retold and re-enacted different versions of why the boy did not stop at the turnpike.

Constructing interpretations through telling and writing stories

Telling a story is a skill which children develop gradually. To begin with, events may be linked in a chain but have no point, purpose or causal links. There may be a setting but no character or problem, or there may be action but no setting (Temple *et al.* 1982: 154). Children only gradually learn to understand the structure of a story and to see the links between problem, cause and action. They find it easier to listen to stories than to make up their own.

Anderson (1993) suggested how museum artefacts could stimulate young children to make up their own versions of stories which explain them. They could, for example, look at incomplete carvings and 'guess' the rest of the story, or make up stories about how they had been damaged. (How did St Michael lose his wing?) They could make up stories to explain what someone in a carving or stained glass picture might be saying. (To whom is Christ speaking in the sixteenth-century carving of Christ riding on a donkey and what might he be saying?)

Medieval carvings, statues and stained glass often depict different versions of the same story. (St George sometimes kills the dragon, and in others he captures it.) This is because folk tales about the saints were accepted by the church as a device for explaining to people their lives and beliefs. These stories were part of the oral tradition and so many versions existed, which became frozen in statues and carvings. Children can retell the different stories depicted. Or they could compare the dragon painted on a Medieval altarpiece with a Chinese dragon embroidered on silk (postcards W205 and FE196, Victoria and Albert Museum).

Constructing interpretations through model-making, painting and drawing is as central to the early years curriculum as stories and 'let's pretend' play. The opportunity to play with building bricks, constructional toys and a range of junk materials is clearly linked to the development of abstract and divergent thinking. In the context of history, children can make models of sites or buildings they have visited, and paint and draw images of stories they have heard. They can compare them, discuss how they relate to what they saw or heard, what they have added, and why. Friends of the school may be enlisted to build models of old ships, forts, shops or dolls' houses (Honeychurch Toys Ltd; The Dolls' House Emporium), with which children could develop play about the past, stimulated by stories they have heard. Or children could make their own models based on (postcards of) a toy (shops, dolls, trains, forts, dolls' houses, an Indian Prince's carriage) in the Bethnal Green Museum of Childhood. *The Model Village* (Fisk 1990) might encourage imaginative play with their models.

Six-year-olds also draw to describe events which occurred over time. They build up the narrative as they go along. It unfolds on the surface of the paper, often showing the same characters at different points of the story. They retell their own versions of it with sound accompaniments as they record it using their own marks; lines often represent movement through space and time.

Chapter 6

Deductions from sources

THE DEVELOPMENT OF THE PROCESSES OF HISTORICAL ENQUIRY

Historians find out about the past from sources, traces of the past which remain. Gradually the range and status of the sources available to them has increased and the process of interpreting sources has developed. Medieval chronicles tended not to make inferences, and not to analyse, evaluate or reflect on statements about events. Bede was unusual in that he did list the written sources he used and attempted to evaluate the oral tradition. With the Renaissance, however, there was a new emphasis on the original documents of Greece and Rome. This led historians, from the sixteenth to the eighteenth centuries, to place greater emphasis on research, and on the use of a wider range of sources: Camden's *Britannia* was based on 'evidence', and Hume's *History of England* traced changes in prices, wages and dress. In the nineteenth century, documentation, and the particular rather than the general, became increasingly important. Documents of varying status were considered relevant: Macaulay used broadsheets, songs, maps and party propaganda as well as political documents. For the first time the research techniques of history were taught in universities, in the Sorbonne and in Berlin, at Oxford and Cambridge. By the twentieth century, history involved an even wider range of sources and areas of enquiry: archaeology, cartography, folk songs, children's games, old sayings, folk lore, oral history, place-names and statistics. Traditions from the past which continue into the present, such as traditional farming methods which may reflect on the past, are studied. Therefore, when children find out about the past from old newspapers, songs, games, photographs or oral history, this is not simply because such sources may be accessible to them; they are also the sources used by academic historians.

However, sources can only tell us about the past if we know the kinds of questions to ask about them, and how they may be answered. This process was clarified by Collingwood in his *Autobiography* (1939). As a young philosophy teacher he rejected the methods of the 'realists' who proceeded from logical propositions which could be proved true or false. Collingwood saw enquiry as being a complex of ordered, specific questions in the tradition of Plato, Bacon, Descartes and Kant. He said that philosophy had found it necessary to accommodate a revolution in thinking about the natural world, based on empirical observation and deduction in the seventeenth century, and that history must encompass a similar revolution in the way man is studied in constantly changing societies. Collingwood worked out his philosophy of history through constant application in archaeology. He proceeded from specific questions about the significance and purpose of objects to the people who made them. How was it made? Why? What was it used for? By whom? Where was it found? Are there others?

Sometimes a question can lead to a premise followed by a deduction. We know that these are Saxon place-names, therefore Saxons settled in this area. We know that these are the laws of Aethelbert of Kent or of Ine of Wessex. Therefore we know that the Saxons made laws about homes, cattle and crops, that most people had rights as well as duties, and some freedom to move around. We know (from archaeological evidence) that certain banks indicate Iron Age fields. Therefore we know the size and shape of fields in the Iron Age and can estimate the population they could support. We know Iron Age people had coins with horses on. Therefore we know that they had horses, brass, tin, copper and used money. We know they had spindles and loom weights. Therefore they spun and wove cloth. Neolithic stone sickles, hoes and grinding mills tell us that Stone Age people grew crops. Therefore they lived in one place, in a community.

Yet often deductions cannot be made from sources. Evidence is often incomplete. Its status may also be uncertain; the walrus or whalebone pendant found in the Barnack Grave may be just an ornament, or it may be a ceremonial or cult object representing ideas or social practices we can only guess at. An account of the defeat of the British by the Saxons written by the sixth-century monk Gildas may be not so much a chronicle of events as an allegorical exhortation to the British to resist the Saxon invaders.

Diaries may be biased; they may or may not have been written for publication. Newspaper and other accounts may be prejudiced. Portraits or photographs may not be typical. The evidence of the past which remains cannot tell us for certain about the thoughts and feelings of the people who made or used it.

Therefore inferences, reasonable suppositions about historical sources, are more frequent than deductions. Inferences must be supported by arguments, and they must conform with what else is known of the period. Yet often within these criteria more than one interpretation is possible. There are no fixed rules which generate a correct conclusion. For example, in the recently discovered tomb of an Egyptian pharaoh at Abydos, some of the oldest examples of hieroglyphic writing were found. This led Dr Vivian Davies to think that the components of later Egyptian writing were present several centuries earlier than previously supposed. However, Dr John Ray disagrees, because the writing does not have phonetic values. However, they both agree that the new evidence suggests that the idea of writing came from Sumer or Elam, and reopens the questions as to what extent Egyptian culture was an independent invention (Hammond 1993).

Historical imagination is the capacity to make a range of valid suppositions about evidence. If the pupil does the supposing with real insight and makes perceptive selections from the wealth of possibilities open to her/ him, given the evidence she/he has, we may say the supposing is done 'with imagination' (Lee 1984).

Through suggesting how a source may have been made and used, and what it may have meant to the people who made and used it (whether it be a piece of writing, a place-name, a picture or an artefact), the historian may attempt to understand and to explain the possible thoughts and feelings which the evidence represents. Collingwood (1946) stressed the importance of trying to understand the feelings and thoughts which resulted in actions and in artefacts which remain, for otherwise they are unintelligible. History, he said, is the history of thought. We cannot say how it felt to make a Stone Age cave painting or wear an Iron Age helmet or to be Eva Braun in the Berlin bunker, but we can speculate about the motives which account for the painting, the helmet and her death in the bunker. The job of the historian is not to duplicate the lost world of the past, but to ask questions about the traces of the past which remain. In the question and answer sequence, the 'right' questions are the ones which lead to a larger complex and do not draw a blank. There is no limit to the number or kinds of questions or to the relevant evidence. It is also important to recognise that some questions can never be answered.

Making inferences about sources, then, involves asking questions about how they were made and used, and how they may have affected the lives, the feelings and thoughts of the people who made and used them. It means accepting that there may be a number of equally valid inferences.

Young children, in making suggestions about historical sources, need to learn that there may be no one correct answer (and also why some inferences may be more likely than others). This gives them confidence in forming, justifying and discussing their own opinions and listening to those of others. It develops children's sense of control over their own thinking in a way that closed questions cannot.

> There are lots and lots of people who are always asking things,
> Like Dates and Pounds-and-Ounces and the names of funny Kings,
> And the answer's either Sixpence or A Hundred Inches Long,
> And I know they'll think me silly if I get the answer wrong . . .
> ('The Friend', in Milne 1979b)

Christopher Robin would have enjoyed 'proper' history. History in the National Curriculum at Key Stage 1 requires children to find out about the past from sources of information, to learn to answer questions about the past using sources, and to begin to select information from sources to answer specific questions about the past.

TEACHING CHILDREN TO MAKE DEDUCTIONS AND INFERENCES ABOUT SOURCES

Oral sources

Good story-tellers' accounts of their childhood are irresistible. Roald Dahl's autobiography (1986: 11) begins, 'this grandfather of mine was born, believe it or not, in 1820, shortly after Wellington had defeated Napoleon at Waterloo'. He then launches into a vivid account of how his father accidentally lost an arm which was 'pulled off' by a drunken doctor who arrived in a horse-drawn buggy, who had been summoned to treat a fracture. The very old and the very young often have a natural rapport, conveyed more poetically by A.A. Milne (1979b) in 'The Charcoal Burner'.

> The charcoal burner has tales to tell. . . .
>
> The springs that come and the summers that go,
> Autumn dew on bracken and heather,
> The drip of the forest beneath the snow
> All the things they have seen
> All the things they have heard. . . .
>
> Oh the charcoal burner has tales to tell!
> And he lives in the forest and knows us well.

Yet teachers cannot assume this rapport. They need to create situations in which it can flourish. They need to consider:

- whom they should invite to talk about their past;
- a focus and stimulus for the discussion;
- how to help children to generate and structure their questions;
- how to organise the session; and
- how to follow it up.

Choosing interviewees

Oral history provides rich sources, because it is concerned with the unique, diverse and personal lives of ordinary men and women, from different backgrounds and cultures. Yet people may be wary of talking about their personal lives, especially to children!

> Hear, Land o' Cakes and brither Scots,
> Frae Maidenkirk to Johny Groats!
> If there's a hole in a' your coats
> I rede you tent it;
> A chield's amang you takin' notes,
> And faith, he'll prent it!
>
> (Robert Burns, 'On the Late Captain Grose's Peregrinations
> Through Scotland, collecting the ambiguities of that kingdom',
> in Beattie and Meikle 1977: 161)

In deciding whom to invite, it is important to consider whether the person will want to talk about their personal experiences to children, and whether they are able to take account of children's interests, vocabulary and limited attention span.

Focus and stimulus

It is best to focus on a specific aspect of a history topic. 'Living Memory' or 'Family History' could focus on toys, clothes, school, games or food. A topic such as 'The Locality' may investigate the fair, the railway station, the library, shopping or occupations. A topic on stories may begin with asking older people how they learnt to read, then what their favourite books were and why. The guest may be able to bring, or the teacher to provide, photographs or artefacts to initiate discussion.

Preparation

The children

Cramer (1993) described classic interview techniques used by oral historians: a number of introductory questions of a closed nature to set the framework and establish a relationship with the subject, followed by a high proportion of open-ended questions about the area being investigated, then a closing frame to bring the subject back into the present.

Children need to be taught how to structure an interview in a similar way. Vass (1993) described how a father was interviewed as part of a local study about the recreation ground, where he had played as a boy. The first interview was dominated by closed questions which led nowhere. 'Did you go there a lot?' 'Did you like it?' 'Yes.' Before a second interview, the children discussed how their questions could be improved to obtain more information. They then found that questions such as 'What did you have to play on?' and 'What happened then?' led to a story about how the umbrella cradle had been removed after an accident, which was followed by a wider discussion about safety, vandalism and pollution.

Cramer suggested that, first, children decide, either as a class or in groups, on five initial questions to ask; for example, 'Where did you live?' 'Who lived in your house?' Then they should practise tape-recording interviews with each other, listen to the tapes, and discuss what makes a good interview. They need to discuss why an 'mmm' or a silence may be better than continuous questions, and how to follow up questions by asking what happened next, why, how did you feel, how do you know? They need to consider why listening and turn-taking are important. Children can then decide, in groups, on an area of their topic they want to investigate during the second stage of the interview, but not necessarily prepare lists of questions as they may focus too closely on these rather than on the topic they are engaged in.

There also needs to be discussion about the language used for the interview and for conveying the information to another audience. This can be an ideal opportunity for bilingual children to demonstrate their skills. The final stage, bringing the subject back to the present, can be the role of the teacher.

The interviewee(s)

An interviewee needs to know something of the age and abilities of the children, the work they have done on the topic and in preparing for the interview, the kinds of questions they may ask, and the expected length of the discussion. They should also understand the kinds of historical thinking and the oral skills the teacher is trying to develop. Vass (1993) described an interview by a class of 6-year-olds, of a mum in her late 20s who had attended their school. The interview was imaginatively prepared in advance. Stories of milk monitors and the demolition of the outside toilets led to a question about whether she had been taught in the same classroom. 'Yes', replied the mother, 'and I sat at your desk.' She told the (true) story of some spilt ink which had marked the desk. After a search, the stain was found by the enthralled children. They were unaware of the time spent by the teacher and parent finding the right desk!

Organisation of the interview(s)

Thought needs to be given to a number of questions. Will the discussion be with the whole class, with a small group or with pairs of children? Will one person talk in turn to several groups? How many adults can be invited? Should their visits be staggered over a period? Where will the interviews take place, and what are the best seating arrangements? What is the role of the teacher?

Follow-up

Children need to clarify and make explicit their findings in order to present them to others. They could, for example, draw a sequence of pictures to illustrate events described, make tape-recordings of what they found out, write labels explaining photographs or objects they were shown, or act out some of the incidents described.

Discussion of the interview after the visitor has left can also lead to considering the reliability of oral evidence. Children need to know that individual perceptions and stories do not necessarily correspond with the accepted view. This can lead towards an understanding of the relationship between story telling, oral sources, myths, legends and history. Vass (1993) described how a North Devon fisherman came every year to talk to children about life between the wars. Every year his stories became more elaborate and inventive as he got to know which stories went down best. The whale, originally a porpoise, which attacked his fishing boat, became an epic of *Jaws* proportions! After he had left, the children asked: 'Was the story about the whale true?' This led to a discussion about whether the story was true, whether the fisherman had been openly lying, whether he intended to deceive or whether he was elaborating in order to create a good story. Young children are capable of sophisticated analysis if the context interests them.

Visual sources

Visual sources have become increasingly important to historians since the Romantic Age when art became regarded as a magic carpet to times past, to the 'spirit of an age'. History became regarded as a means of decoding images of past events, places, personalities and emotions. Clark (1969) hoped that by studying art the historian might be involved in historical enquiry more truthfully than is possible using other sources, and Gombrich saw art as a central historical source. He said that 'between art and history there is no contest; as soon as a work of art is made, it becomes part of history'. Gombrich (1977) saw art as a key to understanding the ways in which different ages and different nations represent the world.

However, visual sources provide their own complexities of interpretation. Paintings present a particularly selective, sanitised and manipulated view of the past. The Dutch historian Huizinga pointed out that the idea which works of art give us of an epoch is often far more serene and happy than that which we find in other sources. Interpreting paintings as an historical source involves major issues. Can styles, for example, be regarded as the moral reflection of an era? Does Gothic represent a pure expression of faith and Baroque represent authoritarianism? Should primitive art be taken as reflecting a primitive society or ornate art be associated with decadence (Haskell 1993)?

Photographs have been recognised as an important historical source since the 1960s. Samuel (1993) described his discovery of photographs as a source.

> These were the first photographs that had ever impressed themselves on me as a visual document . . . their unexpectedness giving to the anonymous the kind of reverent attention normally reserved for politicians and literary celebrities. . . . [They] promised intimacy between historians and their subject matter, allowing us if not to eavesdrop into the past . . . at least to rub shoulders with it.

In 1972, the National Portrait Gallery appointed its first photographic curator. Photographs are more likely to reflect the lives of 'ordinary' people but, like paintings, they are often, in different ways, selective, biased or contrived.

Visual sources also include cave paintings, whether from the Mpongweni mountains of Lesotho or from Lescaux in France. They include painted, printed, woven and embroidered textiles, stained glass and statues, advertisements, postcards and book illustrations.

Young children can learn to look at, discuss and make inferences about pictures. A picture gives form to ideas and is something to which they can attach their own ideas. Interpreting a picture involves dynamic interaction between the creator and the viewers. By playing with ideas provoked by a work of art, they create something of their own from it, and in that play they have to deal with concepts – logically, intuitively and imaginatively.

More research is needed into how children perceive images and what they can cope with at different ages; it seems that from 3 to 6 years old children prefer increasingly complex visual patterns. Once a child discovers how much there is to be gained from looking at pictures, reading a picture becomes wonderfully taxing. Looking at pictures represents a puzzle and our attitude to them must be open. There is no guarantee we can make sure of all we are shown. We have to begin with, 'maybe it is about . . .' (Doonan 1993: 11). Doonan went on to say that if we

> discover too many enigmatic details to support an hypothesis, we may have to abandon it and start looking all over again. We also have to tolerate ambiguity. We may settle for several interpretations and be satisfied with them all – or none. What is crucial, through all the sensitive testing and hypothesising, is that we remain open-minded and prepared to give the process plenty of time.

Book illustrations may be a good way to introduce children to the skills of decoding paintings and photographs. Children can first learn to talk about the ideas, moods and feelings they represent, and how they have been achieved, through lines, shapes and colour. Young children can infer from facial expressions and body language what people may be thinking, feeling and saying. Later they can use these skills in talking about illustrations in books about the past. Unwin (1986) suggested that children may prefer to see things as they may have been, in illustrated reconstructions of past times, rather than as archaeological remains. Children can also use illustrations in old children's books as a primary source; Beatrix Potter's *Mrs Tiggywinkle* contains much information about washday. Eventually they can transfer their decoding skills to paintings and photographs, and discuss the moods, feelings and ideas represented in them.

Paintings

Paintings can provide an historical dimension to a variety of themes: folk tales, food, clothes, houses, children, pets. They can reflect a range of cultures. Paintings such as *The Negro Page* (Aelbert Cuyp 1620–91) or *Michael Alphonsus Shen Fu-Tsung* (*The Chinese Convert*) painted by Sir Godfrey Kneller (1646–1729), both in the Royal Collection and reproduced as postcards, can provide visual evidence of the long-standing links between Europe, Asia and Africa. Chinese or Indian paintings could be reproduced from books for older children (e.g. Gleisner 1992: 38–9; Goalen 1992: 12, 14; Roberts 1992), or from postcards in the Victoria and Albert Museum collection.

Children can extract information from paintings, and make deductions and inferences about events, clothes and artefacts. They can discuss the validity of a painting as an historical source. How was it made? For whom? Why? Did they always look like this? Did most people dress like this? Paintings can develop historical imagination. What might it feel or sound like to be in that picture?

Lulu and the Flying Babies (Simmonds 1988) delightfully illustrates the process of a child becoming involved in and enchanted by paintings in a gallery. Angry because she is not allowed to play in the snow, Lulu finds herself talking to two cherubs in one of the paintings in a gallery. They take her to fly with them into the snowy world of Breughel, to ride on horseback behind a king in another painting and to taste the fruit in a Dutch still life. *Smudge* (Dickinson 1989) shows how 'a very scruffy boy' finds himself part of the Bayeux Tapestry, a Greek vase and a Lowry scene.

Arnheim (1974) suggested how we can help children to look at a painting with us in a more organised way. First of all we describe the whole picture. Next, safely guarded by the structure of the whole, we try to recognise the principal features, then explore the dependent details. Gradually the entire work reveals itself, falls into place, and begins to engage all the powers of our mind with its message. Finally, we might ask whether the picture tells a story, what might have happened before or afterwards, or what sounds might be heard if we were there. We can discuss the picture as an interpretation, and whether it makes us feel happy or sad, whether we like it or not, and why.

Through the 'Images of People' project at the Russell-Cotes Art Gallery and Museum in Bournemouth, activities were developed which help young children to see that the way illustrations represent people may only be one interpretation and may not be reliable. For example, children can choose a collection of objects to represent themselves, guess the meanings of each other's displays and explain how they felt when others interpreted their objects; or a teacher can choose an object to represent the class and children can say whether they feel it represents them (Batho 1994).

Box 6.1 Looking at paintings: a possible sequence of questions

---

Find out about the past and answer questions using the source

1 Overview of the picture

- What people can you see?   Who do you think they are?
- Where are they?   Why?
- What are they doing?   Why?
- Are there any letters, numbers   What do they tell us?
    or crests?

2 The details

- What are they wearing?   Are they rich?
    What are they holding?   Are they powerful?
    What sorts of hairstyles?   Would they wear these clothes
                                        every day?
    What colours are their clothes? Is there a special reason?
- What buildings can you see?   Why are they in the picture?
    What furniture, plants, pictures, Why are they in the picture?
      pets, lighting?
    What is in the background?   Why?
- What do the people's actions,   Who is the most/least important?
    gestures suggest?   What might they be saying, feeling?
                                      What does the picture tell us about
                                        women, children, age, race?

This example shows how children in a year 2 class were able to make deductions and inferences about portraits of Queen Victoria and of Queen Elizabeth I. At first the children were given four pictures of Queen Victoria painted at different times of her life. They quickly recognised that the same person was present in each picture and put them into chronological order. They then guessed who she might be. One child said a queen, because she had a crown in one picture. They next tried to work out why the different pictures had been painted, using the evidence in the pictures. They suggested various important life events, including birthdays, wedding, her coronation and retirement. They used elements in the pictures to make sensible guesses as to which pictures might relate to what. They discussed why she was wearing black when she was old. Some of the children knew it was the colour of mourning.

Then the children looked at a selection of portraits of Elizabeth I. There was some debate about whether she was the present queen, then they discussed how long ago she had died. They compared the pictures with those of Queen Victoria, even though these had been removed from sight, and quickly identified the coronation painting. They made many detailed observations, looking at hair, clothes and jewellery as well as the backgrounds. They identified which pictures the crown, sceptre and orb appeared in (they had to ask what these objects were), even when they were in the background. They later said that they had been included to show that she was a queen.

The children talked about Queen Elizabeth's age in each picture. They stated that she must be youngest in her coronation picture because that was the start of her reign. They discussed why she had so many jewels in the pictures. They suggested it was 'because she wanted to show she is rich' or 'because she was greedy'. When looking at Marcus Gheeraerts' portrait, which shows the queen standing on a map of England, the children realised that she could not really have been standing on England, that it must have been only in the picture and that she was standing on the map to show that she ruled England.

When asked why she was painted so often, they suggested 'because she was queen of England', 'because she was famous', 'because she wanted everyone to know what she looked like'. They expressed various opinions about her character. The children were quite certain that she was not as thin as she was portrayed. They knew that she had 'hoops' under her skirt.

The work covered a range of levels in the National Curriculum and the discussion was recorded to make assessment possible.

The children had opportunities to consider time and change, the differences between past and present in their own lives and in other people's lives, by comparing the pictures and seeing how Elizabeth and Victoria had changed during their lives, and to recognise similarities and differences between different periods in the past, by identifying features common to more than one picture and the differences between them.

They considered how and why images of the past are created, recognising that they were working with pictures of real people and that particular messages were being expressed in the paintings. They used the pictures as sources of information about the past, talking about what they could see in the paintings and asking questions about the pictures and the people in them, looking at the pictures for the answers to their questions, and making deductions from the paintings. They selected and put together information from more than one painting to answer specific questions.

Photographs

Photographs as an historical source include personal photographs, photographs from books, newspapers, or postcard views. They may be linked to themes such as 'Ourselves', 'Our Street' (or school or village), 'Jobs People Do', 'Holidays', 'Clothes' or 'Transport'. Old photographs are also often used with young children because they are a graphic representation of 'otherness'. Dates, addresses, messages and titles often extend the visual dimension, especially on postcards which pre-date the telephone.

Joanne Edwards, a student working with year 3 children who had studied the Second World War the previous term, showed them a photograph of her grandparents' wedding in 1943. They immediately deduced that it was taken during the war.

A They've all got uniforms on. He's a pilot.
JE How do you know?
A You can see the wings on his uniform.
K They're wearing soldiers' outfits.
B They didn't have much money in the war. They couldn't have new dresses. She's wearing a normal dress like you'd wear at a party. She's got a small bunch of flowers and no veil. They had short dresses so they could run down the shelters.

All the children were able to transfer their knowledge about the war to the photograph; it is interesting that the girls talked about the women's clothes and the boys about the pilot's wings and the men's centre partings.

The children were also able to make inferences about the people's feelings and motives, by drawing on their knowledge about adult behaviour from soap operas!

A They wanted to be happy and make more out of their lives. They wanted to have happy memories in case they died. It's like *Home and Away* when Blake wanted to marry Meg before he died.
B And Ted and Rita in *Coronation Street* . . .

In a second session these children were shown a sequence of five family photographs and the teacher recorded what they noticed about them. She found that the questioning about the earlier pictures gave them a framework for discussing the later pictures without prompting.

The synopsis in Box 6.2 of the children's descriptions, questions and deductions shows how they developed each other's points and responded to each other's questions.

Box 6.2 Looking at photographs

1880 photograph
Why is the address on the photo? So other people would go back for a photo?
You don't see ladies now with buttons from the chest to the neck.
There are beads on either side.
The dress would cling to your neck.
I think the boys' collars would be uncomfortable – it's sort of stiff material.
They got dressed up to have their picture taken. Oh yes.
And the photographer's put them in order for the picture. In the olden days
    they didn't say smile.

1912 photograph
It's winter. He's wearing his coat and gloves.
I think he was going for a walk in the park with his dog.
He's got bloomers and a dress on and socks, like girls, and frilly things on
    his shoes.

1946 photograph
This picture isn't very old because you still see girls with their hair like that.
It's an old-fashioned pram. Nowadays babies sit up in them. They don't lie
    down like in that one.
It may have been taken because they have a new baby.

1960 photograph
It looks like the time of the teddy boys – you know – like in *West Side Story*.
They might be on holiday.
I don't wear *dresses* on holiday. I wear shorts and tops.
It's not far away. It's Butlins or Eastbourne maybe (both are places known
    to K). It's a holiday camp or hotel.
It's summer; the flowers are out.

1970 photograph
They're sort of hippies in 1970 – you know, flower power.
They're at a wedding. You can see the church – the arch.
Are they getting married?
They all look relaxed and happy.

Curtis (1993) suggested strategies for using visual sources with low
ability and developing bilingual pupils, which could also be used with
young children to help them to understand that different sources lead to
different views of the past.

Two groups of children are given different sets of pictures which convey
contrasting messages; for example, poor and rich Victorian children or
children in a town and in the country, or leisure and work in Victorian
times. The teacher could work with each group in turn. Each child in the
group chooses a picture and tells the others what he or she thinks is
happening in it. Other children may say whether they agree, if not why
not, and whether they can see anything else in the picture. Then the group
decides what it thinks its set of pictures tells it about the period, and
records this in one or two sentences of shared writing. Each group later

reports back to the whole class on what it has found out from its set of pictures about the period. The teacher discusses with the whole class why the findings of the two groups were different.

Other work with photographs could examine concepts of evidence and validity.

Evidence

Children could take photographs of their school, street, shop or village and work out what people in the future might know or guess from them. This would develop the idea of the photograph a a document, and that 'now' will become part of history.

Validity

To explore notions of validity, children could collect photographs of themselves and sort them into 'everyday' and 'special occasions': birthdays, weddings, festivals, first day at school, the school concert, formal group photographs of the class. They could then discuss how pictures in the two categories are different (clothes, food, place, composition), and which tell you more about everyday life. They could discuss whether people only take photographs on happy occasions. (Are you ever crying in a photograph?)

Another way into this area would be to look at old photographs, which were posed and only taken on formal occasions. Did these people always look like this? (Even photographs of Victorian working people had to be posed.) Why was the photograph taken? What did these people want us to think about them?

The following example shows how children are able to recognise that the circumstances in which, and reasons why, photographs are taken can influence the messages they convey and must be taken into account in interpreting them and generalising from them.

A group of year 3 children were shown photographs of two family groups taken at the beginning of this century; one was taken by a professional photographer and one by an amateur. They immediately noticed this difference in status:

K   This was taken by a friend or a member of the family. Otherwise he wouldn't have his head cut off! And the lady isn't ready. She's looking down. The other one was taken by a proper photographer?
B   Yes. They're all in order. It wouldn't be like that if they weren't ready.

The children recognised that therefore the photographs conveyed different messages.

B The Harrisons are rich. You can tell because of their house behind them, and the jewellery the lady's wearing.

E They're trying to look posh people. When we have our photograph taken we just cuddle up for it.

K I don't think the Parsons are *that* poor. The others have got a proper photographer so they put on their nicest clothes. But this lot have just gone out into the garden. It's just a family photo.

Advertisements

Old advertisements are another good way of discussing how reliable a source is, because children are familiar with advertising. The Robert Opie collection of advertisements, in the Museum of Advertising and Packaging, Gloucester, is published as postcards which could be enlarged. They range from a very clean blacksmith and family outside his forge (Hudsons Extract of Soap; Hudsons leaves no smell, saves your linen), and a naked infant beside a basin on a chair (Good Morning. Have *you* used Pears Soap?), to a grand Victorian lady on a train (Bovril. The Main Line to Health), and groups of children at the seaside, by the river and at a party, their play enriched in each case by the uses they make of a large Colman's Mustard tin. The clothes and situations are an historical source; their validity could be investigated by comparing them with a similar advertisement today. What does a modern advertisement tell us about clothes and houses today? Why was it made? What do the people who made the advertisements want us to think? Would advertising today give a true picture of how people live now?

The local environment

> [History] gives an interest and a meaning to things which perhaps we should not have noticed before, not only villages and towns and buildings, a church, an old house, a bridge, but even the landscape itself; prehistoric tracks, monoliths, barrows . . . the romance and pathos of industry, the mines that were once hives sounding with the activity of hundreds of men . . .
>
> (Rowse 1946: 31)

Tawney (in Rowse 1946: 42) said that what an historian needs is not more documents, but a stout pair of boots. Almost all localities have some old buildings and sites which children can visit.

Buildings

These may be listed buildings, of which there are 400,000 in England, a local church or any unexceptional but old buildings in the locality.

Children living in old houses could find out about their own homes, using street directories, and make books based on Our House (Rodgers and Rodgers 1991). This tells the story, in pictures, of different children living in the same house in 1780, 1840, 1910 and 1990. An English Heritage Key Stage 1 video (1992) shows how to prepare for, organise and follow up a class visit to an old house. It is a case study based on a seventeenth-century merchant's house in Great Yarmouth.

First, children could observe, then record in drawings or photographs:

- how the walls are made: timber frame filled with wattle, brick, plaster, stone;
- how the roof is made: thatch, slate, tiles;
- doors and hinges, windows, chimneys;
- decoration, writing, figures;
- number of rooms, upstairs/downstairs;
- fireplaces, ceilings, floors, bells, ovens, pump.

Then they could discuss questions about the past, for example:

- Has the building been changed? Why?
- How did people heat and light the house, cook, get water?
- How many people probably lived here?
- How were the rooms used?

Finally, they could follow up the visit by presenting for an audience the deductions and inferences they had made about what it may have been like to live in the house in the past, and how and why it had changed. This could be in the form of labels for photographs, a model, a slide show or role-play, and would involve explaining causes and effects of changes over time and interpretations.

Sites

These may include sites where evidence of occupation has been found:

- archaeological sites in the process of being excavated;
- incomplete structures (a Roman villa or part of a Medieval town wall);
- industrial sites (wind or water mills for grinding, drainage, spinning or weaving);
- warehouses (or a blast furnace or chainmaker's workshop);
- traces of communication systems (old tracks indicated by hedges, walls, a milestone, a horse trough);
- old streets (indicated by street names, mews, inn signs, lighting, coal holes, post boxes, plaques;
- canals (with bridges, locks, towpaths).

Children can observe clues about the site and record their observations in drawings and photographs. They can use these records later to list questions about how the sites were made and used, and why. This could lead to finding out more from books, and oral and other sources, and to presentations, in different forms, of what they have found out. This could include 'an archaeologist's talk' illustrated by slides, a display of drawings and plans with descriptions and explanations, models and play reconstructions. The processes of archaeology could be demonstrated to the audience, for example by describing a dig in the school grounds, either to see what children could find or to discover 'evidence' preselected and buried by the teacher. Alternatively, children could demonstrate to their audience how archaeologists work by burying an artefact in layers of sand/earth/gravel in a fishtank to display a section, or they could build a model and bury it in the sand tray for others slowly to rediscover, record and interpret.

Artefacts

Britain has 2,500 museums. Since 1960 new ones have sprouted up at the rate of thirty a year (in Fakenham there is a Museum of Gas and Local History, while in Jarrow there is 'Bede's World'). We owe our great museums to the Victorians, but their ideas are not ours; art, relics and facts were presented in dusty cases, without context or passion, to be observed in silence. However, the museum education services which should make museums more accessible today have not been enhanced in recent years. Access to museums increasingly depends on ability to pay, on sponsorship and on cynical, spurious and snobbish assumptions about what would be popular. It is therefore essential that children learn how to observe, enjoy and ask historical questions about artefacts, both in and outside museums.

Bruner (1966) said that to explore through touch how things are made and how they work is an important way of introducing the key ideas of a discipline to young children. He called this 'enactive representation'. Children can have the opportunity to touch objects from the past in 'handling sessions' in museums, through loan collections, through sessions such as 'Mrs Tanner's Tangible History' (see p. 196), or by making their own collections in school, either temporarily in connection with a particular topic or by building up a school 'museum'. Collections of artefacts, replicas and children's historical costumes are also available commercially (e.g. History in Evidence, Articles of Antiquity – see p. 196). Tanner and Wood (1993) have written excellent books to support such Key Stage 1 collections, and children would also enjoy *My Class Visits a Museum* (Grifiths 1987) and *Me and Alice go to the Museum* (Rodgers 1989).

If a school decides to make its own collection of historical artefacts, it needs to decide on criteria for selecting these.

1 Core criteria:

- Is there a modern equivalent, which is different in several ways, so that children can compare the two and explain the changes?
- Does the object have a purpose the children are familiar with?
- What can children work out from it about how it was made and used, and how it affected the lives of the people who made and used it?

2 Other considerations:

- Will the collection include objects which relate to other curriculum areas (rocks, fossils, bones, books, etc.)?
- Will replicas be included?
- Will objects be collected only if they relate to themes the school has decided to study; if so, will they be categorised in sub-themes (e.g. Victorian kitchen, nursery, living room)?
- Will objects be collected because they represent key events or changes, so that children can extrapolate from the particular to the general?
- Is it important that the objects represent different social groups, the lives of children, men and women?
- Is it important that the collection includes artefacts which reflect religious beliefs?
- Should the collection reflect different cultures, through such themes as food, clothes, homes, possibly with the labels in more than one language?

3 Criteria for rejecting artefacts:

- Is it valuable?
- Is it too fragile to care for properly?
- Is it too dangerous for children to investigate?
- Is it too large to store permanently?

4 Storage and use:

- Who is responsible for organising the collection and for its use (a teacher, parent, friend of the school, children)?
- Is there a written rationale for the collection which can be given to possible donors?
- Is there a method of planning and evaluating children's learning from the collection which will assist future planning?

Excellent guidance on setting up a school museum for Key Stage 1 children is given in *School Museums and Primary History* (1994) published by the Historical Association.

Two recent DfE surveys found that both visiting museums and creating a school museum are important ways of introducing young children to history. Where children had visited a museum, the youngest pupils in Key Stage 1 described contrasts between life now and in the past. They could describe different features of the past and changes over time (DfE 1992a: 4). Where schools were building up a museum, 'even the youngest pupils were acquiring a sense of "now" and "then" and all the pupils were given the opportunity to develop ideas about the pace of change and to make deductions from historical sources' (DfE 1992a).

Many of the historical sources involved work in other curriculum areas. One class of year 1 and 2 pupils looked carefully at two reproductions of nineteenth-century paintings of the seashore to compare clothing then with what they wear on the beach now; they described the details and highlighted the differences between then and now. This involved both language and art. In another school, year 2 pupils' work with wooden artefacts was directly linked to an assessment exercise in National Curriculum science. They had examined the material and discussed guidelines for its display, writing instructions such as 'do not leave in bright sunlight' (DfE 1992b: 5).

Bowyer (1992) described how a cluster group of small schools produced two 'Time Boxes' with sixteen articles in each for under £200. Artefacts which were inexpensive to replace were purchased from museum shops, flea markets and replica shops. One box contained everyday objects and the other 'mystery' objects. The objects were not connected with each other except by the idea of 'time'. They included old keys, wooden toys, a button hook, Roman lamps, old coins, Tudor cutlery, an amphora, medicine bottles, a Viking game piece, Victorian lenses, a sundial, replica tin cars, pill boxes, an Egyptian charm, a needlecase, a flat iron and a candle-holder. Teachers met to discuss how the boxes could be used. They devised a structured programme of questions for those who wanted an introduction to using the boxes of artefacts with a whole class, a group or with individual children. These questions included:

- Can you draw the object? Put measurements on your sketch.
- What is it made of? Why was it made?
- What does it feel like?
- What do you think it was used for?
- What kind of person might have used it?
- Is it decorated? How?
- Which object do you think is oldest? Why?
- What else would you like to know about it? How could you find out more?

The boxes also contained a rope and pegs for making a sequence line, and lenses and magnifying glasses for close observation.

Mathieson (Batho 1994: 15–21) describes in another case study how she collected boxes of artefacts for a cluster group of first schools, and suggests good ways of introducing them to children: pretending she found an object while spring-cleaning her grandma's house, or wrapping up an object in a treasure chest, so that children first guess what it might be. She found the treasure chest worked particularly well with a mixed age range, as older children shared expertise and younger children's concentration span was extended. Mathieson is also developing a local history box for the cluster group, on such general themes as 'Local People', 'Farming', 'Transport' and 'Industry', to which individual schools add examples from their immediate locality. She then plans to add slides and videos to the boxes. This project was funded by the local education authority.

Eno (1993) has pointed out how perceptions of an artefact are influenced by cultural background: Muslim children do not have photographs or statues at home, but the Sikhs do have models of their gods. What might be obviously an old Roman lamp to some people is like an oil lamp others may see at festivals today. Whereas a Morris Oxford car may seem old-fashioned to us, it is the height of modernity in some Indian cities. When she showed a replica of an English Civil War period flat metal plate to year 2 children, two Sikh boys and three Muslim girls, she was conscious that it was similar to the sort of tableware most of the children used at home. They therefore impressed her by saying it was 'something very old'; it would be interesting to know the reasons they gave, particularly since one of the boys then peered at a replica Stuart coin, trying to decide what football team it represented!

Drawing artefacts

Observational drawing of details, or of entire objects, in a museum or in school, encourages children to look closely, over a prolonged period. The act of drawing involves selecting the significant features and forming a personal perception of the object. In this way, a relationship with the object is created, based on internal and external ordering of experience. An image of the object is internalised and remembered. Their drawings are concerned with what they know, with what interests them and with spatial relationships rather than with perspective, but even very young children are beginning to formulate a language which is concerned with representation.

Remembering the image makes it easier to remember the discussion, the deductions and inferences made about the object, to transfer them to similar examples seen later, and to extrapolate from the particular to the general. Bruner (1966) said that this prevents a 'mental overload' of facts. Drawing historical artefacts also focuses attention on basic materials (wood, stone, metals, clay), which have been central to all civilisations throughout human history. It raises awareness of the similar and the

different ways in which they have been used. Careful observation encourages children to describe objects accurately and to ask questions about
them.

Strategies for questioning

Smith and Holden (1994) described a range of strategies they used to
encourage children from Reception to year 3 to ask questions about objects:

- *Open-ended questions:* in small groups children handled all the artefacts,
  then selected one to draw. They then found out more from reference
  books and used the artefacts in role-play.
- *Focused questions:* children sat in small groups with one artefact per
  group. With no guidance from the teacher, they wrote key questions
  about their artefact. The groups then shared their questions and the
  teacher gave them further information for extending their enquiry.
- *Focused research*: children in pairs selected an object related to their
  history topic. They discussed its origin, use and evidence of authenticity,
  then planned further research.
- *Artefacts circus*: groups sat around their tables with one artefact per table.
  Each group wrote one question about the artefact, then moved to the
  next table. There it tried to answer the previous group's question and
  added another question. The session ended with a class discussion led
  by the teacher.

Here are some examples of children's deductions (information acquired
from an historical source):

- *Kettle*
  This is a kettle that a Victorian would use. I noticed there was a white
  handle. It has a black holder and the holder is a funny shape and very
  bendy . . .
- *Stone hot water bottle*
  It wouldn't be very comfy. It would hurt your feet. I wouldn't like that
  one because it's too fat and too big. I like my own.

By year 2, children were following their deductions with further inferences
about what the artefact meant to the people who used it (using historical
sources to answer questions about the past):

C They had to use horses for pulling carts. They didn't have cars in those
   days so they didn't go very fast.
M The milk churn was used to carry milk in. When it was empty the milk
   collector came to collect it to put more milk in.

Also they were considering a range of possible inferences:

D It's for storing things . . . ?
K No. For carrying things . . . ?

W It's to put wine in . . .
N A drinker what you drink out of?

The following example shows a sequence of work with a vertically grouped year 1/2 class. The aims were:

- to introduce the children to the idea of objects and their value as learning materials;
- to encourage children to look, and develop good concentration and observational skills;
- to introduce the notion of touching and handling objects.

In *Stage 1*, children felt and described everyday objects in a 'feely bag' then took them out to see how accurate their descriptions had been. In *Stage 2*, they compared an everyday object, a modern iron, with an iron from 'beyond living memory', a Victorian iron.

With only gentle encouragement and key questions, the discussion that followed centred around how the modern iron made steam and how it worked. The children examined and handled the iron with great interest and curiosity, pressing buttons and switches and at one point pulling it apart. Next they passed around the heavy Victorian iron and the children immediately referred to it as an 'iron from the olden days' and, without prompting, went on to state that it was probably used by a 'Victorian maid'. This was quite astounding when one considers that the children had previously done very little in the way of history topics.

They were fascinated by the iron's weight and colour, and by the words that were printed on the warmer plate. Again, they were eager to touch and feel.

The children posed questions such as 'How old is it?' and 'Where did it come from?' They were encouraged to try and answer their own questions by looking for 'clues'. They did this with enthusiasm and interest, and began to formulate opinions and to try to answer the questions they had posed. They went on to compare an old telephone and a modern one. Then they sketched the objects. They became quite enthralled at having to focus on details. A feature of all the sketches produced from these sessions was that the children drew what they could see, what they observed, rather than what they thought a telephone or an iron should look like.

Stage 3 involved work at the Museum of London with five selected Victorian artefacts. The aims were:

- to apply the handling and observational skills already practised in earlier classroom sessions;
- to look at and examine authentic historical artefacts from beyond living memory;
- for children to begin to formulate their own worksheets in order to complement and record their observations.

The adult working with each group recorded the observations on the museum handling sheet to allow the children to concentrate on using observation skills fully. Using the adult helpers in this way enabled the children to engage in free discussion and uninterrupted exploration of the object in front of them. Then the Museum Education Officer asked the children to record their findings by making a detailed sketch of the object they had focused on, drawing it as they saw it, not as they thought it should look.

The children were more than able to 'sketch as they saw' and to include the finest details. This was a marked improvement from when the work programme began and B, who regularly informs people 'I cannot draw', produced a remarkably detailed and accurate artistic impression of the metal toasting implement his group was focusing on.

It was noticeable that the children's observation and enquiry based skills had progressed and developed over the previous few weeks. So, too, had their overall ability to concentrate and focus on the learning. Their teacher pinpointed this as a direct cause of advances in learning in other curriculum areas.

It was also significant that when the children came back together to share their views and sketches at the close of the session, they were able to sit without stirring for at least 30 minutes, listening and contributing to the on-going discussion. This applied to all children, but again, children such as A and J, who usually had difficulty concentrating and listening, were controlled and enthusiastic throughout the session. Work in the classroom and at the museum has shown that looking at objects, and an enquiry-based and tactile approach to history, enabled all the children, including those exhibiting special learning or behavioural needs, to benefit, and, more importantly, to feel that they *were* achieving.

In *Stage 4*, five selected objects from a loan collection of Medieval artefacts were used in school. The aims were:

• to focus observational and recording skills on artefacts from a particular historical period (Medieval) and to apply knowledge already gained from topic work on 'Castles';
• for children to use their own formulated worksheets to record their observations of the artefacts used.

In preparation for this session, the children were asked to think about the sorts of question they might like to ask when examining and handling 'old' objects and artefacts. This was the first stage in getting the children to prepare their own evaluative worksheet, to be used at museums and other historical sites. The Museum of London sheet was not re-shown or discussed by the children; thus the outcome is even more remarkable as they produced a list of investigative questions which were very well structured and, from an historical point of view, extremely relevant. The children were then asked to categorise these questions into five sections, to give them some sort of logical sequence: questions such as 'What does it feel like?' or 'What is it made of?' preceded 'What is it worth?', thereby building up a descriptive picture of the object before having to formulate judgements about the object's age or worth. In this way, answers to the earlier questions could inform the later questions.

The children examined the objects assigned to their group and attempted to answer the questions from their observations. All groups had one child who acted as scribe and some groups actually shared the 'scribe' task. It was very obvious that the children were working more comfortably when answering questions they had devised than when they were using the museum worksheets, even though the objects were by far the oldest that they had examined so far and were unfamiliar. The class teacher and the museum teacher agreed that this definitely had a connection with the fact that they were working to a recording format that had come from them and was, therefore, wholly familiar and relevant.

The children were again encouraged to spend much time drawing their objects and it is significant that they were now so skilled at observing and looking closely that they sat for longer and produced some of the most detailed sketches of the whole work programme.

The final period of the session was taken up with a class discussion and by sharing answers to the sheet questions. The teachers were acting only as facilitators. It was the children who instigated, led and participated in the discussion and some of the informed guesses as to what the Medieval objects were used for, and by whom, were quite accurate.

The children had progressed from having little or no knowledge of history and, in some cases, poor concentration and observational skills to producing highly detailed sketches and a sequenced and categorised, evaluative, historical worksheet, through their work with historical arte-facts.

The class teacher observed improvements, during the 6-week pro-gramme, in children's concentration and confidence, both in work related to the topic and in other areas of the curriculum.

Follow-up activities could include finding out from museum staff how they catalogue, label and care for their collection, and how they interest the public in it, in order to create a school museum or temporary class collection.

Another case study by Matthews and Shaw (Batho 1994: 22–5) describes how cross-curricular work with a year 2 class evolved from a class museum, set up as an economic awareness project; they considered problems of access, who should pay and what the money should be spent on. There were opportunities for speaking and listening, using reference material and information retrieval as children took turns as curators and guides, and for writing, keeping a visitors' book, sending invitations and making descriptive labels. In science, they considered different sources of light and heat, candles, oil, gas and electricity, then observed, predicted and set up experiments. A visit from a brewery dray led children to making their own carts, and studying 'forces'. In technology, children designed and made Victorian toys, spinners, tops, peg dolls and dolls' houses.

An alternative way of structuring work with objects might be:

Stage 1 Looking at, feeling, using and talking about one familiar object.

Stage 2 Looking at and talking about two familiar objects widely separated by time, comparing and sequencing them.

Stage 3 Looking at two objects closer together in time, comparing and sequencing them.

Stage 4 Looking at three or more objects from different times. The closer they are in time to each other, the harder it is to contrast them. But the more familiar they are to the children, the easier it is. (This is a helpful contradiction.)

Stage 5 Using other sources, e.g. old photos, old books, living memory, to date artefacts.

There are several points to remember about this scheme:

• These stages may overlap; for example, a child in year 2 working on Stage 1 may well wish to use the library to research an object.
• What is familiar to the teacher may not be so to the child and vice versa. Artefacts are an excellent way of ensuring that our classrooms reflect ethnic diversity.
• Support with questioning will enhance children's understanding.
• This diagram of progression is one-dimensional. Other aspects of progress will relate to the complexity of children's deductions, their ability to synthesise, the depth and breadth of their background historical knowledge, their experience of handling artefacts.

The third set of examples of work with artefacts comes from a school where the topic for year 1 and 2 classes was 'Our Houses'. This involved art: prints and rubbings from bricks, stone and wood, and pottery slab models of house fronts with lift-up flaps to find who lived in each house. There was science (testing the strength of model houses made with plastic bricks of different thicknesses, by blowing with straws) and mathematics (pictograms showing how many people lived in each house or flat). The teachers would not have added a history dimension had it not been required by the National Curriculum. However, they made a small collection of old domestic artefacts and were delighted by the children's responses. Some children wrote labels for a display. In some cases, the labels simply communicated information.

Bahadir The carpet beater is for beating the carpet.
Grant In olden days there was some old things.
Nikki I drew a hot water bottle and it had patterns on it.
Katy This is an old iron.
Ayra In the olden days they used a washboard.

Other labels explained what the artefacts tell us about the past.

Tainoo In the olden days there was no washing machines, so they had to use something like plungers.
Hasna In the olden days they had no rubber, so they had to use hard hot water bottles.
Deepa In the old days they had no washing machines so they had scrubbing boards. They had no electricity, so they put the cloth on the scrubbing board. The washing board was hard. It is made from wood and glass.
Sarah In the old days they did not have hoovers, so they had carpet beaters. They took the carpet up and put the carpet on the washing line and bashed the carpet and all the dirt came off.

Written sources

Frank Smith (1989) has made it clear that writing should not involve repressive discipline, deadening instruction or blind drilling, lest:

> Under a cruel eye outworn
> The little ones spend all the day
> In sighing and dismay.
> (from 'The School Boy' by William Blake 1757–1827)

Fortunately, written historical sources can provide opportunities for fun! Suitable sources which communicate information and raise questions about the past include:

- a child's own documentary evidence – baby book, clinic book, birthday cards, birth and marriage certificates (although this can be a sensitive area);
- the school log book, recording why children were absent, what they were punished for in the past;
- local street names, referring to famous people (Chaucer Road) or events (Trafalgar Road), to places which have disappeared (Station Road, Market Road) or to connections which no longer exist (Jamaica Road, Canary Wharf);
- children's own names, associated with places or occupations (Smith, Patel);
- advertisements on old walls or stone lettering listing departments in now defunct stores;
- writing on street furniture – pillar boxes, coal holes, lighting;

- inscriptions on memorials, statues, brasses, plaques, gravestones;
- old newspapers, stamps, coins, letters, postcards, recipes;
- inn signs (Rotheroe 1990).

Children can also consider the nature of language as a symbolic communication system which is central to all societies. Donaldson (1978) said that if children understand the abstraction of language as an objective tool, they are helped to make inferences from an early age. Children can learn about the nature and importance of written language as a symbolic code through looking at a variety of scripts: an Arabic text from the Koran, a Medieval illuminated manuscript of the Bible, an agrarian calendar, a Roman tombstone or Egyptian hieroglyphics.

They can discuss what the meaning of the writing may be, the sorts of things that people needed to write down, and why. In the following extract, children were discussing Stone Age petraglyphics (found in *How Writing Began*, Macdonald Educational Starters Long Ago Books).

B   They could communicate. [This was a 'hard word' the children had been introduced to as a key concept in the topic.]
S   And they could talk to each other, because they could draw pictures.
N   They had signs as well, to communicate.
B   To tell each other things and to help each other.
S   They would have helped each other . . . not one person done it all.
W   They shared ideas. They left messages.
N   An 'animal' and a 'man' might have been 'going hunting'.
S   This looks like an arrow.
W   It could be a help sign . . .
B   They could use symbols. [This was another selected, taught, concept.]
S   I think the old Stone Age did very well at cave painting, but the new Stone Age thought it took too long to do a message quickly.

Even if children cannot understand examples of earlier styles of writing in English, because of difficult script and their limited reading ability, they can search for some letters which they recognise, and understand that forms change over time. Listening to brief extracts, to unfamiliar vocabulary and syntax, can help them to understand that language itself changes.

Children can also listen to extracts about childhood from contemporary diaries. *Lark Rise to Candleford* (Thompson 1989: 87, 121) describes school, play, games and songs, and festivals in the 1880s. Laurie Lee (1989: 35, 53) describes his childhood in the 1920s, in the village school, in the kitchen, at outings and festivals, in summer and winter. Children will probably most enjoy Helen Bradley's illustrated account of her childhood at the beginning of this century. In *Miss Carter Came with Us*, for example, she shows preparations for Christmas, and a visit to the seaside, which they could compare with their own experiences (Bradley 1974: 22–3, 30).

Music

> It is true that the appreciation of music is, of its own kind, a musical experience ... but over and above that ... there is always the allusion to its own time and period, of which it is the most intimate and secret revelation possible.
>
> (Rowse 1946: 124)

Musical sources include old sheet music, records and record players, songs, instruments, and music-making depicted in old paintings. From musical sources, it is possible to find out about:

- work in the past – the tasks and rhythms of spinning, weaving, sailing and harvesting which were accompanied by work songs;
- events – described in ballads and folk music, and in military music;
- celebrations of beliefs and religious festivals;
- leisure – in folk songs and dances from a variety of cultures, and in more recent, popular, music;
- music typical of different periods (e.g. Medieval, Elizabethan).

A musical dimension can be included in any history topic. Children can listen and participate in song and dance, in a Medieval joust, an Elizabethan ball, in sea-shanties or Victorian songs around the piano.

Grandparents enjoy teaching old playground games. Parents enjoy contributing their old popular records. Bilingual children and parents welcome the opportunity to teach songs in other languages and traditional dances from other places.

Part III

Organisation, planning and assessment

Part I considered the kinds of knowledge children may have about the past and the levels of thinking they may bring to bear on it when they start school. Part II suggested how different aspects of historical thinking may be developed in school. Part III discusses how coherent units of study may be planned which take account of progression in content and in historical thinking.

Criteria for effective planning and organisation in history have been identified as dependent on a consistent approach to planning and assessment throughout the school, based on documentation produced through consultation (DES 1989b). This should reflect clear aims, in terms of knowledge, skills and attitudes. Effective learning was found to involve discussion and questioning, beginning with children's existing knowledge, then introducing new facts and ideas related to first-hand experiences. Teachers showed children how to investigate primary sources in order to find out about the relationship between past and present, or what it might have been like to have lived in another time. Investigations were recorded in a variety of artistic, creative and mathematical forms. The non-statutory guidance in *History in the National Curriculum* (DES 1991) and *Teaching History at Key Stage 1* (NCC 1993) includes suggestions for implementing these criteria. Within these suggestions a variety of approaches is possible.

In this section, three levels of organisation and planning are considered: whole-school (or Key Stage) organisation, topic planning with in-built assessment opportunities, and detailed plans for activities within a topic. At each level, possible formats are given and decisions to be made are examined.

Chapter 7

Whole-school or Key Stage planning

The aim of the revised National Curriculum is to provide a framework around which teachers can use their professional judgement to construct a coherent and meaningful curriculum to suit the needs of their children, in their locality, in a creative and flexible way. This involves making judgements about breadth and depth and how to manage time most effectively. There is, however, a danger that history, which many teachers have begun to see as appropriate to early years education, will be marginalised if overlap with other curriculum areas is not exploited.

The first important area to clarify is the relationship between nursery education, the reception class and the first two years of school. It was argued in Part I that, from their earliest years, children are capable of embryonic historical thinking and are aware of the past in their environment and experiences. Part II considered how teachers may explicitly build on this experience. However, the transition from home to school is not the same for all children. Children begin school at different times of the year preceding their fifth birthday; only some have had nursery experience, and this in a variety of settings. Nevertheless, schools want nursery and reception classes to be part of their whole-school planning. It is important, therefore, in spite of an appropriately different emphasis in the rationale, content and structure of the pre-school curriculum, to recognise the links in the continuum between this and planning for years 1 and 2. The Rumbold Report (DES 1990) stressed this progression, showing how the 'areas of experiences' recommended for children under 5 (DES 1989d), which combine cognitive, motor and social skills with linguistic, mathematical, scientific and aesthetic experiences, could be devloped through activities such as using the local environment, and visits to places of interest, as a stimulus for role play. The constructivist high scope curriculum (Holmann *et al.* 1979) is organised around similar key experiences. Suggestions for whole-school planning (Figure 7.1) are therefore shown as a continuum.

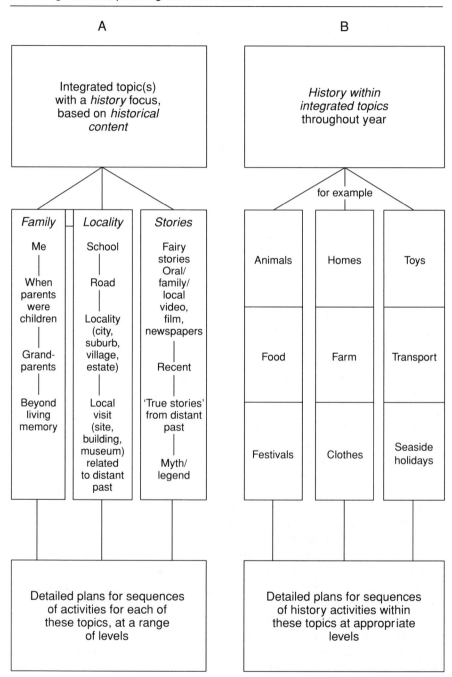

A

Integrated topic(s)
with a *history* focus,
based on *historical*
content

B

*History within
integrated topics*
throughout year

for example

Family | *Locality* | *Stories*

Me

When
parents
were
children

Grand-
parents

Beyond
living
memory

School

Road

Locality
(city,
suburb,
village,
estate)

Local
visit
(site,
building,
museum)
related
to distant
past

Fairy
stories
Oral/
family/
local
video,
film,
newspapers

Recent

'True stories'
from distant
past

Myth/
legend

Animals

Food

Festivals

Homes

Farm

Clothes

Toys

Transport

Seaside
holidays

Detailed plans for sequences
of activities for each of
these topics, at a range
of levels

Detailed plans for sequences
of history activities within
these topics at appropriate
levels

Figure 7.1 Outline of approaches to planning examined in Part III

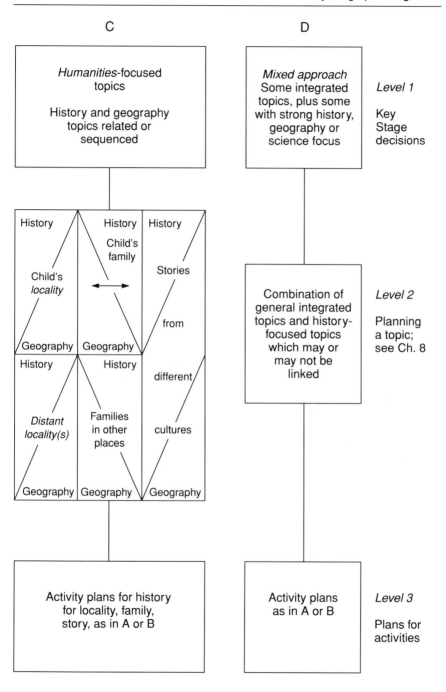

The first decision to be made is how history should be linked to other curriculum areas:

- will history be taught through some topics during the year which have a strong history focus;
- or through a clearly defined historical dimension within topics such as clothes, food or toys;
- or through humanities-focused topics in which history and geography are either combined or sequenced;
- or through a mixed approach of integrated and subject-focused topics? (See Figure 7.1.)

HISTORY-FOCUSED TOPICS

Over each year one term, or two half-terms, could be spent on topics based on historical content, for example family history, Victorians, castles. Mathematics, English, science and technology, and music could then be related to the period studied. This approach enables teachers and children to become immersed in a period in the past, to investigate it in greater depth, ask questions and pursue investigations over a long period, to become familiar with the thinking processes which are at the centre of the discipline and to achieve a coherent understanding of another period. This would be a good introduction to a more detailed study of the period at Key Stage 2.

Mathematics and English are systems of investigation and communication which need to be used and applied in a variety of meaningful contexts, and therefore should continuously permeate all areas of the curriculum. It could also be argued that history is an umbrella discipline which involves all aspects of past societies, and therefore includes art, music and religious education. There is, therefore, a strong case for a curriculum based on a series of integrated topics, led by history, geography or science, in sequence. However, a disadvantage could be that young children may forget what they have achieved in historical thinking if it is not continuously reinforced.

HISTORY WITHIN INTEGRATED TOPICS

Traditionally, Key Stage 1 topics have not been subject led; they have been based on such themes as 'Animals', 'Homes' or 'Toys'. If such a topic is planned so that it has a clear historical dimension, both in content and in thinking, children can see that the past is an important dimension of any theme. If the history aspect is linked to a clear chronological framework through a time-line, children can begin to build up a map of the past over a long period of time. *Teaching History at Key Stage 1* (NCC 1993: 11) suggests how history can be taught through such topics as 'Me', 'Games and celebrations', 'Places', 'People', 'Food and clothing', 'Travel and exploration'. However, 'topics' have been criticised in the past because activities have been included in a random way because they are linked to the topic by content. The thinking processes of each discipline and progression within them has not been recognised as the basis for selecting and planning activities.

HUMANITIES-FOCUSED TOPICS

There is a great deal of overlap between history and geography. Both investigate the same kinds of sources (pictures, film, artefacts, music, stories, oral and written sources) to find out how people live, their work, leisure, beliefs, homes, food and clothes. They are based on the same organising concepts which run through societies: agriculture, manufacture, trade, communication, social structure and belief systems.

There are also differences between history and geography. History focuses on interpreting the causes and effects of changes over time. Geography is more concerned with the interactions between people and their natural and man-made environment, with the influences of landforms and climate on settlement and daily life.

However, there may be good reasons for planning topics in which the geographical and historical dimensions are either parallel or sequenced. Since societies in different places and times are based on the same organising concepts, children develop a framework for making connections, for recognising similarities and differences. The links between history and geography may be made in a number of ways.

Children might use maps, pictures and sources to find out about their locality today: its churches, houses, workplaces, transport. Next they could find out how they have changed and why. Then they could use the same categories to compare and contrast how people live in a more distant locality, in Britain, Europe or in a developing country.

- A topic on family history may lead to finding out about places where parents or grandparents were born or other family members live.
- A study of a local shop could lead to finding out more about where some of the goods came from, how they were grown there and why.
- A study of the school could lead to a comparison with a school elsewhere in the world.
- A topic on 'Me' could focus on children's personal history over five or six years, then go on to find out about children in another place.
- A visit to a workplace (a farm or post office, for example) could lead children to trace its links with other places, then to find out how it has changed and why.

- A topic on stories could trace similarities and differences between themes of folk tales from different countries: heroes, cunning, power, jealousy; stories about weather, animals, food, journeys, markets.

Bruner (1963: 10) believed that studying early societies is the best way to learn about the nature of society, the human condition and the continuity of evolution.

A MIXED APPROACH

A combination of subject-focused topics, with perhaps one half-term each year spent on a science- a geography- and a history-focused topic, and three half-terms spent on 'themes' would allow the two approaches to curriculum planning to be evaluated. Whether history-focused topics or more general themes are planned, it is important to recognise the potential links between history and other areas of the curriculum.

English

However history is taught, it provides an excellent and natural context for language development. Indeed, the National Curriculum for English at Key Stage 1 (DfE 1995) states that children should be given opportunities for telling stories, both real and imagined, for imaginative play and drama, and for listening to nursery rhymes. They need to explore, develop and clarify their ideas, to predict outcomes and discuss possibilities, to describe events, observations and experiences, to give reasons for opinions and actions, to show an understanding of what they see and hear, to participate in drama and improved activities, using appropriate language in a role situation and also to respond to drama that they have watched. Through stories, artefacts, pictures, oral history and visits to old buildings, explored through play and discussion, history fulfils all these requirements.

Mathematics

Historical enquiries may involve number calculations and data presentation. Objects can be sorted into sets according to age, materials and/or function, and recorded in Carroll and Venn diagrams. Questionnaires and surveys can be recorded in pictograms and bar charts. Calculations can be based on time-lines. Investigations may involve observing and recording tessellations and repeating patterns in windows, roof-tiles, bricks and ceilings, and decoration on artefacts or fabrics. Observing shapes in buildings, and making models, can involve the vocabulary of two- and three-dimensional shapes. Maps and plans involve direction, shape and space. There are many opportunities for measurement – of time (hours, days, months, birthdays, seasons, years), of length (the length or thickness of a castle wall), of weight (of artefacts or ingredients in recipes) – and for using money and barter (in role-play).

Science and technology

History is concerned with the ways people in the past obtained and used materials: leather, wool, silk, cotton, stone, clay, wood, thatch, gold, lead, iron. It is concerned with how people grew, harvested, stored, preserved and prepared their food; how they obtained water and light and heat. Changes in tools, technology and energy sources are key causes of wider changes in society. There are many opportunities for children to investigate how people in past times kept warm, dry and fed, the jobs this involved, the tools they used, and why these changed. Stories and rhymes introduce children to cobblers, smiths, weavers, spinners, woodcutters, farmers, millers and dairy maids, markets and journeys. Through examining artefacts, they learn about materials and about how things work. By visiting, observing and making models of old buildings, they find out about structures (How tall can you build the tower? How wide can you make the arch? Can you make a timber-frame house with strips of wood or rolled paper or straws?). They can learn about energy through pictures and stories, about sailing ships, windmills, balloons, watermills, coal fires, steam trains, clockwork toys, carriages, early cars and planes. They can discuss how these worked and how they affected people's lives. Children can experiment, heating clay to make pots, making natural dyes, spinning and weaving, making models with natural materials (stone, wood, thatch).

Art

History provides a context for children to look closely at artefacts and paintings, to learn that they express the ideas, feelings and ways of life of the people who made them. By recording their observations of artefacts in their own drawings and paintings (possibly extended into collages, sewing and printing), they notice their shape and texture. Through making models of buildings (a castle or a Victorian dolls' house), or drawings of events in the past, children are developing their historical imagination and making their own interpretations, based on what they know.

Music

A painting, story or visit can be used as a stimulus for simple compositions. Children could make up music to accompany a story or they could investigate, select and combine sounds which describe a visit to a windmill, a steam railway or sailing ship. They could try to recreate the sounds which might be heard in a picture, for example of a Victorian street scene or railway station, a picture of harvest, or of a market or fair.

Children can sing together songs from other times: nursery rhymes, playground games, folk and popular songs. They could match traditional songs with folk tales from other countries. They can listen to old instruments and to music from other times; Medieval music, for example, can accompany 'let's pretend' play in a castle, or sea shanties can be linked with adventures on sailing ships.

SELECTION OF CONTENT FOR HISTORY AT KEY STAGE 1

History in the National Curriculum requires that, at Key Stage 1, children should find out about the past through stories from different periods and cultures, and through a range of historical sources. They should find out about changes in life, work and leisure within their own lives and the lives of their families and other familiar adults, and in the lives of people beyond living memory. This should include learning about men and women with different backgrounds and about different types of memorable events, in Britain and in other countries.

Clearly, it is important that these areas of knowledge are structured and integrated in a meaningful way. Yet there is no evidence for a clear pattern of progression in structuring content. It may seem logical to start with a child's own history, then go on to when grandparents were children, and then to a period beyond living memory. But there is no evidence that this is the best way to develop children's concept of time or of chronology; young children love stories about distant times and stories which begin 'Long, long ago . . .'. It may also seem logical to begin with a child's immediate environment, home or school, then to move outwards to the locality, the street or village, then beyond to distant places, through holidays, friends and television; but young children love stories which begin 'In a land far away . . .'. From the beginning, children create their own imaginary places and times in play.

Poster (1973) and West (1981) argued that children learn most about their own time and their own place by being confronted with stark comparisons, with dramatically different times and places, which can clearly be contrasted with their own experiences, and that recent emphasis on direct, concrete and sensory experiences has underestimated the power of this argument. However, it would seem logical to plan a sequence of units which either move outwards in time and place, from the family and school, to distant times and places, or vice versa.

Before deciding on which sequence of content, it might be helpful to brainstorm the resources in the locality, which will link the programme to first-hand experience and to children's own interests, and create valuable interaction and shared understandings between school and community. Some resources may be more suitable for a particular group, because of distance or the kinds of related activities they stimulate. For example, are there old houses or shops or a church in the immediate vicinity which young children could observe on a short walk? Is there a museum loan collection which could be borrowed for them to use in school; what period does it relate to? Would it be better to invite people from the local community or story-tellers to talk to younger children? Is there a castle, a great house, a museum, a gallery or 'living history' reconstruction which would be more suitable for older children to visit?

Figure 7.2 suggests how topics which cover a large time-span might be sequenced moving from the present outwards or vice versa, and how the range of resources available for each broad period could be noted.

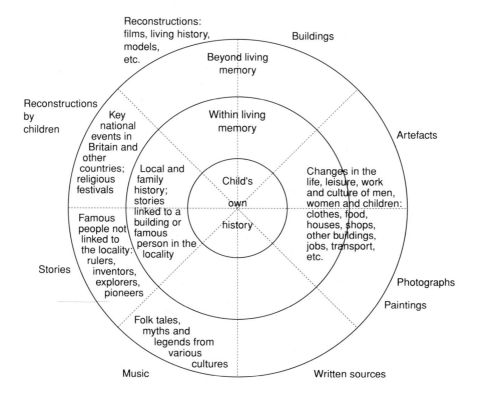

Figure 7.2 How topics may be sequenced and related appropriately to local resources

CROSS-CURRICULAR THEMES AND DIMENSIONS

Next we need to consider how cross-curricular dimensions and themes relate to history at Key Stage 1 (NCC 1990). The cross-curricular dimensions are concerned with developing personal qualities and values, with social development, with understanding cultural diversity and with equal opportunities, irrespective of gender or ethnic or cultural background. Through making inferences about historical sources, children learn to form an opinion, to support it with a reason, to listen to the views of others and to accept that there may be no one right answer. They can learn about social and cultural diversity through different children's family histories and through stories, myths and legends from various cultures. They can find out about the roles of women and girls and attitudes to them, and how and why they have changed.

The cross-curricular themes are economic and industrial understanding, environmental and health education, careers education and education for citizenship. In local and family history, stories and folk tales, children can consider how tools and other artefacts were made and used, how people kept warm and dry, how they grew and cooked their food, the jobs they did, the journeys they made and why. They can find out about health care in the past: how babies were cared for, granny's childhood illnesses or old wives' tales. They can find out about how and why jobs in their locality have changed, and about famous local people. Local links with particular themes could be indicated on the Key Stage plan.

PLANNING FOR PROGRESSION

Progression in historical understanding involves interaction between increasing knowledge about the past and increasingly complex historical thinking. It develops through experiencing a variety of primary and secondary sources and learning to ask appropriate questions about them. This depends on language development, on learning to say 'because' and 'perhaps', to use time language and historical vocabulary.

Historical understanding also grows with maturity because it involves understanding human behaviour. It is a broadening as well as a hierarchical process. It is particularly difficult to plan for progression in historical understanding because variables interact. It is possible to make a simple deduction from a complex source, or to develop complicated reasoning about a simple source.

There is some commonsense progression in the things young children can do. There is a broad progression in the kinds of stories they enjoy. Simple fairy stories such as 'The Three Bears' or 'Little Red Riding Hood' can form a basis for discussing motives, perspectives and interpretations. Fairy stories with more complex motives, plots, such as 'Snow White', and myths and legends involving more powerful emotions, come later on. Stories about the life histories and families of other, familiar children may precede stories about children or events long ago. Free play in an historical context dominated by fantasy can gradually come to depend more on what is known or can be found out; it can be the basis for later role play and hot seating or freeze-frame drama. As children's knowledge and concept of time develop they can progress from making sets of 'very old' and 'not very old' to sequencing photographs of themselves, then of their families, then impersonal photographs over several generations. They progress from sequences to standard units of time. Children may make deductions from increasingly impersonal or abstract sources; written sources may progress from a baby tag, then an old seaside postcard to Tacitus' description of Boudicca. Deductions may be increasingly well argued and numerous, increasingly concerned with ideas rather than descriptive.

ASSESSMENT AND RECORD-KEEPING

The level descriptions are useful in ensuring that the routine activities children undertake involve them in genuine historical thinking. Through observing children in a variety of ways, it is possible to record to what extent they have achieved the intended learning outcomes. For example, writing samples might record children's level of response to the use of historical sources. They may be asked to write a label (for a drawing, a model, an artefact, photograph or a reproduction of a painting in a display) describing the exhibit, suggesting what it tells us about the past and/or what it tells us about the people who made and used it. Children's developing awareness that the past is represented in different ways might be recorded as brief notes, after discussing different versions of a story with groups of children, or it might be recorded through observing and discussing different groups' interpretations, in play or model making, of an event or a story. Their understanding of sequence in events might be achieved through making a picture story, by displaying familiar objects in chronological order, by recording personal belongings or incidents on a sequence line, or by listening to a group's presentation of a display it has made. To show awareness that the past is divided into periods of time, they might sort pictures into sets of, for example, Victorians and Romans.

The National Curriculum level descriptions attempt to provide a broad description of the development of each aspect of historical thinking, but they cannot monitor this in a precise way because historical thinking is not hierarchical and because the variables (sources, questions and inferences) are complex and interacting. For example, ordering in sequence events in a story can be achieved by a 4-year-old if the story is simple, but it can also tax a professional historian. Placing objects in chronological order depends on whether the objects are familiar, how many there are, how great a time-span they cover and what changes they represent, how much knowledge is required, and whether the sequence is ambiguous. Montioring change over a period of time may require describing changes represented by a slate, a fountain pen and a word-processing disk in sequence, or describing the economic and social changes they represent. There are many levels of understanding how and why the past is represented in different ways. For a 5-year-old, this may mean comparing two different illustrations of the same event; to an historian, it may mean discussing whether Macaulay's description of James II as 'obstinate and imperious' (1969: 569) is a 'fact' or a 'point of view'. Questions about sources and deductions from sources can be made at many levels of complexity. The checklist based on formative assessments of work that children have achieved can then be used as an informed basis for describing the level that each child has consistently achieved, either at the end of a topic, a year or a Key Stage. Although only the end of the Key Stage assessment is a statutory requirement, to be reported to parents, this does not negate the value of keeping on-going records. (However, the introduction to the revised National Curriculum stresses that there is no need for *elaborate* tick lists.)

Assessment, unless the product of extensive and detailed research, can never be more than a rough bench-mark. 'The quest for the perfect test is like a search for fools' gold or the philosopher's stone, though rather more fools than philosophers embark on it' ('A–Z of Education', *Observer*, 5 Sept. 1993: 57).

The three interacting strands of historical thinking can all be identified at successive levels in the National Curriculum: interpreting sources, analysing changes over time, and constructing and evaluating accounts of the past. However, the progression within each strand is necessarily far from clear (see Box 7.1).

Box 7.2 shows how assessments made through normal, on-going class activities, as shown in the study unit plans, can be recorded at different levels of specificity for a variety of audiences and purposes.

Box 7.1 Three strands of historical thinking

Areas for historical study (History in the National Curriculum Programme of Study Key Stage 1 (DfE 1995))	Level	Deductions and inferences from sources	Interpretations: understanding why accounts differ	Understanding causes and effects of changes over time			
		Strand 1	Strand 2	Similarity/ difference	Sequence/ chronology	Language of time	Motive/ causation
						Strand 3	
Everyday life, work, leisure, culture (i) in children's own lives and in the lives of adults around them	1	Awareness that they can find out about the past from sources of information		Awareness of the distinction between past and present in their own and other people's lives	(i) Recount from stories about the past (ii) Develop ability to sequence a few events and objects	Use everyday terms about the passing of time	Some implicit awareness of motive and cause in sequencing accounts of events, and of people's lives
(ii) and of life in Britain in a period beyond living memory Different kinds of famous men and women	2	Beginning to answer questions about the past using sources of information	Beginning to show awareness that the past is represented in different ways	Make distinctions between aspects of their own lives and past times	Use terms concerned with the passing of time to order events and objects	Use terms concerned with the passing of time	Suggest reasons why people in the past acted as they did
Past events of different types in Britain, and in other countries	3	Use sources of information beyond simple observation to find answers to questions about the past	Identify some of the different ways in which the past is represented	Recognise some similarities and differences between periods	Awareness that the past can be divided into different periods of time	Use dates and terms referring to periods in the past	Begin to identify reasons for and results of key events and changes

Box 7.2 Recording assessments

Possible audiences	Purpose	Method of assessment	Recording	Pupil profiles	Checklist of statements within the description
Class teacher and subsequent teacher	To recognise and plan for individual differences; to monitor progression	(a) Discussion: class, group, individual (b) Listening to conversations as children draw, paint, play (c) 'Let's pretend' play (d) Writing: books, labels, brochures (e) Formal presentations, slide show, etc.	(a) Teachers' notes (b) Collection of work reflecting specific statements within level descriptions	✓	✓
Child	To understand purpose of activities and to what extent they were achieved	Self-assessment through discussion with teacher / parent (self-assessment booklet?)	Drawings, models hand-made books		
Parents / guardians	To promote partnership, liaison, dialogue, understanding, interest between home and school	Discuss with teacher / child. Contribute through working in school, offering resources, accompanying visits	Child's work taken home	✓	
Present school	Plan, monitor, develop whole-school teaching and assessment.	Staff meetings	Selected samples of work for analysis and		✓

Possible audiences	Purpose	Method of assessment	Recording	Pupil profiles	Checklist of statements within the description
	Collect resources, agenda for discussion. Mutual support		discussion		
Next school	Facilitate differentiation; continuum in learning experiences and thinking	Formal and informal liaison		✓	✓
Cluster groups	Agenda for discussion. Sharing ideas about strategies, resources, assessment	Discussion group	Selected samples		
Research	Possibility of formal large-scale or long-term research	Focused, funded projects			
School governors, LEA, Ofsted	Responsibility for monitoring National Curriculum entitlement	Governors' meetings, inspections			
Others, e.g. workplaces, visitors to school	Promoting understanding between school and wider community	Liaison with teachers			
Museum educators	Planning relevant programmes				

Chapter 8

Planning a unit of study

Planning a study unit involves planning activities which will allow children to acquire historical knowledge through the processes of genuine historical enquiry. Therefore it is necessary to devise activities which relate particular aspects of historical thinking at appropriate levels to the content of the topic. It is then possible to assess children's historical thinking as part of their on-going work in a variety of ways.

Planning involves a sequence of stages: a consideration of the needs and qualities of a particular group of children, of the school's curriculum plan and of the teacher's specialisms and interests; an overview of resources; selection of focuses for investigations; selection of key concepts; consideration of possible activities related to each focus; long-term plans showing how activities relate to level descriptions and how they can be assessed; more detailed, short-term plans for each activity.

Figure 8.1 describes the planning process. It is a modification of a model designed by the Professional Studies Team in the Department of Teaching and Education Studies at the University of Lancaster, which is used very successfully by students. The whole-school curriculum plan was discussed at the beginning of Part III. The following stages of the planning process will be considered now in more detail.

OVERVIEW OF RESOURCES

Primary sources

In the whole-school plans, local resources were reviewed: museums, galleries, sites, churches, great homes, municipal buildings, theatres, cinemas. Themes for study units were selected which related to these. Before planning the study unit in detail, it is important to make a preliminary visit to find out (if possible, through discussion with on-site staff) how preparation for a visit and follow-up work can be planned which reflects strands of historical thinking. Some suggestions are given in Boxes 8.1–8.3, which show (in the first column) the historical questions

Figure 8.1 The planning process

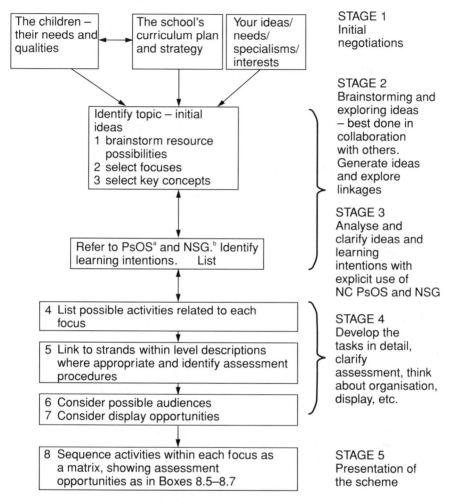

Notes: ᵃProgrammes of study. ᵇNon-statutory guidance.

which children may be asked and (in the second column) how these may be related to each kind of historical resource.

The local community

What opportunities for local history can be provided by the local library (maps, street directories, census returns, newspapers, photographs); how can local community centres, workplaces, parents and friends contribute to oral history?

Box 8.1 A picture gallery

Are there pictures related to the topic? Will they interest children? Are there pictures of children, of men and women, from different cultural and social backgrounds?

Can they develop awareness that the past is represented in different ways?	Are these pictures about real people and fictional characters?
Are there opportunities to recount episodes from stories?	Is there more than one picture about the same place, event, person? Are there pictures which tell a story?
Are there opportunities to make a distinction between past and present?	Is it possible to compare past and present, in clothes, artefacts, buildings, daily life?
Are there opportunities to find out about the past, and ask questions about the past, from sources?	What questions about the past might the pictures raise? What can children work out from the pictures?

Box 8.2 A museum

How will children be able to recognise similarities and differences between past and present, and between different periods in the past?	Are there collections of clothes or artefacts of the same kind from different periods? Can children compare/identify differences between past and present from the artefacts? Can they explain why they changed?
Will they be able to see how representations of the past are made?	Is there a museum reconstruction?
What questions could children investigate using these exhibits? Can they suggest reasons why people acted as they did?	What could children work out from the exhibits about how they were made and used, and how they affected people's lives?

Artefacts

These could be collected, or borrowed from friends, a museum or library.

Extracts from contemporary writings

Use old children's books, advertisements, posters, or even short extracts (for example, from Julius Caesar), diaries (e.g. Pepys, or the diary of a 12-year-old Kentish girl (Kent Archive Office, 1986)) or accounts of Victorian children (Adams 1982).

Box 8.3 An archaeological site, castle, windmill, church, great house

Will children be able to listen to, find out about, retell and reconstruct events linked to the site?	Is there a story associated with the site? Why was the place constructed?
Can children consider why the building, road, etc. was constructed here and why it may no longer be used, or why its purpose has changed?	What differences could children find between past and present? How has the place changed over time? Why?
What was it like to live and work here? How can children use the site to answer questions about the past? What questions might they investigate?	What questions might children ask about the place? What could they find out about the life and work of the people who lived here?

Videotape

Collect old news items about key events or extracts from old films shown on television which illustrate aspects of daily life in the past: houses, clothes, streets, shops.

Music

Collect sheet music and recorded music related to the period.

Simulations and reconstructions

Collect extracts from films or plays on television related to the period. Are there any Living History Reconstructions (see *English Heritage Events Diary*)?

Stories

Collect children's books – stories set in the past, stories about real events (myths and legends if appropriate), old children's books – to use as primary sources and to compare different versions.

Secondary sources

Collect children's information books, both recently published books and old history books, to compare different interpretations in text and illustration. Another Tale (see p. 196) has produced Key Stage 1 history packs of both fiction and non-fiction, and teachers' notes on such themes as 'Homes and Buildings', 'Clothes and Children'.

History 'schemes'

The National Curriculum has resulted in a spate of books which purport to relate suggested activities to attainment targets and assessment. There is a great danger, in using them uncritically and exclusively, that children's and teachers' work will not be rooted in their own interests and enquiries, and that assessment will be crude and unreflective. Often they are most useful as a source of information and ideas, which teachers can select, modify and develop to support their own topic plans.

SELECTION OF FOCUSES

Having decided on resources which are available to their own school, teachers can select focuses within a history topic. Each focus may reflect a particular strand of historical enquiry: sources, time and change or interpretations (Box 7.1). This will ensure that each strand is adequately covered, and make assessment and record-keeping more manageable. Work on castles, for example, may focus on a visit to a castle, castles in stories and the castle today and in the past (Box 8.5). A topic on clothes may focus on clothes in stories about the past, and clothes in photographs (Box 8.6). The history dimension of a topic on a farm (Box 8.7) may focus on inferences about sources, on differences between past and present as illustrated in stories and artefacts, and on different interpretations of life on farms in the past as shown in stories and pictures. Groups of children can work on different focuses then present their work to each other. Alternatively, organising the work in a series of focuses paces it and gives it coherence: work can be drawn together, presentations made and conclusions drawn at intervals.

SELECTION OF CONCEPTS

It is important for teachers to select key vocabulary within a topic so that they can decide, in their planning, when and how to introduce new historical concepts to the class, then how to encourage children to use them independently in writing labels, or captions to pictures, in their own discussions and in play. Teachers will then be clear as to what opportunities they are creating to monitor to what extent children are learning these new concepts. Concepts may be related to the topic (black-out, gas mask, ration book) or to the process of historical enquiry (evidence, maybe, perhaps, because). They may involve the concept of time (now, then, earlier, later) or abstract vocabulary central to all societies (trade, power, defend, attack).

POSSIBLE ACTIVITIES

In order to plan a variety of activities through which children can explore each focus, it may help to review possible opportunities for active learning before deciding which are the most suitable for a particular class and theme. Possible activities include:

- collecting information through use of surveys, questionnaires, interviews, databases (recording a gravestone survey, for example, using OUR FACTS database), primary and secondary sources;
- considering the causes and effects of change (e.g. making and explaining sets and time-lines);
- making deductions and inferences;
- writing archaeologists' or historians' reports and explanatory labels for class displays and museums;
- reaching interpretations through free play, role-play, models, drawings;
- presenting results of enquiries in drama, exhibitions, oral and video-tape, and slide presentations.

ASSESSMENT

Assessment opportunities must also be built into the long-term planning. If activities are planned which reflect strands of historical thinking at specified levels, evaluating the resulting work is on-going and formative throughout the unit of study. Work must be planned with clear, expected learning outcomes which can then be recorded. Assessment is an integral part of planning. It could be based on writing a label explaining a time-line, a museum label, an 'archaeologist's' report, a story or poem. It may be made by observing imaginative play, or by listening to children's discussion in a group as they make a model or a painting, discuss a source, or sort into sets of 'old' and 'new'. This could be related to children's self-assessment of their work, either written or oral. It is extremely important that the purpose of activities is made explicit to children (and to parents) so that they are involved in deciding to what extent these have been achieved. Many sequences of activities involve all three strands of historical thinking, but it can simplify assessment if one strand in particular is assessed in each focus (Figure 8.2).

POSSIBLE AUDIENCES

It is helpful to decide at the planning stage on possible audiences for each focus of a topic and how the children may present their work to them. This will give a purpose to the work, for children and their teacher, and encourage motivation, quality and quantity. It also makes links between school, home and the wider community, and offers an opportunity for

Box 8.4 The history component of an integrated topic, 'Clothes' (the focuses are (1) 'My clothes'; (2) 'Clothes in other places'; (3) 'Clothes in other times')

Science	Art	Religious Education	Mathematics
• Sort according to materials, winter/summer, natural/man-made • Design and carry out tests for washability, durability, warmth, water resistance (Health Education – need to keep warm, clean, dry. Protective clothing matched to occupations)	• Collect fabrics from a variety of countries, decorated using different techniques (e.g. West African print, Batik, woven patterns, embroidery, tie-dye). Discuss how they were made. Collect illustrations in books • Print own fabric with wax-resist fabric crayons, junk, potatoes; tie-dye, weave, knit	Visitors from churches explain special clothes worn by priests in their church, and what they symbolise	• Surveys (e.g. favourite sorts of shoe) • Time investigations (e.g. which type of fastenings are quickest to do up) • Measures: shape and space – make outfit for teddy; money (clothes shop) • Algebra: design a sequence for a bead necklace and record it; make necklace to friend's formula. Is pattern correct? • Number counting (e.g. for durability test; how many rubs before there is a hole?)

History: Time and change

- Retell true stories or stories set in the 1930s, 1900s, beyond living memory
- Collect photographs, sequence and describe, and try to explain changes in one item of clothing
- Sort newspaper photographs of these periods into 'ordinary people' and 'celebrities'
- Survey: 'Were clothes in — easier to keep clean/smarter than clothes today?'

Geography

- Collect pictures of people in hot, cold, temperate climates. Sort into sets. What does each set have in common? Why? Identify on globe/map
- Invite a visitor familiar with locality which has a climate different from Britain to explain/demonstrate traditional clothes and modern modifications
- Do clothes show job or status? How are they suitable for the lives people live in this place? For the climate? What are they made of? How?

Technology

Design and make an outfit for a very dirty/ragged/cold/hot or wet teddy or doll

Cross-curricular themes

- Citizenship: collect pictures – who are these people? What do they do? Why? Why do they wear special clothes? (e.g. Queen opening Parliament, lords, baronesses, bishops, judges, local mayor, aldermen, members of voluntary organisations, police, firefighters, nurses)
- EIU: house corner play – a clothes shop
- Equal opportunities: (a) traditional dress of various cultures; (b) jobs women do which they did not do in the past, and clothes they wear, e.g. firefighter, police, pilot, bus driver, engineer, scientist

English

- Talking and listening. Interviewing visitor about traditional clothes from another country (geography)
- Reading: labels for fabrics (art), or for photographs (history); stories (e.g. 'The Emperor's New Clothes' and 'The Emperor's Dan-Dan', a West Indian version (see Agard 1992))
- Writing: a (picture) story about a teddy who gets very dirty/ragged/cold/hot or wet

Box 8.5 Example of a history-focused topic showing how activities are planned which reflect history level descriptions and how they can be assessed: Key Stage 1, 'Castles'

Focus	*Historical strand*	*Resources*
Visit to a castle	**Deductions and inferences from sources** Level 1: find out about the past from sources of information Level 2: answer questions about the past using sources of information Level 3: select information from sources to answer specific questions about the past	Visit to a castle. Record in photographs, drawings. What do we know? What reasonable guesses can we make? What would we like to know? Secondary sources – reference books Information about other castles (e.g. Red Ford, Agra, Mughal miniatures, Victoria & Albert Museum, castles in Europe)
Castles in stories	**Interpretations** Level 1: (a) recount episodes from stories in the past; (b) understand that stories may be about real or fictional people Level 2: (a) retell stories about people and events and use terms concerned with the passing of time to order events; suggest reasons why people acted as they did; (b) show awareness that the past is represented in different ways Level 3: (a) demonstrate knowledge of events, people and places they have learned about; discuss causes and consequences of a choice and results; (b) show developing awareness of why past is represented in different ways	Extracts from films (e.g. *Ivanhoe*, *Robin Hood*) Illustrated fairy stories (e.g. 'Rapunzel', 'Cinderella', 'Puss in Boots') True stories about castle visited
Now and then	**Understanding time and change** Level 1: awareness of differences between past and present Level 2: can make distinctions between their own lives and past times Level 3: can recognise similarities and differences between different periods in the past	Secondary sources; reference books Old recipes (e.g. Renfrew *et al.* 1993), picture cards (postcards, or cards made from brochure) of castle at different periods (e.g. Norman, Medieval, Tudor, 18th Century, today)

Concepts	Activities	Method of assessment
Attack Defend Moat Tower Hall Dungeon Drawbridge Feast Armour Jousting	Make a model; label and explain parts Write booklet or poster for other visitors Draw pictures of parts of castle; label, explain	From model, brochure or picture can: Level 1: describe Level 2: ask questions; refer to other sources to find out more Level 3: make reasonable suggestions based on evidence about how castle was made, used, and why
	Free play (e.g. make flags, 'drawbridge', 'moat', to turn house corner into castle tower; hobby horse tournament). Write proclamations; invitations to feast Teacher observes questions, checks anachronisms, provides resources to find out more, extend Play continues based on new information Story-writing	Level 1: (a) retell story; (b) discuss whether stories are true. How do we know? Level 2: (a) discuss different groups of children's play based on evidence seen in the castle, or in 'true stories' Level 3: (a) can retell 'true stories'; (b) can use vocabulary such as 'I think', 'perhaps', and 'We don't know because...'
Now The present Today New	Paint a background for the model of the castle today, and one for when it was new Or make a tape of things you may have heard then and things you hear today, at the castle Or cook food they may have eaten then, and now, or listen to music they may have heard then and music today Put in order/draw pictures of the castle at different periods	Level 1: can contribute background paintings appropriately Level 2: can describe differences between the old and the new and attempt to explain them Level 3: can put pictures of castle at different periods in order; suggest reasons for changes; name periods

Box 8.6 The history dimension of an integrated topic, 'Clothes'

Focus	Understanding changes over time, using sources	Resources
Clothes in other times	Level 1: (a) recount episodes from stories of the past; (b) show awareness of differences between past and present; find out about the past from sources	Illustrated true stories set in the 1930s, 1900s, beyond living memory
	Level 2: make distinctions between own lives and past times. Order objects; suggest reasons why people in the past acted as they did; answer questions about the past using sources	
	Level 3: recognise similarities and differences between different periods in the past. Select information from sources to answer specific questions about the past. Can identify reasons for and results of changes. Awareness that the past is divided into two periods	Photographs over three generations (and beyond living memory)
	Interpretations Level 2: beginning to show awareness that the past is represented in different ways	Collect from newspapers photographs of people at work (ordinary people) and filmstars, politicians, etc., of same date

Concepts	Activities	Method of assessment
Old, new Before, then, next, after, in the end	In a group, take it in turns to tell next stage of story	Level 1: can sequence events correctly Level 2: can refer to factual knowledge of people and events in detail
Edwardian, Victorian, Tudor Fabric: wool, cotton, fur, silk, leather, straw, lace Decoration, jewellery Other special vocabulary as appropriate	Collect photographs of parents (great) grandparents, pictures of people beyond living memory Display them in sequence. Write captions for each photo saying 'I am wearing . . . because . . .'. Select one item (e.g. hat or shoes) and copy them from each picture. Present sequence as a fashion commentary to an audience describing changes and suggesting reasons why clothes changed	Level 1: can describe clothes in photographs Level 2: can describe differences, can sequence photographs. Can suggest why people wore these styles of clothes. Level 3: can identify differences between particular items of clothing at different periods. Can select information from pictures to answer specific questions (e.g. do you think this woman had a job? Why?). Can suggest possible reasons for changes, and effects on people's lives. Can label clothes as, e.g. Victorian/ Tudor/Roman
	Sort photographs of 'ordinary people' and 'celebrities' into sets. In groups, describe what each set tells us about this period	Level 2: Can explain why deductions from 'ordinary people' and 'celebrities' sets give different versions of the period

Box 8.7 The history dimension of a humanities-focused topic, 'The Farm'

Focus	*Historical strand*	*Resources*
	Making deductions and inferences from historical sources	
	Level 1: find out about the past from sources of information. Recount episodes from stories of the past	Photographs and drawings made by children on visit (e.g. doors to barn wide enough for cart, iron ring in wall for tying up animals, drinking trough, stile, date over door, name of farm)
	Level 2: answer questions about the past, using sources of information	
	Level 3: select information from sources to answer specific questions	Collection of old implements
		Old photographs
		Diary extracts, e.g. *Ordinary Times: A Hundred Years Ago* (Adams 1982); *Lark Rise to Candleford* (Thompson 1989): harvest pp.132–7, children's games pp. 87–120). Philip (1993) documents the hardships of rural children
		Old paintings about rural life, both idealised (e.g. *Willie Lot's Cottage*, Constable) and realistic (e.g. *Bird Scaring*, George Clausen)
	Time and change	
	Level 1: show awareness of differences between past and present. Recount episodes from stories about the past	*The Tale of Jemima Puddleduck, The Tale of Sally Henny Penny* and Thompson (1989: pp.132–7, 87–120) retold by the teacher
	Level 2: make distinctions between aspects of their own lives and past times. Order objects. Suggest reasons why people in the past acted as they did	Sequence artefacts, e.g. milk-maid's yoke, milk can, milk bottle, carton
	Interpretations	
	Level 1: understand that stories may be about real people or fictional characters	Folk tales from a variety of cultures about growing and selling crops (e.g. 'The Great Big Enormous Turnip', 'Jack and the Beanstalk', *Shaker Lane* (Provensen and Provensen 1992)
	Level 2: show awareness that different stories can give different versions of the past	
	Level 3: increasing awareness that the past is represented in different ways	Collect images of village life in the past, e.g. photographs of people dressed in old-fashioned clothes (reconstructions), old photographs, nursery rhyme illustrations, pantomime, paintings

Concepts	Activities	Method of assessment
Hay, straw, wheat, barley, sheaves, farm, cultivate, plough, sow, mow, harvest, crops, store, hay-stack, herd, flock, domesticate, select, breed (*agriculture*) Buy, sell, market, profit (*trade*) Yoke, cart, wagon (*transport*) Patterns, smock Plough, rake, scythe, sickle, pitchfork, butter churn (*tools*) Dairy, barn, stable	Make careful observational drawings. Write explanatory labels Each child write a question about one of sources collected for quiz. (Display questions next to sources) Leave tape-recorder near quiz display. Children research specific questions posed by teacher or a visitor (e.g. what was it like to be a country child 100 years ago?). Children record any evidence they find on the tape Play back tape to class. Discuss findings	Level 1: can write label (or explain to others) how the artefact/building may have been used. Can recount episode from a diary Level 2: can suggest relevant questions about sources, for quiz. Can suggest or find out possible answers Level 3: can use a range of sources to answer the question
First, then, next; a long time ago, later Old, older, new, newer	Act one of the stories or put separated illustrated pages in order Draw artefacts in chronological sequence	Level 1: can use evidence in illustrations to discuss how the past was different. Can put events in order Level 2: can explain milk obtained now and in the past; why and how this would have affected people's lives. Can order artefacts
	Discuss whether these stories are about real people. Are diary extracts about real people? How do we know? House corner play stimulated by evidence found on visit about farming in the past (props, e.g. stable door, horse trough, milk-maid's yoke, range) In pairs, sort pictures into sets: 'true', 'maybe' and 'not true'	Level 1: can sort names of characters written on card into sets: 'really lived', and 'not a real person'; explain reasons Level 2: different groups can say how they used the 'props' in their play to tell different stories Level 3: can give reasons for placements, support argument, listen to other views

Figure 8.2 Work in other curriculum areas which links with a history-focused topic, 'Castles'

Mathematics

- Vocabulary related to shape and space, direction and comparison (below, above, corner, through, etc.)
- Measures (on site); standard and non-standard (e.g. record in strides the length of the walls, width of the moat, etc.)
- Calculations related to science (e.g. turn wheel 10 times to raise bucket), and to EIU and EE investigations

English

- Talking and listening: stories, discussion throughout activities, presentation to an audience, interviews and questionnaires (EIU, EE)
- Reading: information books (pictures or text), stories, invitations to ball/ tournament at castle

Art

- Collect, enlarge postcards of paintings of castles in different styles and discuss colour, style, brush strokes
- Imaginative painting/drawing based on evidence of visit, and on stories
- Observational drawings of details (e.g. a window) on site, recorded in photographs, developed in models, pastel, sewing, etc.

Science and Design and Technology

Investigate:
- materials – what parts of the castle remain? Why?
- forces and structures, e.g. how can you make a wall stronger? Test bricks of different widths; blow with straws
- levers and pulleys – working models of drawbridge, spit, portcullis, flag pole
- design and make, e.g. a helmet, lady's headdress as in picture, hobby horse for tournament

Religious education

- Values and attitudes
- Myths and legends from the distant past, in different parts of the world
- What are the things people thought worth fighting for?
- Were they right?

History

- Make model of castle based on evidence, ask questions, make references, use reference books
- Play stimulated by visit and stories. Differentiate between what is known and what is imagined
- Consider differences between 'then' and now

Cross-curricular themes

- EIU: How is the castle looked after? By whom? Why? What jobs do they do? Who pays? What does the shop sell? Make a castle shop in school, with postcards etc., or exhibit model of castle as a mini-enterprise with tickets, leaflets
- EE: could too many visitors spoil the site? How can it be protected? Why?

Geography

- Use map, pictures, observation, to work out why site was chosen (water supply? defence?).
- Draw a secret plan for enemy explaining defences
- Draw a plan of inside a castle as it might have been
- Make model from bricks or construction toy. Destroy in play fight. Rebuild using plan

EIU – Economic Awareness and Industrial Understanding   EE – Environmental Education people not necessarily involved in education to learn about and value what is achieved in school. Possible audiences may include another class, the whole school, parents, local libraries and newspapers, teachers' centres, workplaces, and local or national organisations (for example, the Historical Association Young Historian Scheme). Investigations may be presented through structured role-play, songs, music and dance in historical contexts, through exhibitions, displays, handmade books, children's presentation of slides, video tape of a visit (with preparation and follow-up work), or audio tape made by children to explain a display.

DISPLAY

It is important to consider at the planning stage how displays can be developed, throughout the project, which are an integral part of the learning process and of the dynamic classroom environment. (Teachers may therefore like to add a column on 'display opportunities' to the planning matrix.) Display can develop and reflect learning as active and interactive. It is important to plan for initial stimuli at the beginning of a unit of study which will interest, involve and raise questions – maybe simply a large artefact related to the topic. Children can then develop increasing ownership of their environment by adding their own contributions, not only of their work, but old toys, things found on 'a dig', or old photographs, as appropriate. These will inevitably stimulate other children's questions and further work. On-going displays might include collaborative model-making or pictures, which evolve as a result of the comments they provoke, the questions they raise and children's resulting research. The learning environment may continue to change as 'props' are made for role-play areas based on the children's own ideas as their play develops, for example, in a castle, a cave or a museum. Children's increasing opportunities for ownership of their environment make it flexible and constantly changing and challenging. They make the learning environment an integral component of a constructivist approach to learning which stems from Piaget, Vygotsky and Bruner.

LONG-TERM PLANS

After extensive brainstorming, it will be possible to select and refine ideas as long-term plans on a matrix (Boxes 8.5, 8.6 and 8.7).

   Box 8.5 gives plans for a history-focused topic on 'Castles'. Box 8.6 shows how history was taught as part of an integrated topic on 'Clothes', involving three curriculum areas: my clothes (science), clothes in other places (geography) and clothes in other times (history). Figure 8.3 and Box 8.7 show plans for an integrated humanities topic, 'The Farm', which links history and geography.

Figure 8.3 How art, music, maths and science make connections between the history and geography components of a humanities-focused topic, 'The Farm'

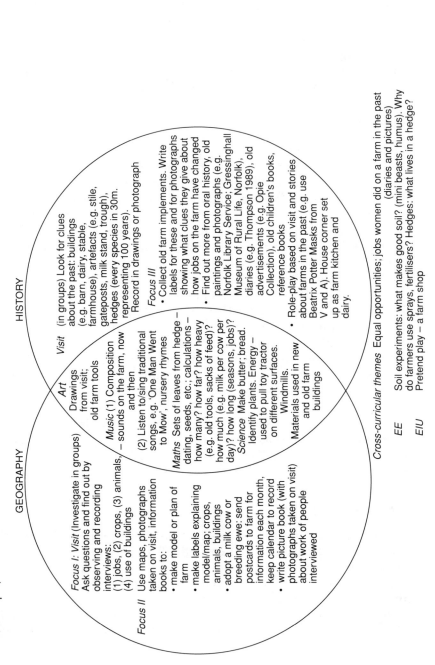

GEOGRAPHY

HISTORY

Focus I: Visit (Investigate in groups)
Ask questions and find out by
observing and recording
interviews:
(1) jobs, (2) crops, (3) animals,
(4) use of buildings

Focus II Use maps, photographs
taken on visit, information
books to:
• make model or plan of
  farm
• make labels explaining
  model/map; crops,
  animals, buildings
• adopt a milk cow or
  breeding ewe: send
  postcards to farm for
  information each month,
  keep calendar to record
• write picture book (with
  photographs taken on visit)
  about work of people
  interviewed

Art
Drawings
from visit;
old farm tools

Music (1) Composition
– sounds on the farm, now
and then

(2) Listen to/sing traditional
songs, e.g. 'One Man Went
to Mow', nursery rhymes

Maths Sets of leaves from hedge –
dating, seeds, etc.; calculations –
how many? how far? how heavy
(e.g. old tools, sacks of feed)?
how much (e.g. milk per cow per
day)? how long (seasons, jobs)?
Science Make butter; bread.
Identify plants. Energy –
used to pull toy tractor
on different surfaces.
Windmills.
Materials used in new
and old farm
buildings

Visit (in groups) Look for clues
about the past: buildings
(e.g. barn, dairy, stable,
farmhouse), artefacts (e.g. stile,
gateposts, milk stand, trough),
hedges (every species in 30m.
representing 100 years).
Record in drawings or photograph

Focus III
• Collect old farm implements. Write
  labels for these and for photographs
  showing what clues they give about
  how jobs on the farm have changed
• Find out more from oral history, old
  paintings and photographs (e.g.
  Norfolk Library Service; Gressinghall
  Museum of Rural Life, Norfolk),
  diaries (e.g. Thompson 1989), old
  advertisements (e.g. Opie
  Collection), old children's books,
  reference books
• Role-play based on visit and stories
  about farms in the past (e.g. use
  Beatrix Potter Masks from
  V and A). House corner set
  up as farm kitchen and
  dairy.

Cross-curricular themes Equal opportunities; jobs women did on a farm in the past
(diaries and pictures)

EE   Soil experiments: what makes good soil? (mini beasts, humus). Why
        do farmers use sprays, fertilisers? Hedges: what lives in a hedge?

EIU   Pretend play – a farm shop

FROM LONG-TERM PLANS TO WEEKLY AND DAILY PLANNING

First, from the topic web and grid, a weekly planner can be made, showing which part of the study unit can be covered each week, in each curriculum area. This ensures that the amount of work planned is feasible and that there is curriculum balance, although every curriculum area does not have to be included each week. This is also a tried and tested approach which prevents teachers driving themselves crazy trying to do too much! For example, the first two weeks of a unit, or 'Castles', might be planned as in Box 8.8.

Second, activities planned can then be fitted into the class timetable at the beginning of each week. Plans will probably be modified, depending on how much was actually achieved. The weekly timetable can be colour-coded to show concurrent group activities as in Box 8.9.

Third, experienced teachers may not need to write detailed plans for each activity, but they will inevitably remind themselves of learning objectives and assessment opportunities set out in the long-term planning matrix, and they will consider how activities and whole class sessions will be initiated and organised, the sequence of questions they will ask, their own role in extending focused activities, and intervention opportunities.

Fourth, experienced teachers do not usually do a detailed written evaluation of each activity, because this process becomes an innate and integral part of professional reflection. This process is essential in order to inform and modify planning in the light of children's responses. Sometimes this will be part of a formal discussion with colleagues, more often an informal exchange siezed in odd moments. Most often it is, *faut de mieux*, an internal dialogue, in the car or the bath! At whatever level, it is part of a cycle (see Figure 8.4).

Figure 8.4 Cycle of teachers' self-evaluation

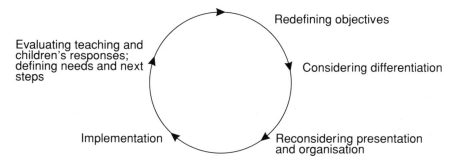

However, even the most experienced teachers will need to record what key activities each child has undertaken, and what they have achieved, on some kind of checklist each day or week (see Box 8.10).

Box 8.8 Planning a unit

Week	History	English	Maths	Science/ Technology	Geography	Art	RE	Music	PE/Dance
5–9 Sept.	Castle visit	Label parts; story about castle	Draw plan	Begin model		Drawings (castles)		Listen to Medieval music. Make up dance	Based on castle story/visit
12–16 Sept.	Use evidence from visit to begin brochure or poster	Role-play	Measure in strides on playground	Continue model			Discuss motives/ values in story about castle		

Box 8.9 Example of a timetable

	8.50–10.30	10.50–12.15	1.20–3.15
Thurs. 7 Sept.	REGISTER — Discuss visit (Weds), introduce group work x o ⊞ *	PLAY x o ⊞ *	LUNCH Music STORY
Fri. 8 Sept.	x o ⊞ *	PE	x o ⊞ *

4 activities

x Draw and label parts
o Draw plans
⊞ Begin model
* Free play – castle area

Focused groups for assessment can be highlighted

Box 8.10 Teachers' checklist of each child's achievements

Week		Record of individual progress	
Learning intentions	NC reference	Children's initials	Special/urgent action notes

Finally, teachers will be able to collect and record more detailed assessments from focused groups they have worked with periodically. This may well allow opportunities for assessment in another curriculum area as well as in history: history and mathematics, history and English, or history and science. Since the introduction of the National Curriculum, assessment has often been seen as the tail wagging the dog. However, when it is an integral part of planning, when curriculum overlap is built into the planning, when formative assessment is recognised as an informal and on-going part of a teacher's inevitable and continuous professional judgement, which is reflected only at intervals in in-depth records, assessment refines teachers' work in an economical way; it gives them confidence because they have evidence that children are progressively achieving a rich variety of objectives in skills, attitudes and knowledge. This was often previously regarded as unquantifiable. Such accountability empowers teachers. It provides a language for valuing, defining, defending and sharing their professional expertise.

Part IV

Four case studies

This section consists of three case studies of work in inner-city schools, and one of history work in a school for children with severe learning difficulties. In each case, history had not previously been included in the curriculum. They describe work planned for a vertically grouped year 2/3 class, a year 2 class, a year 1 class and a class of older children with special educational needs. They illustrate different approaches to planning and to assessment, and different curriculum content and teaching strategies.

Case study 1 is a history-focused topic, linked to art and English. The long-term planning web was the basis for a weekly 'menu' and detailed activity plans were written for each week. Assessment was based on teachers' notes, recording discussions with individual children about their writing and drawing.

In case study 2, the teacher had clear ideas of the kinds of historical thinking she was trying to develop, but the work evolved and differentiation was built in through observing children's responses to activities and allowing them to develop their own ideas. As the teacher observed and evaluated, she noted possible alternatives and extensions for a subsequent class. By the end of the term, children themselves were able to suggest a variety of ways they might respond to an activity. Assessment was on-going and formative, based on observations, discussion, writing and drawing.

Case study 3 was the historical dimension of an integrated topic on buildings. A sequence of activities was planned which reflected strands of historical thinking within level descriptions, and assessment was based on the teacher's notes of conversations with the whole class, groups and individuals. Extracts from these notes show how open-ended tasks reflect the complexities of children's thinking and so the need to return constantly to the same statements of attainment in different contexts.

The first two case studies involve finding out about the past through artefacts, photographs and oral sources. The third case study is based on finding out about the distant past (castles), through secondary sources (story) and play.

Case study 4 describes the history dimension of a topic on 'work'. The teacher made a reconstruction of a Victorian kitchen, including a range made from painted cardboard boxes and a collection of artefacts. She devised ways of helping children who had a range of severe learning difficulties to understand how cooking and washing were done differently in the past. Her careful individual records show the ways in which each child responded to these experiences.

Chapter 9

Case study 1: year 2/3 – 'Memories of Childhood'/'The Victorians'

This was a history-focused topic lasting half a term, taught by Helen Ingham. There is a whole-school approach to planning for science, mathematics, history and geography. Within this framework, teachers of year 2/3 children mapped out the following sequence of topics for six half-terms. They focused on one curriculum area in each topic. (This was the first topic with a history focus planned for Key Stage 1.)

Autumn Term
- 'Journeys' (geography focus)
- 'Festivals of Light' (science and religious education focus)

Spring Term
- 'Memories of Childhood'/'The Victorians' (history focus)
- 'Growing Plants' (science focus)

Summer Term
- 'Minibeasts'/'Wild Garden' (science focus)
- 'Local History' (history/geography focus)

PLANNING FOR YEARS 2/3

Three year 2/3 teachers planned the topic web together but weekly planning was done by individual teachers, as it depended on the objects and photographs children brought to school.

Because of the specified programmes of study for Key Stage 2, year 3 children in the class also used *Grandma's Attic* (Coate 1991) in order to be involved in the study unit on Victorian Britain, which the rest of the school was working on.

CLASSROOM ORGANISATION

There were five mixed age/ability/gender groups, each consisting of five or six children, for topic-based work. In any five-day period they worked

Box 9.1 Long-term plan devised collaboratively by the three year 2/3 teachers

Extensions for year 3	*Non-topic work*
Grandma's Attic (Coate 1991)	• Maths: differentiated work on place value, data handling
Escape from the Workhouse (Barnard 1989)	• Science: interactive display, investigating magnets
Lady Daisy (King-Smith 1993)	• Language: reading activities, spelling and punctuation
	Art: self-portraits
	PE/games
	Music/drama

Visit to Bethnal Green Museum of Childhood Visit from local history librarian	Memories of Childhood/ The Victorians. First half Spring Term. Yrs 2/3 Classes H, C, L/M	BBC TV 'How We Used To Live' and 'Watch' as a springboard for discussions

Artefacts	*Time-lines*
We hope to choose 2/3 focuses (e.g. toys, domestic artefacts, clothes) and encourage children to bring in artefacts, then work on the following activities: • Label an artefact • Research a question (e.g. why a marble in an old bottle?) • How did it affect people's daily lives? Try using object • Put a collection of objects in order of age What do we use today? How/why is it different? Why has it changed?	Children collect photographs of themselves (display, label, order). Make a zig-zag book of things they can remember. Play 'This is Your Life' based on zig-zag books. Photographs and artefacts brought in Collection of family photographs; what do they tell us? Interview older people about toys when they were little. Are all their memories similar? How have toys changed? *Interpretations* *Peepo* (Ahlberg and Ahlberg 1983) *Once There Were Giants* Waddell and Dale 1989) *Granpa* (Burningham 1984) *My Great Grandpa* (Waddell and Mansell 1991)

around five activities, one per day, for the first session of each morning (until break). The teacher focused on one of these activities and worked with each group in turn, over five days. A support teacher also focused on one activity for two days each week. There were also whole class workshops, for 'Teddy Bear Day', and to follow up the museum visit.

The topic was supported by a visit to the Bethnal Green Museum of Childhood for a handling session on 'A Day in the Life of a Victorian Child', by a visit from the local history librarian, and by the BBC Television programme, 'Children in History'.

The focus of the topic was a display of objects and photographs brought to school by the children, which were discussed daily, and a series of school assemblies provided an audience for their work.

Box 9.2 An example of one teacher's weekly plan derived from the topic web

Activity plan – Me now!		
Area	*Activity*	*Resources*
English (my focus)	'This is Me Now' – who I am and what I am like 1st–2nd drafts, give words, etc., as appropriate	Writing book Pencils Paper
Maths	With a partner find out about each other – age, height, etc. Record in a database format	Scales Tape measure Forms Pencils
Science	Magnets – what is attracted to a magnet/what isn't? Record in an appropriate way	Magnets Magnetic/non-magnetic objects Paper
History	Choose an object from the display and investigate using the questions as a basis, work with partner	Objects Paper
Art	Self-portraits – using oil pastels, paying extra attention to colour mixing/shading	Cartridge paper Oil pastels Mirrors

Boxes 9.3–9.5 show examples of activity plans for history, developed from each weekly plan.

Box 9.3 Activity plan – Objects on display

Resources	Flat iron Candlestick Slate (anything they bring in)
Purpose	To get them to look closely at one object, and use questions as a form of enquiry
Activity	Working individually or with a partner, choose an object. Look at it closely then read the questions (provided as activity is not supported). Use the questions to investigate the object
	Encourage them to ask the owner about the object
	Report back to the whole class at the end of the session

Box 9.4 Activity plan – Ordering photos

Resources	Photocopies of photographs, scissors, glue, paper
Purpose	To practise ordering, also to justify why decisions have been made
Activity	Cut up photographs and stick in right order – write a sentence about each one. Extension – 6 photos – justify why in that order – looking for clues in the photographs

Box 9.5 Activity plan – My life

Resources	Class time-line Dates of birth Zig-zag books
Purpose	To order events in their own lives,
Activity	Talk about things that have happened in their lives especially those which have a specific date, e.g. being born, starting school, siblings being born, etc.
	Put these in order in a zig-zag book. Extend to putting dates on

ASSESSMENT

The teacher added to children's own drawing and writing remarks which they made, as they talked to her about them. They were able to say far more than they were able to write. Stevie's book about teddy bears was made after visiting the Bethnal Green Museum of Childhood, watching a television programme and discussing the class collection of old toys. The excerpts in Box 9.6 show how Stevie's writing (S.Wr) and the dialogue recorded by the teacher (T.Wr) were assessed.

Box 9.6 Assessment

Place familiar objects in order	S.Wr	Teddy bears have been out for a long time. In the museum we saw lots of teddy bears in glass and information about them.
	T.Wr	Mrs Steif invented teddy bears in Germany ages ago. She made them because she was in a wheel chair. There was that cartoon we saw on 'Watch' of the USA President saying he wouldn't shoot the bear. Teddies were named after him. Teddy was short for his first name but I can't remember what that was.
Communicate information from an historical source	S.Wr	Paddington Bear is old. Paddington is not as old as a Steif teddy bear, but he is a lot older than SuperTed. Woody told us his date on TV but I can't remember, but it was about 50 years ago maybe.
	S.Wr	SuperTed is old. He was out in the olden days. He was on TV in 1978. That's before I was born, so it's the olden days.
Understand stories may be about real people or fictional characters	S.Wr	Micky Mouse does not look like he does now. If you look at Micky Mouse now you can see the difference.
	T.Wr	He was a lot thinner then, they've made him more cuddly and fun, better for cartoons really. I prefer the new one.
Identify differences between past and present	S.Wr	Bears are valuable in shops.
	T.Wr	Steif bears are the most valuable. You know if it's a Steif bear because they have a button in the ear and some make a growling noise.
	S.Wr	Some have split from where it was very well loved.
	T.Wr	My Mum's teddy was filled with sawdust. Now they're filled with soft foam. They are more cuddly now. I guess if all teddies were filled with sawdust you'd cuddle them because you wouldn't know any different.

Chapter 10

Case study 2: year 2 – A class museum

This was a history-focused topic lasting one term taught by Angela Kinsett. It involved sequences of activities investigating artefacts, photographs, and written and oral sources which evolved through enquiries initiated by children and were developed by the teacher.

Throughout the school, work was topic-based. Although this topic had a history focus, other topics had no clear curriculum focus (e.g. air, designing a house, road safety). The ethos of the school centres on collaboration and on co-operative teaching and learning; children are encouraged to plan their own work. Children work in groups or pairs for each task; groups are selected according to children's ability to cope with a specific task. During the course of the day the class meets to share ideas.

This case study was not planned in detail before it was begun as the work developed in response to questions and new evidence. However, the teacher was clear throughout about the aspects of historical thinking she wanted to develop and activities were focused on these.

After discussion about the ways in which people find out about the past, the children unanimously decided to have a museum. Although the teacher had hoped that the museum would be about parents when they were young, the children, who had little experience of working on personal history, were far more interested in their own past and decided to collect information about 'Us as Babies'. They were soon inundated with photographs and artefacts, which gave rise to questions, to looking for differences and making comparisons, using a great deal of time vocabulary.

All the photographs and artefacts were put on display and labelled by the children. They took responsibility for the museum, for keeping it tidy, changing displays, ensuring exhibits were handled carefully and explaining them to visitors.

Children's interest in their own past led them to ask questions about the childhood of their parents and grandparents, and they brought in a variety of older objects and photographs.

Ebony and Sarah wrote explanatory labels for the photographs of their parents as children. They all showed an awareness of change over time and communicated information derived from the photographs. Sarah's photograph raised questions beyond the information in the picture. The children's writing describes parents' different experiences of the past.

This is my Daddy with my Granny. My daddy is young. Granny is bout 35 in this Picture. My daddy iS about 1 month old in thiS Picture. it iS Summer.

(Emily)

When my Mummy was young She lived in Jamaica WiTh her grandMa and her two broThers. She had tWo PiCTures Taken in JaMaica tWo OF The PiCTures show a difference about My Mummy. In one of the pictures she is little and in the othew one She is big.

(By Ebony)

When my Mummy was young
I lived in the country. The milk was delivered by horse and cart the large urns were on the back oF the cart. We went to the door with a jug and walter he drove the cart. He measured the milk into the jub. With a ladle. the horse was called dolly. When I was 10 years old I went to secondary school I taravelled by bus through the Country lanes and it took Over an hour. Every year the river Flooded . . .

When my daddy was young
I Lived on an estate. athe At the bottom ofmy garden was a railWay line and a river. Every day whe I Walked to School I went past a Cotton mill called hardmans Where lots of our neighbours worked. on Saturday mornings I went to the Odean cinema with my brother and our friends.

(Sarah)

The teacher then planned sequences of activities related to other sources: artefacts, photographs and postcards, written and oral sources.

ARTEFACTS

Activity 1: communicating information about an historical source (level 1)

The children were given a selection of objects. They looked at them, handled them, talked about them and shared their ideas. (A tape-recorder was used to record descriptions and for assessment purposes.) Once they were very familiar with the objects, they drew them. The children needed to handle objects to develop observational skills. This activity was repeated a number of times to encourage such development.

Activity 2: using sources to stimulate questions about the past (level 2)

Once children were familiar with handling, observing and talking about objects, they were asked to devise a sheet of questions relating to the investigation of objects. This was an activity for groups. One child in each group had the task of scribing and also of leading the group, thus encouraging active involvement in discussion and relieving the less confident writers of a headache. Sheets were trialled by other groups, followed by discussion and the drawing up of a class sheet for use throughout the project. This was always open to revision.

Activity 3: selecting information from sources to answer specific questions about the past (level 3)

A group of children was given a number of related objects. A box filled with 1950s kitchen utensils led to questions, discussion and guessing (it could have been developed to compare kitchens now and in the 1950s). Once the children were familiar with the objects, they drew them and wrote observations.

Children's questions about sources led them to use information books to help answer their questions. Emily, aged 6, brought in an old bottle. She showed the bottle to the class and told them what she knew about it. The children put forward their own ideas and suggestions. Emily then went off to the library to research the bottle and came back with a book showing an identical bottle and some information, which she shared with the rest of the school in an assembly.

Activity 4: putting together information from different sources (level 3/4)

A very successful activity resulted from a suitcase of artefacts being sent in by a parent. All the artefacts related to her childhood. The suitcase contained two swimming certificates, an identity card, a key, two different sized bracelets, a small brown leather purse containing coins and a box camera. The task of investigation was given to a mixed ability group of children. They were given the suitcase to open and to talk about. They were given the task of recording what was inside, as it was not theirs to keep. The children decided between them who would do what. They decided they could find out about Mrs C by asking her questions about the objects in the suitcase and the best way was to write letters. The children set about drafting and redrafting their letters. Questions were not always fruitful, but there was a keen sense of wanting to know.

Within a few days, Mrs C had replied to all the children. She really went to great lengths to answer all the children's questions, to supply the information they wanted, so that they could piece together a small part of her past.

Letters written by Mrs C to the children were a source of information but could also have been used as a basis for distinguishing between facts and points of view, and this could be an area for development.

Activity 5

Children were again able to ask questions about a variety of sources when they visited the Reminiscence Centre run by Age Concern in Blackheath (level 3/4).

The centre is divided into the oil shop, wash day and the parlour. Children were able to investigate these three areas, ask questions of the elderly people, listen to their reminiscences, make observational drawings and fill in worksheets if appropriate. They were able to present some of their findings to parents and other children, through drama, as part of their Christmas celebrations.

Natalie became Margaret, one of the ladies who had talked to them. She sat with other children around her and they asked her questions about Christmas when she was young.

Q Did you have Christmas decorations?
A We were too poor to buy decorations, but I remember making paper chains out of newspaper.

A book of Christmas memories at the Reminiscence Centre was also a source of information. It would also be a useful resource in the development of the ability to understand interpretations of history. 'Merry Christmas: greetings in the mother tongue of nine minority groups' (see p. 196) could have added a bilingual dimension.

Activity 6

An adult visiting the school left a Victorian writing slate and a class reading board. This was the beginning of an investigation into 'The Victorian School Room'. A large group of children undertook this task and between them found out how different schools were in the past. They set up their own small class, sat in rows with hands behind backs, and stood up to talk to the teacher. They found out about the clothes they would have worn and the work they would have done, used pen and ink for handwriting (with no blots!), tried out some cross stitch, had a go at learning tables and found out how difficult it is to do the things we do today when confined to a desk.

Activity 7: making deductions from sources, identifying differences between past and present, and placing objects in chronological order

Favourite artefacts turned out to be cameras and teddies.

Cameras

Groups discussed similarities and differences between these and listed lots of questions that needed answering: how do you take a picture with an old camera? Where does the film go? How does it open?

Old photographs or postcards

These formed the basis for observation and questionnaires about what had changed: types of shops, fashion, street furniture, vehicles on the road. Children engaged in activities, generally in pairs. If two children of differing ability worked together, the more able scribed, encouraging the partner to help with initial sounds, and to give ideas. Problems did occur if two more able children worked together. Often they wanted to work independently and not share their ideas. They wanted to produce their own pieces of work. This presented an opportunity to talk about why we collaborate and co-operate in our work; what can be gained by combining ideas and expertise.

When working with postcards, observation and discussion were the first skills to be developed. Each activity took the children a step forward. Children could jump in at the stage most appropriate for them, some progressing further than others. The children were being directed towards an historical approach to questioning. They had the opportunity to share their work with the rest of the class during one of the times they came together.

Activities relating to postcards

Activity 1: communicating information from an historical source orally

In pairs, the children were given a postcard to look at. They talked with their partner about what they could see. They shared their observations with another group or with the class.

Activity 2: communicating information from an historical source in writing

In pairs, the children were given a postcard to look at. They talked about what they could see and wrote down a list of observations. They shared their observations.

Activity 3: recognising that sources can stimulate questions about the past

In pairs, the children looked at a postcard, talked about it and wrote down any questions they wanted to find the answers to. They shared their questions with the class and others began to think about answering the questions.

Activity 4: recognising that sources can help to answer questions about the past

The children were set the task of trying to find the answers to their questions. They could also help find the answers to someone else's questions. This led to discussion on how they could find the answers.

Activity 5: identifying differences between past and present, and describing changes over time

A natural progression would have been to take a theme – buildings, fashion or transport – and to have given the children a selection of pictures relating to a particular period. They could have looked for styles, similarities, differences, particularly in fashion, between rich and poor. If different groups of children had taken different periods, further discussion could have taken place on developments and changes in time. Work could have been displayed on a time-line.

Activity 6: asking questions about a source

Photographs of the local area formed the basis for discussion on what happened in Lee Green during the Second World War. Photographs showed street scenes, people celebrating, an air-raid shelter in the back-ground, the Union Jack at the window, a bomb site. These raised many questions.

Written documents

A letter written by a former resident of the area was investigated by a group of able children. Their first task was to decipher the writing (no mean task!) and to extract relevant information. They were able to sort the information into that about the area and that relating to the Second World War. A development from this was to gather together the relevant artefacts, pictures and information on the Second World War and present these as a section on their own in the museum. It could easily have been investigated further.

Information about the area
The Pond was crowded with skaters.
We Were out in the park every SPare minute.
They had a park next to their house.
They had huge horse chest nuts.
I hope they put back the cherry tree.

Information about the war
Finding out about War.
Bob had just come in from Washing and shaVing at the sink. a bomb dropped not far away it landed right upon the sink. Had he been there he would haVe been killed. They had the air raid shelter in the big field. They were underGround. This was they used planes. They tried to bomb woolwich Arsenal. becouse they mod bombs and guns there. The people must have felt scared.

(Both extracts from Mrs C's letter)

ORAL HISTORY

An exciting area of this project was interviewing people about their childhood. Various activities took place before interviews to encourage children to think carefully about questions, to consider the person being interviewed and to get the best out of the occasion.

It was necessary to consider whom to invite to be interviewed – men and women of different ethnic groups and backgrounds. Adults who grew up in different countries are able to offer a new dimension, to develop children's perspective of a wider world, of different cultures and ways of life. This provided an excellent opportunity to discuss similarities and differences. It was necessary to consider what the adult would talk about: childhood, in relation to a specific topic – wash day, evacuation, or a particular artefact, 'My favourite toy'. Would the children understand the visitor? Would the visitor hear the children? Had the children planned the questions they wanted to ask? How would the interview be recorded? Was a permanent record of the interview wanted?

Activity 1: a class activity

Once it had been decided to invite a particular person, the children were asked to compose a letter giving some background information about the topic. A few children were given the task of writing out the letter.

Activity 2: a class activity

What questions should be asked? The children were asked for ideas, which were written down. They decided to list their ideas under headings such as home, school, toys, washing, cooking, transport. The children asked questions spontaneously but it was a good idea to have the list available to refer to when necessary.

Mrs C, one of the parents, brought in a wash board, an old iron, a trivet and a carpet beater, all of which fascinated the children. Her interest in anything old resulted in information being at her fingertips and she was able to answer questions prepared by the children. Afterwards, groups of children worked on observational drawings, writing labels for the museum and researching the artefacts further.

Mrs O, a parent from Ghana, brought in a traditional cooking pot and told the children how it was used for cooking, and the types of food cooked in it. The children likened it to cooking on a barbecue. She came in a while later and talked to the children about her childhood in Ghana. The children were delighted to hear that she had lived in a large house, had a swimming pool and servants, and that her mother was a head teacher. After describing life for her family, Mrs O also related how others had lived in entirely different circumstances and still do.

Mrs B was a friend of the school. She was 70 years old and seemed to remember every detail of her childhood. The children had a wonderful time asking her questions. They built up a family tree about her. She remembered the muffin man; beating her carpet on the line each morning; the first time she wore powder; and 'making do' in so many ways!

A variety of activities resulted from these visits:

- Children were eager to word process and desk top publish their accounts and very often worked in pairs on this task.
- Children had a go at developing their own family trees.
- Some children were fascinated by the tale of the muffin man and found out about other nursery rhymes.
- Other children made a display of artefacts Mrs B would have used when she was young, and found information in relevant books.
- Another group re-enacted wash day as it would have been for Mrs B as a child.

Before the class museum was dismantled, children had an opportunity to invite a friend to come and visit it. Letters were drafted and written and replies were received. Year 2 children had the delight of sharing their museum, their work, with others.

i remember when mrss   was youny she was not a allowed to wear make up and was allowed to wear powder she had no carpets no electric light she had to scrub the floors and the table. she had no bath room she had a coal fire. the front room was for best only lee on sunday she had an old kettle she never had a fridge when she was 14 years old she went to wobleworths to buy some clothes and some shoes her father grew some vegetables and they had some stew she had plastic dolls they killed their pet to eat.

ASSESSMENT

Assessment of children's work was on-going. Concepts and ideas understood in discussion were jotted down for inclusion in individual profiles along with special pieces of work which were photocopied.

Children's self-evaluation

The project was rich in opportunities for individual, paired, group and whole-class work, enabling children of all abilities to work together and, in the process of doing so, to discuss, share and evaluate both their own ideas and those of each other. Evaluation of the museum and of activities in progress was continuous. Children's opinions were sought and acted upon; after all, it was their museum.

Teacher's evaluation of the project

The children started to discuss, to compare, to sort and classify, to question, to research, to plan and communicate, to record, in a variety of ways. They became aware of history, of a time before now, that some things are older than others, of chronological sequencing, that changes occur, that things can be similar or different. They realised there is a need to respect 'oldness' and the importance people have in history, that there are many types of evidence which can be used in questioning and developing an understanding of the past.

The class museum generated a sense of curiosity about the past, co-operation between children, perseverance and independence when developing their own work and a keen sense of respect for their own museum and all it entailed. The children were open-minded and eager to find out. They were building on their historical knowledge through their own involvement and growing ability to question.

The development of a class museum was a great success, probably because all the children became so involved regardless of their ability. There were areas which were not developed because time did not allow. Asking for favourite records could have resulted in research into music as far back as the 1920s. Focusing on buildings in photographs could have led to a study of local Victorian houses. Books brought in could have developed work on interpretations of history. The list is endless.

Chapter 11

Case study 3: year 1 – 'Castles'

This case study illustrates the history dimension of an integrated topic, lasting one term, on 'Buildings', including class, group and individual work. The long-term plan is shown in Box 11.1. The class teacher was Julie Giles.

Box 11.1 Long-term plan for history activities showing assessment opportunities

Activities	*Historical thinking*	*Assessment opportunities*
Activity 1: picture reading ↓ Activity 2: class story ↓ Activity 5: collage	*Deductions from sources* Find out about the past from sources of information	Talk about a picture of a castle Listen to children talking as they make their collage, to see how they apply information from picture story and reference books to the collage. Take notes
Activity 3: reinforcing ↓ selected vocabulary Activity 4: draw examples for 'houses now' and 'castles then' (e.g. doors, windows, cooking, lighting)	*Time and change* Identify differences between past and present	Listen to children talking as they identify differences between buildings, and daily life in 'houses now' and 'castles then'
Activity 6: listen to story about Robin Hood	• *Interpretations* Beginning to show awareness that the past is represented in different ways • *Time and change* Place in sequence events in a story	Ask children in small groups • Do you think Robin Hood is a true story? • Can you remember what happened in the story?

• *Motive* Suggest reasons why people in the past acted as they did	• Why do you think Robin Hood killed Guy of Guisborne? Why was Little John arrested? Why did Robin Hood rescue Little John?

The activities allow children to demonstrate, by talking to each other and to the teacher, that they have achieved level 1 in each of the attainment targets (and are working towards level 2).

The plans for activities are followed by notes of children's conversations during the activities, recorded for assessment. The selected vocabulary introduced and used included:

drawbridge, gatehouse, moat, stables, stores, guardroom, latrines, well, arrows, slits, lord.

ACTIVITY 1: PICTURE READING (WHOLE-CLASS ACTIVITY)

Aims
- to identify differences between past and present;
- to communicate information acquired from an historical source;
- to make deductions;
- to develop concept of a castle.

Method
- Show children a large tourist poster of people visiting a castle today.
- Ask them what they can work out from the picture.
- Write children's comments around the edge of the picture – each child adds his or her name to his or her comment.
- Have any of the children seen a castle? Where? Was it like this one? Different? How?

ACTIVITY 2: CLASS STORY – A FICTIONAL STORY SET IN THE PAST

Aims
- to help children to imagine what it might have been like to have lived in a castle a long time ago;
- to understand that stories may be about real people or fictional characters;
- to place in sequence events in a story.

Method
- Read *The Castle* (Rowe 1991). This is an illustrated story about life in a castle from the point of view of a spit-boy who discovers that 'Grey Fox' is planning to attack.

- Use information in pictures to discuss differences between a castle and a house, and what it might have been like to have lived in a castle.

ACTIVITY 3: CHILDREN WORK IN PAIRS

Aim   • to reinforce selected, specialised vocabulary, introduced in discussing picture, story and information books.

Method • Children are given photocopied plans or picture of a castle and set of cards. Each card has a specialised concept written on it which was previously introduced and used in discussing the picture, story and information books.
- Children working in pairs take cards in turn and try to link them to parts of the castle plan or picture.
- Discuss their labels with teacher; modify if necessary.
- Use cards to label their drawing of a castle.

ACTIVITY 4: INDIVIDUAL

Aims   • to help children to identify differences between past and present;
- to learn and use special vocabulary.

Method • Children choose card(s). On each card is written a feature common to a castle and a house (e.g. door, window, wall, light) or an activity carried out in a castle and a house (e.g. cooking, washing, getting water).
- Children draw a picture illustrating their card 'now' and 'in a castle'.

ACTIVITY 5: CHILDREN WORK IN SUCCESSIVE GROUPS AS CLASSROOM ORGANISATION ALLOWS

Aims   • to use information in picture, story and reference books in order to communicate information from an historical source. This will also involve asking questions about the past, making deductions and developing an awareness that filling in the gaps in the evidence makes different interpretations possible in reconstructing the past.

Method • Using what they have learned from picture, story and reference books, first group discusses the site of a castle with the teacher (need for defensive position – on cliff or hill – and for water for moat and daily use). Sketch in chalk on very large paper with teacher's support. Sponge-print background.

- Second group uses books and previous knowledge to find out, with teacher's help, materials available to build a castle (e.g. wood, stone, thatch), and the requirements of a castle (e.g. defensive walls, keep, drawbridge, portcullis, narrow windows, battlements). Children decide how to represent materials in collage (e.g. balsa for wood, polystyrene for stone, dried grass for thatch). Sketch out the castle on to background with teacher's support. Make collage of courtyard, walls and keep.
- Third group discusses with teacher and finds out from books the people who might live in the castle, their clothes, the jobs they might do; draws people for collage.

ACTIVITY 6: WHOLE-CLASS STORY, FOLLOWED BY DISCUSSION BETWEEN TEACHER AND SMALL GROUPS

Aims
  - to help children to place in sequence events in a story about the past;
  - to suggest reasons why people in the past acted as they did;
  - to understand that stories can be about real or fictional characters.

Method
  - Read a story about Robin Hood to the class.
  - Children draw a picture story (or make a zig-zag book) to retell the story.
  - As they do this, teacher discusses the story with individuals or small groups and makes notes on their comments.

Notes from children's conversations are recorded for assessment.

Example 1: communicate information acquired from an historical source

Activity 1: picture reading

K   The castle is made of stone.
M   The windows are narrow.
C   That's to stop arrows hitting them.
M   The windows are rectangles.
K   They don't have glass in.

Deductions:

K   'This may be an island. There is water.'
M   'It's a photograph. A painting would not be so smooth and clear.'

Activity 5: children talk as they make a collage of a castle based on information in picture, story and reference books

D   The men go up there to protect the people. (The baddies would climb over.) They have things on their heads to protect them.

E   Yeah – helmets.

D   The door is so people who live there can get in – and visitors.

E   But if an enemy climbed up the ladder you could pull down the ladder.

M   They'd fall in the moat. There's water all around the castle.

J   I've got a fort at home. It's a proper castle. And you can climb up the walls. And I've seen a real castle . . . with a moat . . .

D   Yeah – that's why the bridge comes up. The people come running up and if they're on the bridge they fall in the water.

E   And if they climb up you could put all hot stuff on, and they get burnt.

M   They had a gate that goes up and down. It's a . . . a – yeah – a portcullis. There are windows for the arrows to go out, and people outside can't hit the people because they're too narrow.

D   And there's water in the pots at the bottom of the tower, and flour in the bags.

E   On the next floor there's fire to keep them warm – and to cook.

D   And there's a thing you turn round. It's a . . . a . . . a . . . a spit fire!

E   And there's a spit-boy that turns the wheel.

D   And they eat animals.

E   They kill a cow.

M   And lambs. They have food for all the people in the houses inside the castle.

E   The things in the top room are for when people attack the castle.

D   At home I've got soldiers, and they fight . . . when I don't even *move* them! And the bridge went up, and they fell in the river! . . . (it's not really the river – it's *hard*!) . . . I got squashed on the bridge when I was there! And one of my soldiers got his head squashed! I said, 'Oh – the blood's coming out . . . '

(This is a good example of how evidence and imagination interact for young children.)

Example 2: identify differences between past and present

Activities 3/4: use selected vocabulary to identify differences between 'houses now' and 'castles then'

The children talk as they draw windows, walls and doors, etc.

L   They didn't have glass.

J   They had wooden, protecting things.

L   They had arrow things. . . . They were called arrow slits.

J   No, L. The arrow slits were in the walls.

D   The glass is bigger in our windows.

L   The castle windows are to protect people.

J   Glass can break. We've got a broken window.

L   Yeah – a thief stole my mum's car radio – he just broke the window.

D   There are lots of windows in a castle, but there's no glass and no curtains . . .

J   They had a drawbridge instead of a door.

L   You pulled it up if you didn't want someone to come in to protect themselves. They wanted the castle and they wanted no one to take it away.

E   We haven't got enemies any more. Castles can be dangerous . . . nobody lives in castles any more . . They're not used any more. People can look at castles now.

L   Even the Queen doesn't live in a castle now.

T   How do you know?

L   I've been past – it's a great big garden . . .

J   There are arrow slits in their walls.

D   Our walls are brick. They've invented bricks now. In a castle they're stone.

J   Stones and cement. They both have cement.

D   Bricks are rectangular – stones are just lumps of rock.

J   In a castle the walls were very big . . .

Activity 1: picture reading

Children's statements are written around the poster, and signed by them:

> The picture is recent.
> We know that because there are cars in it.
> And houses.
> And coaches.
> And caravans.
> And boats.
> The car park is big because all the visitors want to explore the castle . . .

Example 3a: understand that stories may be about real people or fictional characters

Teacher   Do you think the story of Robin Hood is true?

C   I think Robin Hood is true because he does not look like a real person in the books. I've been to Disneyland and I think I saw Robin Hood there. *And* Little John and Maid Marian are true, because they're *good* characters and they would fit in with Robin Hood's team . . .

[after listening to E]

Robin Hood *may* be true, but the picture may not be like Robin Hood was.

A It *is* true – because there was a man called Robin Hood. Because it said in the story.

K Yes, because when Robin Hood was alive, when King John was King. He might have been fighting with Prince Richard – Mrs G told us there was a real Prince Richard.

E I think the story is *not* real because the person who made the book wouldn't be alive when Robin Hood was.

C I don't know. Robin Hood might still be alive now.

E *And also* I don't think Robin Hood is real because it's just pictures – and I don't think Robin Hood is so good as they put in the books.

This discussion illustrates the knowledge children need in order to discuss whether a person in a folk tale really lived. They would have found the question easier in the context of a giant's or Cinderella's castle. Nevertheless, the quality of their reasoning and the exchange of ideas is impressive.

The children who said the story was true all tried to support their statement with an argument: *because* . . . I *think* I saw him; *because* . . . they would fit in; *because* it said so in the story; *because* other events in the story were said by Mrs G to be real. It is interesting that within these arguments there are different levels of reasoning: 'it said so in the story' is less carefully reasoned than C's arguments, and K actually cross-referenced with events she knew to be historical. Although E may be correct, and does seem to be trying to express the idea that the story is a legend or folk tale since she implies that Robin Hood is an idealised character, the argument that the author could not be his contemporary and so the story cannot be true, although showing awareness of time, is less valid than K's argument that if Prince Richard is true, so may Robin Hood be true.

It is interesting that the children were engaged in genuine discussion. C was reappraising her arguments after listening to E, although she later decided to stick with them, while E, when challenged, found more arguments to support her own view.

Example 3b: Place in sequence events in a story

Teacher Can you remember what happened in this story? [Robin Hood]

C Robin Hood was in a wood. Little John got captured. He was going to be hung by the neck. Then Robin chopped the rope and he escaped.

A   Robin Hood got loads of men – and there's bows and arrows and there's Maid Marian, and she's riding a horse, and there's deer there, and Robin rode in the forest with Little John and Little John was going to get hanged, but Robin saved him.

The story had a complex plot, sub-plots and a number of characters. Robin Hood killed Guy of Guisbourne because he said he had come to kill Robin. Little John was captured. He was going to be killed. Robin, dressed as Guy of Guisbourne, told the sheriff he had come to kill Robin's servant, then rescued him.

It is interesting that both these children selected the characters and sequence of key events (Little John was captured and about to be hanged but Robin saved him). They did not offer any causal explanations. However, they were able to do this when questioned more closely.

Example 3c: Suggest reasons why people in the past may have acted as they did

Activity 6: class story – Robin Hood

Teacher   Why do you think Robin Hood killed Guy of Guisbourne?
E   I don't think he was *planning* to. He just shot a bow and arrow and got him, right in the shoulder.
C   I don't think he meant to. He just wanted to do that so he wouldn't do it any more . . . take poor people's food away . . .
K   He was a baddie. Because he was looking for Robin Hood.

Teacher   Why was Little John arrested?
E   He killed the soldier.
C   Because he shot too many of his men. He wouldn't have any crew – any team left.
K   He shot one of the King's men.

Teacher   Why did Robin Hood rescue Little John?
C   He was his friend – one of his team.
E   He dressed up as one of his team and said Robin Hood's body was lying on the ground, but it wasn't really him.
K   Little John was a goody and if he hangs up he's going to die.

Although these answers are factually correct, they reveal different levels of response. E and C are aware of chance as a cause; A implies that Robin Hood could not be wicked because of other evidence in the story; E recounts the circumstances which accounted for the rescue. Other answers were simply based on 'goodies' and 'baddies' as sufficient explanation of motive and events.

Chapter 12

Case study 4: children with severe learning difficulties – 'A Victorian Kitchen'

This case study is of work undertaken by Margaret Taylor in a school for children with severe learning difficulties. Although the children were 8 years old, the study is relevant to early years education because it shows how children with severe learning difficulties can participate in a broad, rich mainstream curriculum. It shows how teachers can plan for their needs through differentiated activities, how children's non-verbal responses can be recorded, and how much such children benefit from this involvement, even if the extent of their purely historical understanding is very limited. The ideas could be used in planning work for young children and for those with special educational needs in a mainstream classroom.

LONG-TERM PLANS

The aims are taken from Curriculum Guidance 6 for Key Stage 1 (NCC 1990):

- to begin to form impressions about themselves (selves);
- to begin to describe ideas about roles at work (roles);
- to develop and describe ideas about work (work);
- to begin to appreciate the nature of change (transition).

In the case of my children I will concentrate on:

- things I can do;
- jobs others do;
- how jobs were done in the past. I will concentrate on the way cleaning was done in the past, comparing old and new artefacts, irons, hoovers, washing equipment. The home corner will be transformed into an old kitchen, which the children will explore (History Programme of Study, Key Stage 1, DES 1991; DfE 1995).

The lessons will focus on:

- a Victorian kitchen;

- learning from objects;
- washing, then and now.

NOTES ON THE CHILDREN

All the children are 8 years old and need help with dressing, feeding and toileting.

Q

- Blind – some minor light perception; partial Aicardis Syndrome.
- Behaviour problems – nipping, biting, scratching.
- Likes – music, singing, rhymes, objects she can hold in her hand.

D

- Epileptic, some visual problems, walks with support at hip or hands.
- Sits unsupported, but 'wobbly'. Uses standing frame, spinal jacket, surgical boots.
- No challenging behaviour.
- Likes – sensory experiences.

L

- Down's Syndrome, fluctuating hearing loss.
- Behaviour – can be stubborn, bossy.
- Language – speaks in sentences – some problems with clarity.
- Likes – swimming, riding, looking at books, helping.

E

- Autistic
- Difficulties – understanding language 'out of context'; talks, but on own terms.
- Likes – television adverts;
    - dough: makes exact copies of letters, words, slogans seen, tries to mould all kinds of substances;
    - computer – matches pictures, words, numbers;
    - swimming, riding.

M

- Epileptic, no known cause of learning disabilities, stands holding support.

- Makes sounds but no speech.
- Needs help with feeding, dressing, toilet.

R

- Challenging behaviour – can't cope with group situations, best one-to-one.
- Aggressive – problems with co-operation at all levels, short concentration.
- Severe dysphasia.
- Likes – cutting with scissors, computer, some stories.

B

- No known cause of learning difficulties; one of most able in group.
- Eager to please, enjoys any activity, easily distracted.
- Uses 1/2/3 key word sentences.

F

- Cerebral palsy; epileptic. Needs support from wheelchair with seat belts.
- Can pick up items, make choices by reaching and eye-contact, nodding.

THE VICTORIAN KITCHEN

Thursday, 24 January

Learning intention

The aim is to use the 'Victorian Kitchen' in the classroom and, by taking the children individually, explore the artefacts and extend their historical knowledge. I will be looking for different outcomes.

Initiation, organisation, conclusion

I will take Q first. While we are in the 'kitchen', the classroom assistant will in turn supervise the children individually to write their names and titles for the displays. There will be three other activities which do not require supervision so that all five children are occupied for the whole time. I will take B, L, E and R in turn.

Learning experience

I will allow Q to explore the artefacts using her hands, smell, etc., and record her responses. I will explain simply what each object is and does, using language appropriate to history – 'old', 'used to', 'a long time ago' – and also record any words, songs, she uses.

Evaluation

Q felt and explored the two hot water bottles and particularly liked the stoppers. She liked the feel of the tin mug in her mouth. She enjoyed the scrubbing board and made sounds with her fingers and with the mug. She loved the feel of the air from the bellows on her face and really made my day when she said 'blew' as I did it.

Q has made her own way into the kitchen at least twice since the session this morning, and sat down and explored the objects on her own.

L has already spent much time in the kitchen and enjoyed showing me how she irons. L is quite stubborn and only co-operated when she was doing what she wanted.

E spent roughly 3 minutes concentrating with me. I think this was quite good for E and he actually spoke in context, which amazed me. He said 'Hold it' when I gave him the old iron to hold.

R wouldn't have anything to do with the kitchen. I don't really know yet how far to insist – it is best to avoid confrontation with R so I left him. I spoke to Ann and she said it was unlikely I would manage to persuade him into the kitchen with me, but why not take the things to R – why didn't I think of that! I will do this next week.

L and B have spent a great deal of time in the kitchen since it was put in place. As I have watched them 'playing' together, I have at intervals said odd things to them such as, 'this is a very old kitchen. This is how things used to be', etc. I also left a big book open at the page that shows an old kitchen similar to mine on washing day. While working with L on Thursday, I realised she had taken all this in. She warmed the iron up by the fire and did the ironing on the table. She sat me down with a cup of tea. Didn't quite understand the toasting fork, so I put a slice of bread on it and showed her how it would toast if the fire was hot.

Thursday, 1 February

Learning intention

The aim is to handle the artefacts in the old kitchen and encourage the use of the senses.

Organisation

I will take the children individually into the kitchen. While I am doing this, the others will be joining in the other activities which have been set up in the classroom. Assistants will be in the classroom leading these.

Learning experience

I will be looking for different outcomes in the session today with D, F and M. Each child will sit with me in the kitchen and explore the objects. I will place them in their hands, encourage them to feel them, give the children opportunities to choose from a selection and feel the air from the bellows. Any observation will be recorded. I will be looking for facial expressions which show interest, likes and dislikes, sounds, etc.

Evaluation

I took D first and he really did seem to enjoy the experience of handling the artefacts. He spent nearly 30 minutes sitting with me and I was pleased with his responses.

F was lying on his wedge – I don't know if this was the best position to be in to explore the artefacts, but he managed well and showed interest in them all.

M wanted to put everything in his mouth. He discovered he could make noises and really enjoyed himself.

I was pleased with this morning – the classroom was a hive of activity and all the children seemed to be enjoying their activities.

LEARNING FROM OBJECTS

Tuesday, 2 February

Learning intention

The aim is to continue with the history side of the topic; use the artefacts with the children to mount a display of silhouettes. Through handling and talking, the children will become more familiar with and aware of their uses.

Initiation, organisation, conclusion

Working with one member of staff, children will individually choose one of the objects, talk about its use and shape, draw around it on black paper – using a luminous colour – and cut it out if possible (if not, R can, if not occupied).

Learning experience

R, B and L will talk about their chosen object – its use, colour, shape, etc., draw around it and cut out if possible. When the display is mounted, they can choose the best place to put their object. They should know what their object is called and its use after this session.

Q and E will choose and draw round their object; both can explore the shape and feel. Staff will cut out. The name will be repeated to them.

D, F and M will be given time to choose and explore their object. Staff will help draw around and cut out.

Evaluation

E

I held his hand and guided it to draw a candlestick. He recognised it at once and sat there comparing the two. He would not entertain the thought os using the scissors to cut it out. He then chose the bellows to draw around and he picked the green pen and drew round the bellows all on his own and then R cut them out for him.

R

Eventually, R came and worked with me. He drew around the mug. He couldn't figure out why it ended up much thinner than the actual mug. He then drew more lines and made it bigger and he even drew in the inside of the handle. He tried to draw around the iron and got himself a bit frustrated because he couldn't manage it. He cut it out but he got confused and couldn't remember which piece it was that he was supposed to cut out.

F

F lay on his stomach over his wedge. He made lots of eye contact with me and smiled many times while exploring the artefacts. He liked the tin mugs and smiled as they ran over the scrubbing board – liked the noise. He lifted his hand to scrape the board himself and smiled as he did it – then looked up at me and smiled.

He liked the feel of the iron – the handle and the smooth bottom.

No response when I blew air from the bellows. He looked at the bread then used his hands to feel it. He listened intently to all the noises I made using the artefacts.

F laughed out loud when M put on the mob cap.

B

B was very co-operative. He looked at the hot water bottles and, when asked what would be put in them, he answered, 'water'.

I asked where the bread would be baked and he answered, 'In there', pointing at the oven. I asked how he thought the oven got hot and he answered, 'Don't know'. I then said, 'Do you think the fire might make it hot?' and he answered, 'Yes'.

B knew what to do with the washing tub. He then lost interest in the kitchen and started looking through the big Oxford history book.

M

M wanted to put everything in his mouth. He liked the sound he found he could make with the tin mug on the copper hot water bottle. He lifted the iron.

He smiled when scraping the scrubbing board. Not interested in the bellows. He liked wearing the mob cap. I showed him himself in the mirror; he got very excited and would have carried on looking at himself if it hadn't been dinner-time.

D

D sat upright in his chair and seemed very stimulated and alert this morning. He soon discovered he could bang the tin mug and enjoyed doing so. Tried to get him to hold two at once but he immediately dropped the first.

He loved the scrubbing board and was lifting it off his knee with two hands. He also used two hands to feel it. He was very active when I gave him the tin plate with the bread on it – loved the feel.

He grabbed at the tablecloth and slid it off.

This is the most alert I have seen D during the past two weeks.

WASHING

Wednesday, 3 February

Learning intention

The aim is to show how the washing was done in the days before washing machines. The children, by using historical artefacts, will develop their awareness of the past. Next week, I will concentrate on the modern way. Comparing old and new washing machines, irons, hoovers, lights.

Initiation, organisation, conclusion

I will organise the washing part of the lesson. I will take the children, if possible individually, and prepare the washing tub, wash, scrub and rinse the painting pinnies. H will start the history display which we didn't get started yesterday.

Learning experience

The children will sort out the dirty washing. I will explain what we are going to do. One at a time, the children will wash the pinnies. They will use the washing implements and scrub the clothes clean. I will emphasise that this is how it was done in the past.

All the children will enjoy handling the washing. B, L and R will gain the understanding of how it was done in the past.

E will enjoy the water play and should participate fully. He will need prompts to keep on task and his responses, if any, will be recorded.

Q will participate fully in the process with my guidance. She will be given the full experience of 'Victorian washing' and any responses will be recorded.

I will video the children and take photographs.

Evaluation

Q

Q, who is blind, was given time to feel the dolly tub, the scrubbing board, the soap and water. I described the articles to her using descriptive language – the slippery soap, the noise the scrubbing board makes.

Q made splashing sounds by pushing the scrubbing board up and down in the water. She then dropped the apron into the water and splashed it about. I then gave her the scrubbing board to rub the apron on. Q was smiling and singing songs throughout. She made no attempt to be aggressive towards me as I worked with her today – she obviously derived pleasure from the activity – feeling, smelling, listening and splashing.

L

L loved the washing. She followed instructions well and enjoyed scrubbing the pinnie. She tried and tried to use the tongs to pick up the washing – couldn't quite push them together at the right time but persevered until she picked up the pinnie. Asked if her mum used a dolly tub at home, she told me, 'No, a washing machine.'

As with B, we discussed what we were doing, watched the water splash and the bubbles appear. L washed three aprons and would have continued for ever. She helped with D as he washed today. She knows exactly what to do.

F

I had a bit of difficulty finding the right place to put F for this activity. A helped me out by holding F over the tub.

F enjoyed the water, the bubbles and feeling and exploring all the objects. By this time, R had added the 'baking cutters' to the water, and F did really well bending over the water and fishing them out with his hands.

F would probably have stayed bent over the tub all day, but A's hands were going numb holding him over the tub. F was cheerful throughout the activity.

Whole group approx. 1 hour

Monday, 8 February

Learning intention

The aim is to give the children the opportunity to compare old and new, using the artefacts the children have been becoming familiar with over the last three weeks, and showing them the modern equivalent.

Initiation, organisation, conclusion

I will begin by taking four children to the lower school washing machine, and the other four to the washing machine in the senior school. H and V, meanwhile, will work with the children in the classroom. At the end of the session, we will go and collect the washing, hang it out to dry or tumble dry it.

Learning experience

I will take four children to the lower school washing machine first and put the washing – 'gym kit' – in to wash. If it is possible without disturbing others, I will discuss how the washing machine works – switches, plugs, soap powder, etc. Back in class, we will discuss the differences between old and new (e.g. could we leave the washing in the old one to wash itself?). I will ask the children for their preferences and why, recording responses if relevant. I will repeat this with the other four children – taking them to the senior school washing machine. V and H will work with individual or pairs of children, comparing the old iron and new iron;

toasting fork and toaster; carpet beater and vacuum cleaner; old pan and new pan, recording their responses.

The resources include the washing activity; an old iron, a new iron, a toasting fork, a toaster, a carpet beater, a vacuum cleaner, an old pan and a new pan.

Evaluation

L and B both told me their mums did washing in machines – not tubs; although they obviously enjoyed 'doing' the washing in the tub rather than putting it in the machine and then leaving it.

Later on in the session, I took R with me to see if the first washing was done. It wasn't but he got very excited watching his shorts going round and round.

We all looked at the clean washing when it came out of the washing machine.

Meanwhile, it was obvious that B, L and R understood the different jobs the artefacts did and understood that the modern equivalent did the same jobs.

Q, M and F felt and looked at the different objects. Their responses were recorded.

B was very keen to 'do the washing'. He and L went first and helped me fill the tub. B grated the soap into the water and swished it around. He then put in the pinnie and used all the implements to wash it.

I asked B what he was doing and he answered, 'Doing the washing.' 'Does your mummy do the washing like that at home?' 'No.' I emphasised that this is how the washing was done a long time ago.

B made bubbles in the water and we looked at these, popped them, etc. B and L washed three aprons each and didn't particularly want to move on to another activity. They helped me show D what to do.

M stood by the tub holding on by himself. He was able to bend over the water and touch it himself. He watched the bubbles and laughed as I popped them. He explored all the different objects, splashed them in the water and used the scrubbing board to make sounds. We scrubbed the pinnie clean on the board. M enjoyed the whole experience.

D stood next to the dolly tub and I let him feel the water, the soap and the scrubbing board. He splashed the water and made bubbles. We put in the apron and splashed the water. We then scrubbed the apron on the board. L and B helped.

D was alert and stimulated during this activity. He did not object to any part of it and held on to the objects as he was using them.

Part V

In-service workshops

Workshops described in this section will draw on information in the previous sections of the book. Children come to school aware of a past and capable of genuine historical thinking. Developmental psychology can inform the development of children's thinking in history. This must be the basis for the planning and assessment of activities in history. History can be an integral part of a broad and rich 'early years' curriculum, based on first-hand, meaningful, experiences. The case studies illustrated how this might be achieved.

The workshops described enable teachers to use this knowledge to develop their own curricula, based on the needs and strengths of their own schools, on the resources of their own localities and on their own interests and those of the children and their families. In this way, teachers can assimilate history within existing good practice, extend their professional expertise and further contribute to our understanding of how young children can learn about the past.

Through participating in the workshops, teachers can work together to write a policy document defining:

1 The nature of history and its importance in the Key Stage 1 curriculum.
2 Activities reflecting aspects of historical thinking.
3 Resources:
   • local organisations, sites, individuals;
   • primary sources; categories collected with criteria for selection and procedures for care and storage;
   • secondary sources; criteria for selection.
4 Planning, assessment and record-keeping:
   • rationale for structuring history topics, with history or humanities focus or as integrated topics;
   • rationale and whole-school plan for topics;
   • long-term teaching and assessment plans for topics selected;
   • procedures for record-keeping;
   • examples of children's work resulting from some activities, at a range of levels.

Useful initial reading for Key Stage 1 history co-ordinators is found in *Primary History 1* (1992: 6–7), *Primary History 5* (1993:12–13) and *Teaching History at Key Stage 1* (NCC 1993: 4–5).

Chapter 13

In-service workshops: some examples

WORKSHOP 1

Aim
- to write an introduction to a school policy document which defines the nature of historical thinking.

Resources
- photocopies of articles (for example, appropriately selected extracts from articles in *Teaching History* or from *Remnants, Journal of the English Heritage Education Service*, or the *National Trust Education Supplement* or *Primary History*) on issues related to different aspects of historical enquiry: making deductions from sources; historical imagination; different perspectives (class, race, gender).

Method
- Individually or in small groups read one of the articles (during or before meeting).
- Give a brief synopsis of the article to the whole group.
- Discuss why each of these aspects of historical enquiry is important. (Keep flip-chart notes.)
- Write collaborative introduction to policy document by completing key sentences, for example:
  - We find out about the past by . . .
  - Historical imagination is part of this process because . . .
  - There is no single view of the past because . . .

The following articles were used very successfully in an introductory workshop on a 20-day history course. They enabled teachers to discuss the nature of history as a discipline.

- Making deductions from sources: 'Evidence in the classroom' (Dickinson *et al.* 1978).
- Historical imagination: 'What is historical imagination?' (Little 1983).
- Different perspectives – class, race and gender: 'Whose class is it anyway?' (Jones 1985), 'A way of looking at history: local, national, global' (Collicott 1993), 'Deconstruction to reconstruction: an approach to women's history through local history' (Welbourne 1990).

Through discussing the articles, the teachers reached the conclusion that although facts may be important, facts in themselves are not history, that accounts of the past are made by selecting and interpreting facts, that imagination based on what is known is an important part of this process, and that accounts are written from different perspectives. As a result of the workshop, several participants said, with starry eyes, that they had never thought about history in this way before, and the course got off to a flying start!

WORKSHOP 2

The purpose of this workshop was to experience the processes of historical enquiry in a variety of contexts, relate them to National Curriculum level descriptions and consider how similar activities may be planned for young children.

In small groups, participants select and undertake one of the prepared activities and later report back to the whole group.

Oral sources

Aim   • to consider how children can use an oral source to describe, find out about the past, ask questions and make deductions.

Method • Listen to tape-recording of an elderly person talking, for example, about her childhood, or her training and early career as a teacher.
   • Consider how you could organise oral history in school.
   • Decide on a KS 1 topic which could include oral history.
   • Write a lesson plan for an oral history session, related to this topic.

Buildings

Aim   • to consider how to use an old building as an historical source with Key Stage 1 children: communicating information, asking questions, making deductions.

Method • Watch English Heritage video, 'The Key Stage 1 Curriculum', noting teachers' preparations, organisation of visit and follow-up work.
   • Outline similar preparations, organisation and follow-up work for a visit to a building familiar to you.
   • Write a lesson plan for one activity related to this visit.

Artefacts

Aim   • to consider how children can find out about the past by describing, asking questions and making deductions about artefacts.

Method • Describe one of the artefacts (in words or by drawing all or part of it).
• Discuss as a group how each artefact was made, how it was used, by whom, and how it affected the lives of the people who made and used it.
• List ideas in three columns: what we know for certain, what we can guess, what we would like to know.
• Write a work plan for a game or activity which would help children to investigate a question about the past through these artefacts.

Pictures

Aim   • to consider how a painting or photograph can be used as an historical source with Key Stage 1 children, to help them to describe, ask questions and make deductions about the past.

Method • Select one of the pictures. These could be enlarged, coloured photocopies of a variety of types of picture, for example, post-cards of:
• toy coach and horses (Bethnal Green Museum of Childhood, London);
• interior of the Butcher's Shop (Blists Hill Open Air Museum, Shropshire);
• the kitchen of D. H. Lawrence's home (The Breach House, Eastwood);
• *A Woman Peeling Apples* (Pieter de Hooch, The Medici Society, London).

Illustrations in books for older children:
• reconstruction of life inside a Medieval merchant's house (Clare 1992: 14–15);
• the birth of Sikri in 1569 (Roberts 1992: 22);
• women musicians in a fairground in Imperial China (Gleisner 1993: 39).

Sequencing family photographs

Aims   • to experience the process of sequencing family photographs as a context for considering motives, describing differences between past and present, and explaining reasons for changes over time;

- to list the knowledge and interests which were brought to bear on the process;
- to consider how a similar activity might be planned for young children.

Method • In pairs:
- exchange sets of photographs;
- sequence partner's photographs on a time-line;
- describe to partner what you know, what you can guess, and what you would like to know about his or her sequence of photographs;
- partner confirms, corrects, supplements information where possible.
- What did you need to know in order to form the sequence? What were you most interested in?
- How would you plan a similar exercise for KS 1 children?

Time and change through stories

Aim • to consider how contemporary fictional stories about everyday life can help young children to examine and understand changes over time.

Method • Select one of the stories.
- Using the format given in Box 13.1, show how it can be used as a basis for introducing historical thinking.

Box 13.1   Introducing historical thinking through stories

Category	Title	Author	Publisher	Date	ISBN
Family history	When I Was Little	Marie Williams	Walker Books	1991	07445 1765–6

Reading level:	Large print (about 15 words per page, with simple speech bubbles)
Illustration:	Humorous, strip cartoon style, plenty of detail
Historical thinking	Granny has rosy recollections of her childhood, when ice-cream tasted of cream and babies never cried
Use primary and secondary sources to consider: • similarities and differences between past and present	Compare pictures: 'We didn't have these . . . but we did have these' How are they different? Why? • Make sets of things granny says which are true, and things which may not be true. (This could be done by children each choosing an example to draw, and writing a caption, on separate cards)

- how and why the past is represented in different ways
  - Sort the things which might not be true (e.g. weather, facts, feelings, rules, play, warnings, food)
  - Why do you think granny said these things?
  Ask your granny about, for example, the weather when she was little, then ask her for photographs of when she was little
  Do they tell the same story?
  Make your own 'Granny comes to visit' book
  Make a page saying 'She didn't have these, but she had these . . .'
  Compare with other people's 'Granny comes to visit' books
  Do all grannies tell the same story?

Cross-curricular extensions

Science

- Weather – keep records: 'It never rained in summer'?
- Energy – steam, electricity
- How long do lollipops last? How is ice-cream made?
- Space travel – first man on the moon – the moon . . .
- Materials (we didn't have these but we did have these . . .)

Mathematics

- Journeys to school: 'We walked 4 miles to school'
- Maths – do *we* do it like this?

Geography

- Journey to school
- Foods, now and then
- Grannies who lived in other places

English

- 'Let's pretend' play: when granny was little
- Questionnaires/interviews
- Book making

Sequencing events in stories

Aim
- to think how fictional stories set in the past may be used to help children to consider the interaction of impersonal and personal factors in shaping people's lives.

Method I
- Read *Minnie and Ginger: A Twentieth-century Romance* (Smith 1990).
- Put the pictures (photocopied on separate sheets) in sequence and retell the story from it in your own words.
- How many words/phrases did you use involving time; cause; effect? How many explanations were concerned with public events; with private feelings; with describing places or everyday activities in the past which were different from today?

- How many pictures relate to the same period of time?
- Which pictures could be put in a different order without changing the story?
- How could you replace one (or more) of the pictures with your own picture to make a different story?
- Could you reshuffle the pictures to tell a different story?

Method II • How could you develop this activity with KS 1 children?

Interpretations through stories

Aims
- to consider how different versions of stories may be created, and the similarities and the differences between versions;
- to consider to what extent young children can begin to understand how and why stories differ, and how you can help them to do so.

Method I
- Select two versions of a folk tale; a traditional and a modern version of a fairy tale; versions of a folk tale from different cultures, e.g. *The Cinderella Story* by Neil Philip (1989); two accounts of a myth or legend (e.g. a Greek myth, or a story about Robin Hood or King Arthur), or a story told in an old and a modern history book.
- How are the stories the same; different? How do you think the different versions came about? What do you think is probably true; untrue?

Method II
- What would children need to be able to do/know in order to discuss whether a story is about real people; in order to compare different versions of stories; in order to understand why there may be different versions of a story?
- How could you help them to do this?
- Is there a sequence in the kinds of stories you would introduce them to in order to do this?

Interpretations through oral history

Aims
- to focus on different interpretations of the past, to understand why different stories can give different versions of what happened, and to distinguish between a fact and a point of view.

Method
- Decide on an event in the past which many people would remember (e.g. the Coronation of Queen Elizabeth II, or the Gulf War). Interview several people old enough to remember the event. Decide on three questions,
  e.g. for the Coronation: Describe the event

  How did you know about it?

  How did it affect you?

for the Gulf War: How did it begin?
What happened?
Why did it end?
- List facts and points of view in interviewees' reports. Consider how the reports are different and why.
- What events might children like to find out about; what topics might such an enquiry be part of?

WORKSHOP 3

Aim • to initiate school-based collection of primary sources.
Method 1 Decide on categories of artefacts which could be collected:
- related to a particular period (1950s, Second World War, Victorian);
- related to a particular (local) occupation (farming, entertainment, fishing, mining, manufacturing);
- which illustrate change in an aspect of domestic life (cooking, washing, cleaning, clothes, toys, games, children's books).

2 List possible sources:
- parents and friends;
- local organisations;
- car boot sales, junk and second-hand shops.

3 Decide on criteria for selection:
- size;
- value;
- interest;
- relevance to topics, possible deductions;
- safety;
- fragility.

4 Decide on storage, care, cataloguing:
- by children;
- a teacher;
- ancillary worker;
- parent or friend of school.
- Is it possible to enlist help of museum staff?

Write a statement for a school policy document on categories of articles being collected, and storage arrangements. Send a copy to possible contributors.

WORKSHOP 4

Aim • to agree a policy for evaluating and selecting secondary sources.
Resources • collection of secondary sources – story books, information books, history schemes.

Method Each group evaluates one category of secondary sources, using criteria suggested.

1 Stories about past times
   - Is there more than one version of the story so that it could illustrate different interpretations?
   - Can the illustrations be used as a source to find out about the past?
   - Do illustrations show how artists convey different impressions through line, form, scale and colour?
   - Does the story allow children to talk about changes over time, why they occurred, why people acted as they did?
   - Does it allow children to talk about how and why a time in the past was different from today?

2 Information books
   - Is there a clear table of contents and simple index?
   - Are there illustrations, photographs or clear drawings from which children can make deductions and inferences?
   - Does the text give didactic information without evidence for it?
   - Are artists' impressions of events based on what is known?
   - Can the book be used at a range of levels (from pictures to text) at different levels of difficulty?

3 Schemes
   - Does it provide information and stimulate ideas for activities which teachers can modify to suit their children's needs?
   - Are there good starting points for children's own enquiries?
   - Are there suggestions for a variety of activities: painting, drawing, model-making, free play, drama?
   - Do the enquiries and activities involve genuine historical thinking?
   - Are there useful sources which would otherwise be difficult to obtain?
   - Is there a variety of sources: paintings, photographs, music, simple written sources?
   - Are there good suggestions about how sources could be used, with and without the teacher?
   - Do the sources reflect social, gender and ethnic differences; different political, economic, social and cultural perspectives?
   - Are there suggestions for links with other curricular areas?
   - Are there ideas for presenting findings in different ways?
   - Are there manageable suggestions for evaluating and recording children's work, which are intrinsic to the activities, and not simplistic?

Decide whether to amend these criteria, before recording them on a matrix against which each new book can be evaluated and uses suggested. Include in resources section of policy document.

WORKSHOP 5

Aim   • to agree on rationale for whole-school planning of history topics.

Resources • current curriculum plan for Key Stage 1 history; *History in the Early Years* (Cooper 1995, Chapter 7); *History in the National Curriculum* (DfE 1995); *Teaching History at Key Stage 1* (NCC 1993).

Method 1 Review existing approach:
- Is sufficient time spent on history to cover adequate content and develop historical thinking?
- Are there opportunities for links between history and other areas of the curriculum, which avoid curriculum overload and fragmentation?
- Are potential resources for history in the local community and environment used to the full?
- Would a new approach to curriculum planning be a useful catalyst for stimulating and sharing new ideas?

2 If there is an agreed need for a new approach to topic planning, consider the advantages and disadvantages for teaching history through history-led topics, humanities topics, integrated topics, a mixed approach.

3 Define the rationale for planning history topics within the curriculum for school policy document.

WORKSHOP 6

Aim   • to agree on themes for history topics (or for humanities or integrated topics with a history dimension) for the following year, as a basis for future development.

Method   In brainstorming possible topics, consider:
- local resources;
- cross-curricular themes and dimensions;
- political, economic, social and cultural dimensions;
- children's ethnic backgrounds;
- seasons, if visits outside school are planned;
- rationale for progression;
- programme of study for history in the National Curriculum, Key Stage 1. Topics must involve:
  - changes in the daily lives of children and familiar adults within living memory;

   – life in Britain beyond living memory;
   – key events and the lives of men and women in Britain and
     other countries;
 • Fill in topic grid in Box 13.2 and check that the above aspects
   are included.

Box 13.2 Topic grid

	Autumn		Spring		Summer	
R						
YR 1						
YR 2						

Examples of whole-school topic grids are given in *Teaching History at Key
Stage 1* (NCC 1993:11, 25–8) and in *History in the National Curriculum* (DES
1991: D5 Diagram 7).

WORKSHOP 7

Aim   • to devise detailed plans for teaching and assessing each of
          topics selected for Key Stage 1, for inclusion in school policy
          document.
Method • Decide whether plans for each year group should reflect state-
          ments of attainment for one level (expecting differentiation
          within the level), or for several levels.
       • There may be opportunities within one activity for assessment
          at a range of levels.
       • There may be opportunities within an activity for assessment
          in more than one aspect of historical thinking.
       • Decide on headings for topic planning grid. Examples are
          given on pp. 130–40 and in *History in the National Curriculum*
          (DES 1991: D3).
       • Teachers work together on long-term plans for their own
          topics.

WORKSHOP 8

Aim   • to decide on form of on-going record-keeping for monitoring
          individual children's progress through Key Stage/school, how
          much detail is necessary, and why. Introductory reading on
          assessing history at Key Stage 1 is to be found in *Primary History*

3 (1993: 5–7, 10), *Primary History* 4 (1993: 13–14), *Primary History* 6 (1994: 11–12) and in *History at Key Stage 1* (NCC 1993).

Method Discuss possible approaches.

- At a minimal level, this could be a tick-sheet listing each strand of each level. Work planned to reflect each statement on topic grids could be ticked on sheet when achieved. Topics and balance of content would be recorded in whole-school plans. This would fulfil statutory requirements.
- Alternatively, Key Stage 1 History Standard Assessment Tasks (SEAC 1993) could be adapted to reflect the content of a topic chosen by the school and responses recorded on a tick-list of statements of attainment. The pictures, artefacts and story used could be selected to relate to the teacher's topic, but assessed in the same way. The advantage would be a degree of standardisation without losing schools' control of topics suited to their needs and interests. A disadvantage could be that reliance on end-of-year Key Stage summative assessment would lessen the need to plan work continuously which reflects statements of attainment, and the processes of historical thinking.
- A third approach would be to write statements describing each strand of historical thinking at each of levels 1–3 on A4 paper, leaving sufficient space under each statement for teachers to fill in the contexts in which work reflecting the statement is planned for a whole year group. When a child has satis-factorily completed the work planned for a statement in a specific context, it is shaded. The advantage of this would be, first, that not all children need cover all the work planned for a year group and, second, that statements could be returned to several times in different contexts over two years. This would provide for broadening and enrichment rather than linear progression which is particularly appropriate in de-veloping historical understanding. Third, it would be pos-sible to investigate which contexts are appropriate at different stages, and so to plan for differentiation within levels. Fourth, it would provide information which reflected individual teachers' plans and individual children's responses, in a way which is not time-consuming.
- Another approach would be to keep individual tick-lists of statements achieved based on work planned for topics, and examples of work on which the assessment is based (both teachers' notes about observations and individual and group discussion, and of children's writing, from explanatory labels and quizzes to brochures), in individual children's profiles.

This would provide excellent data for longitudinal studies, monitoring individual children's development, and for moderating assessments and evaluating teaching strategies. It would encourage reflective and investigative practice and could be used for research and case studies. The disadvantage would be that selecting and copying children's work and keeping detailed teacher's notes of observation and discussion is time-consuming. Emphasis on children's handmade books, displays and presentations for audiences could be overlooked and replaced by emphasis on collecting work which no one will have time to analyse in detail.

If the main purpose of keeping records is for children and their parents to be aware of progress, the emphasis should be on children's possessing and keeping their own collections of work. Records based on this are sufficient to inform a public audience that progress is planned for, achieved and monitored. School-based collections of work in pupil profiles will mainly be of benefit for research and the reflective practice of teachers.

WORKSHOP 9

Aim   • to share and evaluate work plans for an activity and analyse different learning outcomes, as a basis for more precisely informed planning.

Resources • some work plans, based on activities outlined in long-term planning grids and examples of children's work which resulted from them.

Method   Possible focuses for discussion include:

• Compare different responses of individual children to the same task, e.g. 'Suggest reasons why people in the past acted as they did', after listening to a particular story.

• Compare responses to the same strand of a level description in different contexts using variety of sources.

• Compare organisational strategies, e.g. show awareness that different stories about the past give different versions of what happened, using oral sources in whole-class session, with groups and in individual interviews.

• Compare methods of presentation in describing changes over a period of time, by explaining a chronological sequence of photographs or artefacts to an audience, by writing explanatory labels, by continuous prose, by role-play identifying with people in photographs or who used objects, by explaining a video made on a visit to a house,

by playing a sequencing card game, by making a comment-
ary on a chronological sequence of songs or dances per-
formed or listened to.
- Compare assessment methods, e.g., show awareness that
  different stories about the past may give different versions
  of what happened, by talking to children as they make a
  model based on evidence, by intervening in and extending
  play, and by modifying the Standard Assessment task
  (SEAC 1993).

WORKSHOP 10

Aim   • to develop partnership with parents and guardians.
Method Review possible approaches, in order to record philosophy and
method in policy document.
Long-term:
- At the beginning of the year (term or topic), explain to
  interested parents, either at brief meeting or in a letter, what
  is planned, why and how it will be taught.
- Display long-term plans in classroom.
- Explain how possible visits (e.g. to a Roman fort or a windmill
  while on holiday may relate to school history topics).
- Explain, in meeting or letter, requests for photographs, oral
  history, artefacts – what is needed, their purpose, how they
  will be used, how they will be cared for (e.g. will they be
  displayed, can they be touched?).
Short-term:
- preparatory information (workshop?) for adults accompany-
  ing a visit.
- organisational information: timetable for day, toilet, eating
  and safety arrangements; groups, rules, expected products,
  e.g. photographs, interviews, drawings.
- historical information: educational notes, maps, plans, historical information.
- questions to ask to extend children's thinking:
  - general open question for each group;
  - possible ways to investigate it (clues available);
  - two categories of question to ask about clues:
    (a) How was it made? How was it used? How did it affect
        the lives of people who made/used it?
    (b) What do you know for certain? What can you guess?
        What would you like to know?
- reasons for detailed observational drawing.
- Parents could try, in a workshop session, asking their own
  questions and making drawings of artefacts.

- Parents could assist in follow-up work in school: pottery models, embroidery, bookmaking, cooking, weaving, etc.
- Parents and friends could function as informed and questioning audience for presenting results of enquiry orally, or in play and display.

Finally, the curriculum leader needs to devise a rolling programme for:

- review, modification, alteration of topics selected and methods of record-keeping;
- evaluation of resources, storage, extending and updating as appropriate;
- sharing ideas with colleagues in other schools;
- inviting guest speakers to stimulate further ideas;
- less frequent but finely focused staff meetings, for example, to investigate the kinds of inferences children across the three-year age-span make about the same source; how play becomes increasingly based on evidence as children grow older; how children of different ages respond to the same story. Such case studies would be valuable in, for example, *Teaching History*;
- monitoring children's development over the Key Stage, by discussing collected samples of work by the same child;
- extending an awareness among parents, and in the wider community, of the quality and value of young children's work in history, through displays, presentations, children's tape-recorded discussions and adult participation in projects.

Lomas (1994) gives an excellent checklist of questions for monitoring good practice in the teaching and learning of history in the primary school. He also outlines the role of the headteacher and the co-ordinator in developing the contribution that history can make to children's spiritual, moral, social and cultural development and to the broad curriculum, and includes sections on meeting special educational needs through history.

Many teachers began early years history because it became a statutory requirement, then discovered how enjoyable and appropriate it can be. It is to be hoped that this book has sparked off further ideas, possibilities, insights and questions, which, in turn, will stimulate further books. Enjoy it; it's fun!

IN CONCLUSION

I should like to return to my initial acknowledgement of the students and teachers with whom I have worked. For these lines were written with a passion which underlies this book, but which has perhaps been overlaid in the writing of it. I wrote how, after hearing teachers, schools and state education denigrated by an 'academic' colleague, I wept in anger for all the teachers I have known who have given their all, their spirits, time and professional expertise, in often difficult circumstances, because of a strong moral commitment to what they consider to be good and right for *all* children, whatever their background or difficulties.

Among these people I include my grandmother, whom I introduced at the beginning of this book. Aged 5 in 1896, she was awarded a history of the world as a school prize. Later she became headteacher of one of the Board Schools which, for the first time in any society, offered an education for all. Her son, my father, became headteacher of one of the first secondary schools which extended these opportunities beyond elementary education. Both were valued and respected members of their communities. For my part I have been interested in developing a rigorous rationale for a rich early years curriculum. However, it has been a difficult journey for teachers in recent years; they have too frequently been misunderstood, undervalued and undermined. But I believe that there is light on the farther shore for those who survive the crossing. For them I shall end on a lyrical note by quoting Tennyson's *Ulysses*:

> Come, my friends,
> 'Tis not too late to seek a newer world.

Resources referred to in the text

Another Tale (1993), Oastdene, Ismays Road, Ightham, Kent, TN15 9BD.
Articles of Antiquity, The Bury Business Centre, Kay Street, Bury.
Bethnal Green Museum of Childhood, Cambridge Heath Road, London, E.2.
Butser Iron Age Village Farm, Queen Elizabeth National Park, Hampshire.
Dolls' House Emporium, Victoria Road, Ripley, Derbyshire.
English Heritage Education Service, Keysign House, 429 Oxford Street, London, W.1.
Folklore Society, School of Scottish Studies, Edinburgh University, St George's Square, Edinburgh.
Haringey (London Borough of), Multicultural Resource Centre for under fives.
History Box; new and traditional stories from Wales, audio cassettes and teachers' and pupils' books, National Language Unit of Wales, Brook Street, Treforest, Pontypridd.
History in Evidence, Unit 4, Holmewood Fields Business Park, Park Road, Holmewood, Chesterfield.
History Standard Assessment Tasks, Key Stage 1 (1993) NFER, Nelson.
Honeychurch Toys Ltd, Woodlands, Lodge Hill, Market Lavington, Wiltshire.
Ironbridge Gorge Museum Trust (*Under Fives and Museums: Guidelines for Teachers*), The Ironbridge Gorge Museum, Ironbridge, Telford, Shropshire.
MEGSS, 'Merry Christmas: greetings in the mother tongue of nine minority groups', Minority Ethnic Group Support Service, Lancashire Education Authority.
Morwellham Quay Copper Mine, Tavistock, Devon.
Mrs Tanner's Tangible History, Gill Tanner, 9 Selvy Road, West Bridgford, Nottingham, NG2 7BP.
National Trust, 36 Queen Anne's Gate, London, S.W.1.
Our Facts database, R.M. Nimbus version, 1988, NCET.
Robert Opie Collection, Museum of Advertising and Packaging, Gloucester.
Science Park, Coventry.
Victoria and Albert Museum, South Kensington, London, S.W.7.
Yorvik Viking Centre, Coppergate, York.
West Stowe Anglo-Saxon Village Trust, Bury St Edmunds, Suffolk.
Women's History Network, Key Stage 1 Biography Project, Department of History, University of York.

Bibliography

Adams, C. (1982) *Ordinary Times: A Hundred Years Ago*, London: Virago.

Agard, J. (1992) *The Emperor's Dan-Dan*, London: Hodder & Stoughton.

Ahlberg, J. and Ahlberg, A. (1983) *Peepo*, London: Puffin.

—— (1984) *The Baby's Catalogue*, UK: Puffin.

Aldred, D. (1993) *Castles and Cathedrals*, Cambridge: Cambridge University Press.

Anderson, D. (1989) 'Learning history in museums', *The International Journal of Museum Management and Curatorship* 8: 357–68.

—— (1993) 'Myth and story telling', Key Stage 1 workshop at the Primary Conference of the Historical Association, Victoria and Albert Museum, London.

Arnheim, R. (1974) *Art and Visual Perception: A Psychology of the Creative Eye*, Berkeley: University of California Press.

Ausubel, D.P. (1968) *Educational Psychology. A Cognitive View*, New York: Holt, Rinehart & Winston.

Baker, J. (1991) *Where the Forest Meets the Sea*, London: Walker Books.

Ball, B. (1989) *Stone Age Magic*, London: Hamish Hamilton.

Barnard, P. (1989) *Escape from the Workhouse*, Saffron Walden: Anglia.

Barnes, J. (1993) 'The saints: close observation and drawing', Historical Association Primary History Conference, Victoria and Albert Museum, London.

Batho, G.R. (ed.) (1994) *Schools, Museums and Primary History*, London: The Historical Association.

Bearne, E. (1992) 'Myth and legend: the oldest language?', in M. Styles, E. Bearne and V. Watson (eds) *After Alice: Exploring Children's Literature*, London: Cassell.

Bateson, G. (1985) 'A theory of play and fantasy', in J. S. Bruner, A. Jolly and K. Sylva (eds) *Play, its Role, Development and Evolution*, London: Penguin.

Bernot, L. and Blancard, R. (1953) *Nouville, un village français*, Paris: Institut d'Ethnologie.

Bhatia, M. (1988) *Happy Birthday Bhini* (English/Gujarati), London: Magi.

Blake, William (1981) *Selected Poetry of William Blake*, New York: New American Library.

Blume, J. (1988) *The Pain and the Great One*, London: Pan/Macmillan.

Blyth, A. (1990) *Making the Grade for Primary Humanities*, Milton Keynes: Open University Press.

Blyth, J., Cigman, J., Harnett, P. and Sampson, J. (1991a) *Ginn History, Key Stage 1 Teacher's Resource Book*, Aylesbury: Ginn & Co.

—— (1991b) *Ginn History Stories*, Aylesbury: Ginn & Co.

—— (1991c) *Ginn History Topic Books*, Aylesbury: Ginn & Co.

Board of Education (1905) *Suggestions for the Consideration of Teachers and Others Concerned in the Work of Public Elementary Schools*, London: HMSO.

—— (1927) *Handbook of Suggestions for Teachers*, London: HMSO.

Booth, W. (1985) 'Narrative as a mould of character', paper given at Language in Inner City Schools Conference, London.

Borke, H. (1978) 'Piaget's view of social interaction and the theoretical construct of empathy', in L. E. Siegal and C. J. Brainerd (eds) *Alternatives to Piaget*, London: Academic Press.

Bowyer, E. (1992) 'Time boxes: an investigation of time using artefacts for Key Stages 1 and 2', *Young Historian Scheme 4*, London: Historical Association.

Bradley, H. (1974) *Miss Carter Came With Us*, London: Jonathan Cape.

Bradley, N.C. (1947) 'The growth of the knowledge of time in children of school age', *British Journal of Psychology* 38: 67–8.

Brown, R. (1982) *If at First You Do Not See*, London: Beaver, Arrow Books.

Bruce, T. (1991) *Time to Play in Early Childhood Education*, Sevenoaks: Hodder & Stoughton.

Bruner, J. S. (1963) *The Process of Education*, New York: Vintage Books.

—— (1966) *Towards a Theory of Instruction*, Harvard: Belknap Press.

—— (1983) *Child's Talk: Learning to Use Language*, Oxford: Oxford University Press.

—— (1986) *Actual Minds; Possible Worlds*, Cambridge, MA: Harvard University Press.

—— (1989) 'Culture and human development: a new look', paper given at the annual meeting of the Society for Research in Child Development, Kansas City, Missouri.

Burningham, J. (1984) *Granpa*, London: Picture Puffin.

—— (1985) *Time to Get Out of the Bath, Shirley*, Oxford: Picture Lions.

Butler, D. (1988) *Babies Need Books*, London: Penguin.

Chukovsky, K. (1968) *From Two to Five*, Berkeley: University of California Press.

Clare, J. D. (1992) *Medieval Towns* (I was There Series), London: Bodley Head.

Clark, K. (1969) *Civilization: A Personal View*, London: BBC/John Murray.

Clements, G. (1987) *The Normans are Coming*, London: Macmillan Children's Books.

—— (1988) *The Truth about Castles*, London: Pan/Macmillan.

Coate, L. (1991) *Grandma's Attic*, Brighton: Tressell.

Cole, B. (1987) *Prince Cinders*, London: Hamish Hamilton.

Collicott, S. L. (1993) 'A way of looking at history: local – national – world links', *Teaching History* 72: 18–23.

Collingwood, R. G. (1939) *An Autobiography*, Oxford: Oxford University Press.

—— (1946) *The Idea of History*, Oxford: Clarendon.

Cook, E. (1969) *The Ordinary and the Fabulous*, Cambridge: Cambridge University Press.

Cooper, H. (1991) 'Young children's thinking in history', unpublished PhD thesis, University of London.

—— (1992) *The Teaching of History*, London: David Fulton.

Cox, K. and Hughes, P. (1990) 'Early years history', unpublished paper, Liverpool Institute of Higher Education.

Cox, M. V. (1986) *The Child's Point of View: The Development of Cognition and Language*, Brighton: Harvester Press.

Cramer, I. (1993) 'Oral history: working with children', *Teaching History* 71: 17–20.

Crowther, E. W. (1982) 'Understanding the concept of change among children and young adolescents', *Educational Review* 34(3): 279–84.

Curtis, S. (1993) 'Constructing tasks for mixed ability groups', *Teaching History* 73: 16–22.

Dahl, R. (1986) *Boy*, London: Penguin.

de Paolo, T. (1988) *Bill and Pete Go Down the Nile*, Oxford, Oxford University Press.

Department of Education and Science (DES) (1967) *Children and their Primary Schools: A Report of the Central Advisory Council for Education*, London: HMSO.

—— (1985) *History in the Primary and Secondary Years: An HMI View*, London: HMSO.

—— (1989a) *Curriculum Matters 14: Personal and Social Education from 5–16*, London: HMSO.

—— (1989b) *The Teaching and Learning of History and Geography*, London: HMSO.

—— (1989c) *History in the Primary Schools of Wales*, Occasional Paper, HMI (Wales) Cardiff: Welsh Office.

—— (1989d) *Aspects of Primary Education. The Education of Children Under Five*, London: HMSO.

—— (1990) *History for Ages 5–16: Proposals of the Secretary of State for Education and Science*, London: HMSO.

—— (1991a) *History in the National Curriculum*, London: HMSO.

—— (1991b) *Starting with Quality. Report of the Committee of Enquiry into the Quality of Educational Experiences Offered to 3 and 4 Year Olds*, London: HMSO.

Department for Education (DfE) (1992a) *A Survey of the Use of Artefacts and Museum Resources in Teaching National Curriculum History*, London: DfE Publications Centre.

—— (1992b) *A Survey of the Use of Artefacts and Specimens in Schools*, HMI, London: DfE Publications Centre.

—— (1995) *History in the National Curriculum*, London: DfE Publications Centre.

Dickinson, A. K. and Lee, P. J. (eds) (1978) *History Teaching and Historical Understanding*, London: Heinemann.

Dickinson, A., Gard, A. and Lee, P. J. (1978) 'Evidence in the classroom', in A. K. Dickinson and P. J. Lee (eds) *History Teaching and Historical Understanding*, London: Heinemann.

Dickinson, M. (1989) *Smudge*, Sevenoaks: Picture Knight, Hodder & Stoughton.

Doise, W., Mugny, C. and Perret Clermont, A.N. (1975) 'Social interaction and the development of cognitive operations', *European Journal of Social Psychology* 5: 367–83.

—— (1978) *Groups and Individuals: Explanations in Social Psychology*, Cambridge: Cambridge University Press.

Donaldson, M. (1978) *Children's Minds*, London: Fontana.

Douloubakas, G. (1985) *Hare and the Tortoise*, London: Luzac.

Doonan, J. (1993) *Looking at Picture Books*, Stroud: Thimble Press.

Dupasquier, P. (1987) *Jack at Sea*, London: Picture Puffin.

Eliot, T. S. (1986) *Collected Poems*, London: Faber & Faber.

Elton, G.R. (1970) 'What sort of history should we teach?', in M. Ballard (ed.) *New Movements in the Study and Teaching of History*, London: Temple Smith.

Eno, P. (1993) 'In touch with the past', *Times Educational Supplement*, Resources III, 10 September.

Erikson, E.H. (1965) *Childhood and Society*, London: Penguin.

Fairclough, J. and Redsell, P. (1987) *Living History: Reconstructing the Past with Children*, London: English Heritage.

Flavell, J.H. (1985) *Cognitive Development*, Englewood Cliffs, NJ: Prentice-Hall.

Friedman, W. (1978) 'Development of time concepts and children', in H.W. Reese and L.P. Lipsett (eds) *Advances in Child Development and Behaviour* vol. 12.

Fryer, P. (1989) *Black People in the British Empire: An Introduction*, London: Pluto.

Furth, H. G. (1980) *The World of Grown-ups*, New York: Elsevier Press.

Gagné, R. M. (1977) *The Conditions of Learning*, London and New York: Holt, Rinehart & Winston.

Garvey, C. (1977) *Play*, The Developing Child Series, edited by J. Bruner, M. Cole and B. Lloyd, London: Collins/Fontana.

Gleisner, C. (1992) *Imperial China*, Oxford: Oxford University Press.

Goalen, P. (1992) *India: From Mughal Empire to British Raj*, Cambridge: Cambridge University Press.

Gombrich, E. H. (1977) *Art and Illusions*, New York and London: Phaidon Press.

Gould, D. (1990) *Granpa's Slide Show*, London: Penguin.

Grafoni, A. (1989) *The Village of Round and Square Houses*, London: Pan/Macmillan.

Greenaway, K. (1991) *Nursery Rhymes Classic*, London: Cresset Press.

Grifiths, V. (1987) *My Class Visits a Museum*, London: Franklin Watts.

Hague, M. (1984) *Mother Goose Treasury: A Collection of Classic Nursery Rhymes*, London: Methuen.

Hammond, N. (1993) 'New discoveries challenge views on hieroglyphics', *The Times*, 24 August: 14.

Harner, L. (1982) 'Talking about the past and the future', in W. Friedman (ed.) *The Developmental Psychology of Time*, New York: Academic Press.

Harpin, W. (1976) *The Second 'R': Writing Development in the Junior School*, London: Allen & Unwin.

Harrison, G. (1993) 'Into battle; an infant archaeology project', *Remnants Journal of the English Heritage Education Service* 21: 1–3.

Harrison, J. (1992) *Timothy's Teddy*, London: Picture Lions, Harper Collins.

Haskell, F. (1993) *History and its Images: Art and the Interpretation of the Past*, New Haven: Yale University Press.

Hastings, S. (1992) *Sir Gawain and the Loathly Lady*, London: Walker Books.

Holdaway, D. (1979) *The Foundations of Literacy*, London and Sydney: Ashton Scholastic.

Holmann, M., Banet, B. and Weikart, D. P. (1979) *Young Children in Action*, Ypsilanti, MI: High/Scope Press.

Hulton, M. (1989) 'African traditional stories in the classroom', in D. Atkinson (ed.) *The Children's Bookroom: Reading and the Use of Books*, Stoke-on-Trent: Trentham.

Hutchins, P. (1973) *Rosie's Walk*, London: Picture Puffins.

Isaacs, S. (1930) *Intellectual Growth in Young Children*, London: Routledge & Kegan Paul.

Isherwood, S. (1987) *Tim's Knight*, London: Hamish Hamilton.

Jahoda, G. (1963) 'Children's concept of time and history', *Educational Review* 15: 2.

Jenkins, K. (1991) *Re-thinking History*, London: Routledge.

Jones, I. (1985) 'Whose class is it anyway?', *Teaching History* 43: 8–10.

Jones, R. M. (1968) *Fantasy and Feeling in Education*, London: London University Press.

Ker Wilson, B. (1990) *The Turtle and the Island*, London: Francis Lincoln.

King-Smith, D. (1990) *The Toby Man*, London: Puffin.

—— (1993) *Lady Daisy*, London: Puffin.

Klausmeier, H. J. and Allen, P. S. (1978) *Cognitive Development of Children and Youth: A Longitudinal Study*, London: Academic Press.

Klausmeier, H. J. and associates (1979) *Cognitive Learning and Development*, Cambridge, MA: Ballinger.

Klein, G. (1989) '"Is going two days now the pot turn down": stories for all', in D. Atkinson (ed.) *The Children's Bookroom: Reading and the Use of Books*, Stoke-on-Trent: Trentham Books.

Lee, L. (1989) *The Illustrated Cider with Rosie*, London: Cresset Press.

Lee, P. J. (1984) 'Historical imagination', in A. K. Dickinson, P. J. Lee and P. J. Rodgers (eds) *Learning History*, London: Heinemann.

Lello, J. (1980) 'The concept of time, the teaching of history and school organisation', *History Teacher* 13: 3.

Light, P. (1983) 'Social interaction and cognitive development: a review of post-Piagetian research', in S. Meadows (ed.) *Developing Thinking Approaches to Children's Cognitive Development*, London: Methuen.

Line, K. (1989) *Lavender's Blue*, Oxford: Oxford University Press.

Little, V. (1983) 'What is historical imagination?', *Teaching History* 36: 27–32.

Lively, P. (1991) *City of the Mind*, London: Penguin.

Loader, P. (1993) 'Historically speaking', *Teaching History* 71: 20–2.

Lomas, T. (1994) *A Guide to Preparing the History Curriculum in Primary Schools for an Ofsted Inspection*, London: Historical Association.

Macaulay, T. (1969) *History of England*, London: Heron Books.

McKee, D. (1980) *Not Now Bernard*, London: Andersen Press.

Maclure, M. and French, P. F. (1986) 'Comparison of talk at home and at school', in G. Wells (ed.) *Learning Through Interaction: The Study of Language Development*, Cambridge: Cambridge University Press.

Marbeau, L. (1988) 'History and geography in school', *Primary Education* 88: 20–2.

Meek, M. (1988) *How Texts Teach What Readers Learn*, Lewes: Falmer.

Milne, A.A. (1979a) *When We Were Very Young*, London: Magnet.

—— (1979b) *Now We Are Six*, London: Magnet.

Ministry of Education (1952) *Teaching of History*, London: HMSO.

Mitchelhill, B. (1991) *Princess Victoria*, History Key Stage One Stories, Set A, Aylesbury: Ginn.

Moyles, J. R. (1989) *Just Playing? The Role and Status of Play in Early Childhood Education*, Milton Keynes: Open University Press.

Munsch, R. (1988) *The Paper Bag Princess*, UK: Hippo Scholastic.

NCC (1990) *Curriculum Guidance 4–8*, York: National Curriculum Council.

—— (1993) *Teaching History at Key Stage 1*, York: National Curriculum Council.

Opie, I. and Opie, P. (eds) (1973) *The Oxford Book of Children's Verse*, Oxford: Clarendon.

Osoba, F. (1993) *Benin Folklore*, London: Hadada Books.

O'Toole, J. (1992) *The Process of Drama*, London: Routledge.

Philip, N. (1989) *The Cinderella Story*, London: Penguin.

—— (1993) *Victorian Village Life*, Spring Hildbury, Oxfordshire: Albion Press.

Piaget, J. (1926) *The Language and Thought of the Child*, London: Routledge.

—— (1928) *Judgement and Reasoning in the Child*, London: Kegan Paul.

—— (1951) *The Origin of the Idea of Chance in the Child*, London: Routledge.

—— (1952) *The Child's Conception of Number*, London: Routledge.

—— (1956) *The Child's Conception of Time*, London: Routledge.

Poster, J. (1973) 'The birth of the past', *The History Teacher*, August.

Prisk, T. (1987) 'Letting them get on with it, a study of an unsupervised group task in the infant school', in A. Pollard (ed.) *Children in their Primary Schools*, Lewes: Falmer Press.

Provensen, A. and Provensen, M. (1991) *Shaker Lane*, London: Walker Books.

Renfrew, J. (1985) *Food and Cooking in Prehistoric Britain*, London: English Heritage.

—— (1993) *Food and Cooking in Medieval Britain*, London: English Heritage.

Roberts, F. (1992) *India 1526–1800*, London: Hodder & Stoughton.

Rodgers, E. and Rodgers, P. (1991) *Our House*, London: Walker Books.

Rodgers, P. (1989) *Me and Alice go to the Museum*, London: Bodley Head.

Rosen, C. and Rosen, H. (1973) *The Language of Primary School Children*, Harmondsworth: Penguin.

Rotheroe, D. (1990) *London Inn Signs*, Princes Risborough: Shire Publications.

Routh, C. and Rowe, A. (1992) *Stories for Time: Resourcing the History Curriculum KS1*, University of Reading: Reading and Language Information Centre.

Rowe, A. (1991) *The Castle*, History Key Stage One Stories, Set B, Aylesbury: Ginn.

Rowse, A. L. (1946) *The Use of History*, London: Hodder & Stoughton.

Ross, R. (1991) *Little Red Riding Hood*, London: Puffin.

Samuel, R. (1993) 'Photography. The "eye of history"', *New Statesman and Society*, 18 Dec.

Sciescka, J. (1991) *The Three Little Pigs*, London: Puffin.

Scott, B. (1994) 'History in the National Curriculum', *Primary History* 6: 11–12.

Scott, D. (1986) *Caribbean Poetry Now*, S. Brown (ed.), London: Hodder & Stoughton.

SEAC (1993) National Foundation for Educational Research publication, Windsor: Nelson.

Shamroth, N. (1992) 'A rolling drama gathers much talk', *TALK, The Journal of the National Oracy Project* 5: 37–42.

Simmonds, P. (1988) *Lulu and the Flying Babies*, London: Picture Puffin.

Singer, D. G. and Singer, J. L. (1990) *The House of Make Believe*, Cambridge, MA, London: Harvard University Press.

Shemilt, D. (1984) 'Beauty and the philosopher; empathy in history and the classroom', in A. K. Dickinson, P. J. Lee and P. J. Rogers (eds) *Learning History*, London: Heinemann.

Shuter, J. and Reynoldson, F. (1991) *Sunshine History Planning and Assessment Guide*, London: Heinemann Educational.

—— (1991) *Sunshine History Starter Pack 1: People in History*, London: Heinemann Educational.

Smith, B. (1990) *Minnie and Ginger*, London: Pavilion Books.

Smith, E. and Holden, C. (1994) 'I thought it was for picking bones out of soup', *Teaching History* 76: 6–9.

Smith, F. (1989) *Writing and the Writer*, London: Heinemann Educational.

Smith, R. N. and Tomlinson, P. (1977) 'The development of children's construction of historical duration: a new approach and some findings', *Educational Research* 19(3): 163–70.

Steptoe, J. (1992) *Mufaro's Beautiful Daughters: An African Tale*, London: Hodder & Stoughton.

Stones, R. and Mann, A. (1987) *Mother Goose Comes to Cable Street*, London: Picture Puffin.

Sylva, K., Roy, C. and Painter, M. (1980) *Childwatching in Playgroup and Nursery School*, London: Grant McIntyre.

Tanner, G. and Wood, T. (1993) *Bathtime; Shopping; At School; Cooking; Toys; Travelling; Washing*, History Mystery Series, London: A. & C. Black.

Taylor, A. (1988) *Lights On, Lights Off*, Oxford: Oxford University Press.

Temple, A., Nathan, R. and Burris N. (1982) *Beginning of Writing*, Boston, London, Sydney and Toronto: Allyn & Bacon Inc.

Testa, F. (1982) *Never Satisfied*, London: Abelard/North-South.

Thomas, E. (1993) 'Irony age infants', *Times Educational Supplement*, 23 April: 5.

Thompson, F. (1989) *The Illustrated Lark Rise to Candleford*, London: Cresset Press.

Thornton, S. J. and Vukelich, R. (1988) 'Effects of children's understanding of time concepts on historical understanding', *Theory and Research in Social Education* 16(1): 69–82.

Tizard, B., Blatchford, P., Burke, J., Farquar, C. and Plewis, L. (1988) *Young Children at School in the Inner City*, London: Lawrence Erlbaum Associates.

Tough, J. (1976) *Listening to Children Talking*, London: Ward Lock.

Trevelyan, G. M. (1919) *The Recreations of an Historian*, London: Nelson.

Tucker, N. (1981) *The Child and the Book*, Cambridge: Cambridge University Press.

Unwin, R. (1981) *The Visual Dimension in the Study and Teaching of History*, Teaching History Series 49, London: Historical Association.

Vass, P. (1993) 'Have I got a witness? A consideration of the use of historical witnesses in the primary classroom', *Teaching History* 73: 19–24.

Vygotsky, L. S. (1962) *Thought and Language*, Chichester, New York: Wiley.

Waddell, M. and Dale, P. (1989) *Once There Were Giants*, London: Walker Books.

Waddell, M. and Mansell, D. (1991) *My Great Grandpa*, London: Walker Books.

Warlow, A. (1977) 'Kinds of fiction: a hierarchy of veracity', in M. Meek, A. Warlow and G. Barton (eds) *The Cool Web: The Patterns of Children's Reading*, London: Bodley Head.

Warner, M. (1994) *From the Beast to the Blonde*, London: Chatto & Windus.

Warton, C. (1993) 'Chalkface assessment and green paint', *Primary History* 4: 13–14.

Wasu, K. (1986) *Bilingual Nursery Rhymes*, Barking: Cheetah Books.

Waterland, L. (1985) *Read with Me: An Apprenticeship Approach to Reading*, Stroud: Signal.

Welbourne, P. (1990) 'Deconstruction to reconstruction: an approach to women's history through local history', *Teaching History* 59: 16–21.

Wells, G. (1981) *Learning through Interaction: The Study of Language Development*, Cambridge: Cambridge University Press.

West, J. (1981) 'Primary school children's perceptions of authenticity and time in historical narrative pictures', *Teaching History*, February.

Wildsmith, B. (1987) *Mother Goose*, Oxford: Oxford University Press.

Williams, M. (1991) *When I Was Little*, London: Walker Books.

—— (1992) *Joseph and His Magnificent Coat of Colours*, London: Walker Books.

Wilson, H. (ed.) (1988) *There's a Wolf in my Pudding*, London: Pan Macmillan.

Winnicott, D. W. (1974) *Playing and Reality*, Harmondsworth: Penguin.

Wright, D. (1984) 'A small local investigation', *Teaching History* 39: 3–4.

Index